Jane Austen's Regency Dashwoods

Sense and Sensibility, India & the Cotswolds

Allen Firth studied mathematics at Southampton University and statistics at University College London, leading to a management career in financial services, before switching in later life to further post-graduate studies at Oxford University and Oxford Brookes University, gaining a doctorate in managing conservation of the historic environment. He recently retired as a Conservation Officer for Stratford-on-Avon District Council. Previous research led to publication of a local history book in 2005 covering the Cotswold settlements of Bourton-on-the-Hill, Batsford and Sezincote.

Jane Austen's Regency Dashwoods

Sense and Sensibility, India & the Cotswolds

Allen Firth

Grosvenor House
Publishing Limited

All rights reserved
Copyright © Allen Firth, 2019

The right of Allen Firth to be identified as the author of this
work has been asserted in accordance with Section 78
of the Copyright, Designs and Patents Act 1988

The book cover is copyright to Allen Firth

This book is published by
Grosvenor House Publishing Ltd
Link House
140 The Broadway, Tolworth, Surrey, KT6 7HT.
www.grosvenorhousepublishing.co.uk

This book is sold subject to the conditions that it shall not, by way of
trade or otherwise, be lent, resold, hired out or otherwise circulated
without the author's or publisher's prior consent in any form of binding or
cover other than that in which it is published and
without a similar condition including this condition being imposed
on the subsequent purchaser.

A CIP record for this book
is available from the British Library

ISBN 978-1-78623-640-1

Contents

Preface & Acknowledgements		*vii*
Introduction		*xi*
Chapter 1	– Jane Austen's Regency Context	1
Chapter 2	– Leighs and Dashwoods – Lord Mayors of London & Silk Merchants	17
Chapter 3	– Fact into Fiction	37
Chapter 4	– Recurrent Themes in Austen's Novels	55
Chapter 5	– The Regency Picturesque	87
Chapter 6	– Regency Icons and Indian Influences	125
Chapter 7	– Passages to India	161
Chapter 8	– Exploring the Indian Picturesque	177
Chapter 9	– Out of India	205
Chapter 10	– 'Hell-Fire Jane' – Sense and Sensibility & the Dashwoods	253
Postscript		*335*
Notes		*337*
Selected Bibliography		*353*
Selected Index		*357*

Preface & Acknowledgements

If it is a truth universally acknowledged that a picture paints a thousand words, then it is equally true that Jane Austen's words paint a picture widely held as a vision of the Regency period. The canvas on which the picture is painted reflects Austen's self-acknowledged restricted focus, and if not quite a miniature, neither is it a broad landscape. However, regardless of scope, acute observation remains a crucial feature of most artistic endeavour and is certainly true of Austen's brilliant writing, which also drew on wider artistic fashion and influences, representing one of the book's key themes. In exploring other interconnected themes, the wider Regency period provides a vibrant background throughout.

The history of the real and high-profile Dashwood family in the 18th and early 19th centuries features prominently, with Indian and Cotswold links strongly shaping the narrative. While the Dashwoods' activities at their West Wycombe estate form an important contextual element, not least through a leading role in the infamous Hell-Fire Club, there is also particular focus on the Dashwood family's home for several decades at Bourton-on-the-Hill in the North Cotswolds, in turn connected with local Austen family links, notably at Adlestrop, Daylesford, and Longborough. Investigation of these real-life Dashwood activities, and their connections with her own family, provides compelling evidence for Austen's choice of the family name Dashwood in *Sense and Sensibility*. A key figure is Sir John Dashwood, 4th Baronet of West Wycombe (1765-1849), whose lifespan encompassed Jane Austen's own (1775-1817). His life story and those of his predecessors are outlined not only as a probable influence on the novel but also in their own right, adding colour and context to Austen's Regency world.

The link between the real and fictional Dashwoods was noted, in passing, in my local history book on *Bourton-on-the-Hill, Batsford & Sezincote* (2005), but was not then a focal issue, and its potential significance was neither fully recognised nor pursued at that stage. However, having followed this up sporadically, mainly through the Dashwood family story and fragmented archive records, it was Janine Barchas's 2009 article, *Hell-Fire Jane*, which really galvanised my interest. As well as providing relevant core research material, her excellent article tied in with my own emerging findings, which in turn add further support and richness to Barchas's theories and assertions, particulary in relation to the Dashwood hunting lodge and activities in the Cotswolds. Her article also overlapped with wider aspects of my research, including closely related connections which are absorbed into the book.

India and its contribution to the contemporary British enthusiasm for 'the picturesque' are specifically represented by sketching the career of the topographical artist Thomas Daniell, RA, whose adventurous Indian journeys and resulting images fed the Regency appetite for all things exotic and oriental, epitomising the period's eclectic and rapidly changing fashions. The Mughal-style country house at Sezincote, with direct Thomas Daniell and Humphry Repton design input, and an inspiration for the Prince Regent's Brighton Pavilion, further pins the action to the Cotswolds.

Alongside the results of primary research, short passages from secondary sources have been incorporated in the text, reflecting related and detailed work done by others. Claire Tomalin's excellent biography, *Jane Austen – A Life* (2000 Ed.), has been a central point of reference, and provides numerous insights which make more sense of my own investigations. Among more recent influential Austen-focused publications, those by Paula Byrne (*The Real Jane Austen*, 2013), Victoria Huxley (*Jane Austen & Adlestrop – Her Other Family*, 2013), and Margaret Doody (*Jane Austen's Names – Riddles, Persons,*

Places, 2015), have been especially valuable sources, alongside a further publication by Janine Barchas (*Matters of Fact in Jane Austen*, 2012); all are highly recommended. Elements of insightful literary criticism by Jonathan Bate (*The Song of the Earth*, 2000) have been incorporated, adding depth to my own commentaries. Among the sources for Indian and Thomas Daniell aspects, those by Thomas Sutton (*The Daniells – Artists and Travellers*, 1954), Katherine Prior (Ed.) (*An Illustrated Journey Round the World by Thomas, William & Samuel Daniell*, 2007), and Romita Ray (*Under the Banyan Tree – Relocating the Picturesque in British India*, 2013) have been indispensable. A few selected passages from these and other authors are quoted and explicitly cited, covering specific points in an exemplary manner; any attempt by me to adapt them would only detract from their quality and coherence, and I hope their inclusion will be taken as a compliment to the authors concerned.

In terms of primary research, I am particularly indebted to the staff at the Bodleian Library for their assistance with accessing the Dashwood family papers, and to Sir Edward Dashwood, 12th Baronet of West Wycombe, for permission to use extracts from those papers, and also to reproduce a number of images. Similarly, I am grateful to the Peake family for various images relating to Sezincote. Permission from the National Portrait Gallery to use a number of their images is also appreciated. While I hold original versions of the majority of other images included and where possible have tried to establish ownership of others, where I have not been able to trace an image's source I hope the owner will excuse the omission and accept my apologies.

The book is dedicated to my wife Catherine, whose occasional invaluable assistance and constant patience have been sincerely appreciated.

Introduction

On 8th November 1790, Reverend Thomas Leigh, a cousin of Jane Austen, sent a letter from Adlestrop in the North Cotswolds to John Dashwood at his hunting lodge in nearby Bourton-on-the-Hill. Thomas Leigh, who greatly influenced Jane in her formative years, lived at the rather grand parsonage in Adlestrop, where Jane stayed on at least three occasions, and he had also visited the Austens at Steventon, their Hampshire home. The recipient of his letter, John Dashwood, was the eldest son and heir of the 3rd Baronet of West Wycombe. Three years later, in 1793, he would become Sir John Dashwood-King (often simply referred to as Sir John Dashwood), 4th Baronet of West Wycombe, inheriting the premier baronetcy of Great Britain. Notwithstanding this inheritance, which included the imposing mansion and estate at West Wycombe, Sir John retained his Bourton-on-the-Hill home with its favourable Cotswold hunting country for another quarter of a century, continuing his active involvement in many aspects of the local community and neighbourhood.

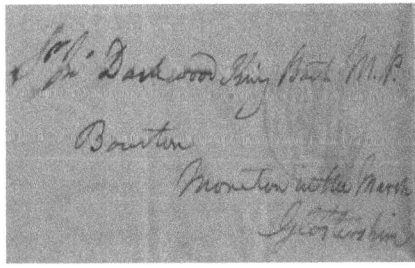

Envelope addressed to Sir John Dashwood King, 4th Bt. at Bourton, near "Moreton in the Marsh", c.1800

Indeed, Thomas Leigh's letter refers to an example of this local community engagement. Its concluding phrase also indicates a closeness and familiarity between the Dashwood family and the Leighs, Jane Austen's close relatives: Jane's mother was Cassandra Leigh before her marriage into the Austen family. As outlined later, the Austen side of Jane's family also had links with the Dashwoods. The letter from Thomas Leigh to John Dashwood reads as follows :-

Dear Sir *Adlestrop Nov: 8 1790*

I beg pardon for giving you this trouble. Mr Tarn tells me that Keck has never done what it was agreed, 2 or 3 years ago, he was to replace on your part at the vicarage at Longbro, and for which I understood you had paid him. Keck has been here this morning, & owns that he delay'd doing the work for a twelvemonth, but then, intending to do it, had counterorders from you. The work remaining undone, he says, was estimated at abt. £3:4s:0d. That must now be done, as Mr. Tarn has let the House. But if you think it was improperly agreed to be done by you, I will take it upon me: as Mr Tarn's finances will not bear its being thrown upon him; altho' his own improper conduct, (which you will be very good to overlook) has occasion'd the inconveniences that have arisen to him in this business.

My wife & Sister desire to present their best respects to Mrs Dashwood & yourself united with those of, Dear Sir, your most obedient & very humble servant

Thos: Leigh[1]

The 'Longbro' referred to in the letter is the village of Longborough, another historic Leigh family location, lying between Bourton-on-the-Hill and Adlestrop, and it is apparent from the contents of the letter that Thomas Leigh and John Dashwood had joint interests there. The Leigh

Introduction

family had long been based in both Adlestrop and Longborough and the south transept of Longborough Church, known as the 'Leigh aisle', houses an impressive Leigh memorial tomb featuring effigies of Jane Austen's great-great-great-grandparents, William Leigh (c.1585-1631) and his wife Elizabeth. During her stays at nearby Adlestrop, Jane would no doubt have been taken to see this impressive family memorial.

The Leigh Memorial Tomb in Longborough Church

The north transept was built much later as a private chapel for the residents of Sezincote, the neighbouring country house and estate lying between Longborough and Bourton-on-the-Hill, and features memorials with other Dashwood connections, outlined later.

Around the time of Thomas Leigh's letter above in 1790, or shortly after, the teenage Jane Austen began devising and drafting *Elinor and Marianne*, an early version of what would become her first published novel, *Sense and Sensibility*. The links between her Leigh relatives at Adlestrop, with whom she and her family had frequent contact, and the nearby Dashwoods at Bourton-on-the-Hill, with their illustrious status and notorious reputation, must at the very least be suspected of influencing Jane's choice of the family name Dashwood for the central characters in *Sense and Sensibility*. This suspicion is explored and investigated in what follows.

The same compact area of the North Cotswolds provides the Indian influences in the book's title, with the Mughal-style country house at Sezincote, unique in Europe, being built in this period, and with Warren Hastings having established his home at Daylesford, immediately adjacent to Adlestrop, after returning from his time in Bengal as the first Governor General of Britain's then disparate Indian territories. The connections are tightened by the fact that Hastings' story is intimately linked with Jane Austen's family. Indian themes are further reflected in the choice of the designer commissioned for the Cotswold country houses at both Sezincote and Daylesford, namely Samuel Pepys Cockerell, brother of Sezincote's owner Sir Charles Cockerell, and later architect to the East India Company. Significantly, Sir Charles had accumulated much of his wealth during his time in India.

Having included in the title the flexible term 'Regency' I feel obliged to clarify the period intended here, particularly as there is no universally accepted usage. Rachel Knowles, for example, provides two references under the heading, '*So when is the Regency era?*'. The first is from Saul David in his biography of George IV, describing the Regency '*in its widest sense (1800-1830)'* as a *'devil-may-care period of low morals and high fashion'*. Her second reference is taken from a notice (now removed) at the entrance to the Regency galleries in the National Portrait Gallery suggesting an even wider time span: *'As a distinctive period in Britain's social and cultural life, the Regency spanned the four decades from the start of the French Revolution in 1789 to the passing of Britain's great Reform Act in 1832'*. Knowles' own view is somewhat similar:

> *'The Regency era is, by very definition, related to the life of the Regent. It is characterised by the freedom and extravagance of George IV compared with the ascetic lifestyle of his father. Although the Regency is a mere nine years long, I am inclined to think that the Regency "feel" starts around the time that George IV came of age in 1783 and continues until his death in 1830'.*[2]

A similar spread of dates is chosen by Charles Jennings, commenting that,

> *'the sweep of the decades from 1780 to 1830 can still be termed the Regency Era. Prince George may have been appalling as the effective head of the Royal Family, but he did establish the perfectly sound notion that art and culture could, and should, be present in every aspect of life; that it was right to be discriminating and to have a sense of the fine and the beautiful. Whatever else he did, the Prince Regent pursued the culture of the aesthetic with energy, taste, sincerity and someone else's money. It was an achievement'.*[3]

As well as providing a wide range of dates for the Regency period, this latter quote helpfully stresses the strong aesthetic strands of Regency life, at least for those with the leisure-time and inclination to consider such things. Austen's readership was made up largely of members of this socio-economic group and, consequently, aesthetics has a large role to play both in her novels and here.

In summary, there is no justifiable precision on dates for the Regency, unless restricting oneself to the narrow period when the Prince was formally acting as Regent; in any event, it is ultimately of little consequence. As Rachel Knowles observes, it is the 'feel' of the period which is more important, and that feel certainly had vague start and end dates. I have therefore opted for a wide definition of the Regency period and, for example, cite primary sources from 1788 to 1831, therefore fitting very closely with the National Portrait Gallery suggestion, perhaps appropriately given that a few of their images are gratefully incorporated in this volume.

Turning to the Cotswolds, the scene of much of the action, the area only really found favour with the wider public from the late nineteenth century onwards, championed aesthetically by writers and architects including William Morris, Guy Dawber and Charles Edward Bateman; it has retained this desirability ever since. This focus on the Cotswolds had a strong affinity at the turn of the twentieth century with the Arts and Crafts movement, itself looking back to an imagined late-medieval golden age for which the Cotswolds, with its characteristic vernacular style of stone buildings, was an ideal model. The Cotswolds had, for centuries, been a generator of wealth, founded substantially on extensive and profitable sheep farming from the medieval period onwards, with numerous glorious churches and country houses - a perennial fascination for Austen - built on the back of this wealth. Although in Jane's Regency period the area had not acquired the wider public exposure it now enjoys (or suffers) it was certainly by then, and had long been, a desirable choice of the wealthy for their country houses and estates. Some such Cotswold country houses feature prominently in the text, often having the character of a place of relaxation, recreation, or retreat, alongside their function as symbols of status and fashion.

Introduction

As pivotal settings for the narrative, key Cotswold locations are those at Adlestrop (where Jane Austen stayed with some of her Leigh relatives), Bourton-on-the-Hill (where the Dashwoods had their hunting lodge), Daylesford (where Warren Hastings repurchased the family's ancestral home after returning from India), Longborough (whose church contains the imposing tomb memorial to some of Jane Austen's ancestors), and Sezincote (which the Cockerell family purchased and radically refashioned in an idiosyncratic Indian style). Both Hastings and the Cockerells had returned to England after service in the East India Company, having accumulated sufficient rewards in the subcontinent to retire to their respective Cotswold country houses. The Indian source of their wealth was displayed in very contrasting ways in the respective architectural treatments of their homes at Daylesford (with subtle and sparingly employed Indian motifs) and Sezincote (featuring unrestrained Mughal exuberance).

Jane Austen's Regency Dashwoods

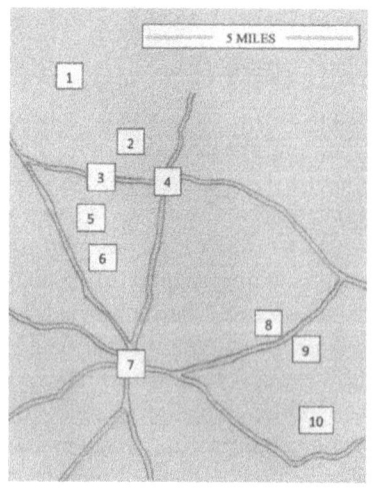

KEY TO INDIVIDUAL SITES

1. Northwick Park
2. Batsford
3. Bourton-on-the-Hill
4. Moreton-in-Marsh
5. Sezincote
6. Longborough
7. Stow-on-the-Wold
8. Adlestrop
9. Daylesford
10. Kingham

Map of Key Locations in the North Cotswolds

CHAPTER ONE
Jane Austen's Regency Context

By the time Jane Austen was born in December 1775, daily life in Britain was already affected, and enriched, by imports from the East, mainly from China, but increasingly from India as well. Tea, coffee, and spices, together with exotic plants, foodstuffs, ceramics and fabrics, had gradually been assimilated into British life, albeit initially only at the upper levels of society, constrained by limited supply and high cost. Associated with these imports was the excitement of new and exotic experiences, accompanied by some inevitable competition among peer groups to keep up with the latest fashions. Over time, however, as trade volumes increased, access to these imports percolated down through most levels of society, so that many became commonplace, tea perhaps being the best example. Language was also enriched by the introduction of new words of Indian origin, such as chutney, bungalow, jungle, loot, juggernaut, and punch. Importantly, some of these Eastern imports had strong visual and design components, expressed for example through ethnic patterns on fabrics and ceramics, with aesthetic influences also encompassing portrayals of buildings and their settings, including landscapes. During the eighteenth century, introduction of Chinese elements into parks, gardens, and country estate landscapes was intended to reflect their patrons' taste, wealth, and awareness of the latest imagery emerging from Britain's expanding overseas exploration and trading interests. At the highest level, the Chinese pagoda at Kew (1762) is an excellent example of this trend.

These exotic and visual influences emerged more strongly in the second half of the eighteenth century in parallel, and in tune, with the cult of 'the picturesque'. Together, they had significant impact on styles and fashions in most spheres of the arts through to the early part of the nineteenth century. This period encompassed Jane Austen's lifetime (1775-1817), with these emerging artistic influences being pervasive contextual factors in her writing, and while Austen's own attitude to the picturesque was somewhat ambiguous, she referenced it extensively. Discussion and consideration of the picturesque by her characters is a recurring and often explicit theme in her novels, frequently intended as a signal of an individual's sensibilities.

The various imported aesthetic influences fed a growing eagerness and appetite for more natural forms from a wide range of sources, broadly as a reaction against the formal, and rather narrow, classical styles which had dominated much of the eighteenth century. Notably, the progression of these exotic and picturesque influences, far from coalescing into a seamless and coherent process, was characterised by a random succession of stylistic waves, part of the general tidal advance of romanticism in the arts. Such exotic influences included Chinese, Indian, Moorish, and Egyptian styles, among others, exploited in various hybrid and idiosyncratic ways, with most having only transient impact. As for 'the picturesque', this was also subject to a succession of imaginative adaptations. Taking the field of landscape gardening as an example, the picturesque was interpreted very differently over time by Charles Bridgeman, William Kent, Capability Brown and Humphry Repton, among others, each bringing a fresh approach, successively latched onto by enthusiastic wealthy patrons. One after the other, these waves of exotic and picturesque possibilities were keenly exploited by a nation with a thirst for new sources of inspiration in an era of rapidly changing fashion. The quenching of this thirst had intoxicating, if often short-lived, effects, epitomising much of the frenetic Regency period.

Jane Austen's Regency Context

The pace of change was matched, and partly driven, by the equally dramatic expansion of Britain's global empire and trading economy, which fuelled the desire for its main beneficiaries to display both their newly acquired wealth and their adopted cultural sophistication. Such sophistication was, however, all too often superficial, representing little more than a blind chasing of the latest fad, and often a futile chase at that. By the time many had invested heavily in their favourite cutting-edge building or landscape projects, these were already becoming outdated, if not immediately, then within a few years of completion. Indeed, some projects were abandoned unfinished, precisely because fashions had outpaced their execution. One consequence of these rapid and overlapping changes, was the emergence of stylistic hybrids. Sezincote, in the North Cotswolds (a classical and restrained Georgian villa internally, but with free-spirited Mughal styling and ornamentation externally) was one example, and another was Brighton Pavilion (its Chinese-influenced interiors contrasting with an Indian-inspired exterior). Neither was an entirely new build; instead they involved major alterations to existing and unexceptional Georgian buildings. Both buildings feature prominently later in the text.

During this turbulent period, incorporating the Napoleonic Wars, several high-profile individuals featured in the book not only influenced the late Georgian and Regency context in which Jane Austen was writing her novels, but also shaped some of the specific allusions within them, notably in *Sense and Sensibility*. Some of these figures had significant influence in the fields of politics, economics and the military but, equally importantly, others were involved in the arts. Such a dynamic period of emerging fashions and styles required two essential components: not only patrons with money, motivation, and enthusiasm, but also artists able to create, develop, and adapt new approaches, whether in landscape designs, paintings, sculptures, literature, theatre, music, architecture, costumes, or other cultural endeavours. Not surprisingly, several individuals whose stories are covered here fall into one or other of these two categories. Prominent among the patrons are the Dashwoods (initially at West Wycombe, and later at Bourton-on-the-Hill), the Leighs at Adlestrop, Charles Cockerell at Sezincote, and Warren Hastings at Daylesford. The artists featured here include S. P. Cockerell, architect to the East India Company, the topographical artist Thomas Daniell, and the landscape gardener Humphry Repton. The diverse stories of these actors, alongside cameo roles for Nelson, Wellington, and the Prince Regent, among other prominent figures, have multiple and often intimate connections to Jane Austen and her family, described in the text in some detail. India provides an almost constant backdrop to these individual portrayals.

Before focusing on India, a brief diversion is made to introduce another important historical character who features in the narrative, and who provides links with other more central individuals, most notably Sir Francis Dashwood. He is Frederick North, later Lord North, the prime minister between 1770 and 1782. It was as part of the settlement of his estates after his death in 1792 that the Cockerells purchased the Sezincote estate in the North Cotswolds at the geographical heart of much of our story, and it was Lord North who had presided over the loss of the American colonies, arguably through his indecision. History has not been kind to his reputation, and it is certainly true that he had only some of the abilities required to be an effective prime minister. North himself was not even confident that he had the abilities to function as chancellor[1], which he had become in 1767. Unfortunately he was also faced with two of eighteenth-century England's most challenging problems, namely America and India, with one key link between the two being tea, which was becoming an increasingly popular and commercial commodity.[2] This link arose from opium production in India being monopolized by the East India Company, with its proceeds used to pay for Chinese tea, which was sent to Britain on East India Company ships, with onward passage in large quantities to the American colonies.

This global trade relied on large vessels which required constant repairs and frequent replacement, putting pressure on the supply of seasoned oak, also needed by the Royal Navy, thereby exacerbating existing political tensions, and increasing pressure for greater government controls over the East India Company operations.

Competition between the Company and the Royal Navy for resources was not restricted to supplies of seasoned oak; securing manpower for their respective fleets was also a source of conflict, as a passage from Christopher Hibbert's biography of Horatio Nelson graphically illustrates. One of Nelson's early commands was of the *Albemarle*, a captured French merchantman, a 28-gun frigate. Hibbert notes that Nelson was happy with both the ship and her crew, even though some had been press-ganged. These unlucky seamen had been on four East India Company ships returning to the London docks. Nelson chased the vessels which initially tried to escape, but when he ordered broadsides from the *Albemarle*'s guns to be fired, the four East India Company ships allowed a number of seamen to be '*bundled aboard the* Albemarle *and two other ships under Nelson's command. They were soon sailing across the North Sea to escort a convoy home from the Baltic*'.[3]

An associated source of tension was the deteriorating relations between the British Government and the American colonists, who were becoming increasingly irritated by what they saw as unfair and penal imposition of taxes, and it was the tax on imports of tea which brought matters to a head. The East India Company was in debt, not helped by the fact that the American colonists' resistance to paying tax on tea led to them purchasing less of it, which in turn meant mounting surplus stockpiles in the Company's British warehouses, mainly in the East India Company Docks in London. Lord North had the ill-conceived idea of selling it to the colonists at such a discount that even with the tax added, it would still be attractively priced. However, the British insistence on the principle of taxation made this compromise unacceptable to the colonists, triggering demonstrations in 1773. That year, an extract from an '*Account of Tea exported by the East India Company to his Majesty's Colonies in North America with the Quantity of Tea conveyed etc*' shows the details of consignments headed for four destinations: Boston, South Carolina, Philadelphia, and New York, the first two consignments being shown below.

Extract from an 'Account of Tea exported by the East India Company to His Majesty's Colonies in North America'

The details above for Boston show entries for a total of 398 chests of tea, split by type including 'bohea' and 'souchon', and invoiced at just under £11,000. In addition, there were 182 chests headed for South Carolina, and 568 chests for each of Philadelphia and New York. The Boston consignments sailed for the American colonies aboard four ships in September 1773 and included the 114 chests aboard the ship *Dartmouth* at the centre of the famous Boston Tea Party incident in which colonists, dressed as American Indians, dumped the chests of tea in Boston Harbour.

This incident reflected the growing tensions which culminated in the colonists' Declaration of Independence three years later in 1776, and during this period the unrest was referenced in various correspondence between Sir Francis Dashwood, the 2nd Baronet of West Wycombe, and the prime minister Lord North. In a letter of 25th January 1775 to Sir Francis Dashwood, North includes the phrase '*As soon as ever the present American business is abated …*'[4], indicating the government's ongoing concerns about the American colonies. A key figure in these American developments was Benjamin Franklin, who has strong links back to the Dashwoods and West Wycombe, outlined later.

The loss of the American colonies in the subsequent War of Independence was an embarrassment to national pride as well as having economic and foreign policy consequences, and its aftermath resulted in India becoming ever more important to Britain. The role and influence of India on British life during Jane Austen's lifetime was substantial, increasing, and central to later imperial and economic development as the nineteenth century unfolded. This is exemplified by Asa Briggs' comments in his volume *England in the Age of Improvement*, covering the period 1783-1867, in which he quotes a Member of Parliament asserting a wider responsibility for MPs than merely representing their British homeland interests – "*We are all of us Members for India*".[5]

This British focus on India emerged from centuries of European infiltration of the East Indies. Romita Ray, for example, notes that from the latter part of the fifteenth-century the Portuguese increasingly targeted pepper, cinnamon, ginger, and nutmeg obtained from the Malabar Coast, these spices commanding high prices in key European spice markets, notably Lisbon and Venice.[6] The Dutch, the French and the British gradually followed this interest in the East Indies, the United East India Company (an amalgamation of Dutch trading companies) being established in 1602, just after the British equivalent received its Royal Charter from Elizabeth I in 1600.

Some idea of the East's diverse and rich sources of wealth, exploitation of which grew steadily from the 15th to the 18th centuries, is directly reflected in the ceiling painting of 1778 for the East India Company House, London, entitled *The East Offering its Riches to Britannia* by Spiridione Roma, which includes several of the goods involved. The term 'offering' is highly contentious. In the middle of the painting, between the elements to the left and right depicting Britain and the East respectively, is an image of a ship on the open sea, representing the main, and sometimes forceful, means by which such 'Riches' were acquired and transported from the East to Britain. Alongside these commercial activities, Nelson's crushing victory at Trafalgar in 1805 secured Britain's global naval supremacy for the remainder of the nineteenth-century and was a key factor in facilitating and protecting expanding trade and colonial acquisitions.

In summary, during the late eighteenth century and early nineteenth, the growing influence of India and all its associations had increasingly impacted on life in Britain, culturally as well as commercially. Seen variously as mysterious, exotic, wealth-creating, and dangerous, India's colourful and ornamental aesthetic and cultural influences extended across a whole spectrum of interests, including botany, zoology, architecture, religion, language, textiles, jewels and spices. Early nineteenth century references to Indian textiles, for example, appear both in Austen's novels and in the retrospective opening passages of Thackeray's *Vanity Fair*.

This great diversity in imports was mirrored by similar variety in the motivations of those venturing out to India. Some went to escape unfortunate circumstances at home, while others went positively in search of adventure, wealth or opportunity. Often it was a blend of several factors, and while a few travelled independently, most ventures were channelled through the East India Company, not least because service in the Company, whether as part of its military, trading or administrative arms, afforded structure and purpose as well as the potential for substantial reward. A letter[7] sent in 1762 to one of our key characters, Sir Francis Dashwood, 2nd Baronet of West Wycombe, reflects not only the influence he commanded in relation to the East India Company, but concisely typifies the motivations and means for venturing to India :-

> *Sir, I ask pardon for troubling you with this, but the bearer Doctor Petrie's brother is an ingenuous young man and has a friend in Asia who has had very good luck, and made a pretty fortune, who offers to settle him in his business before he leaves the place. My request therefore is that you would be so kind to recommend him to the East India Company to let him go out a writer in their service.*
>
> *Which favour will very much oblige your friend and honrble. Servant*
>
> *Vere Broke*   *July ye 6th 1762*

A 'writer' in the service of the East India Company was effectively a clerk, the introductory level of administrative employment, and not in itself a particularly lucrative post. However, the reality was that once in India most such 'writers' were able to supplement their income with private off-the-books business, and this individual clearly had ready-made opportunities awaiting him. Provided the East India Company was operating efficiently and securing profits it asked few, if any, questions about such moonlighting, or indeed about any associated ethical or legal niceties.

While commercial and trading impacts were crucial, art and artefacts emerging from India, whether produced by European or native artists, played a major role in shaping perceptions of the sub-continent, and fuelled the excitement and fascination associated with newly established imperial frontiers. Part of this enthusiasm went hand in hand with a growing confidence about Britain's place in the world and the generally optimistic view reflected in Briggs's *England in the Age of Improvement*. Such 'improvement', which included the industrial and agricultural revolutions, and their social consequences, extended to attempts to impose Western religious and cultural values on new colonial acquisitions. This philosophy of improvement was carried through in India with, at least initially, positive and assertive feelings in Britain towards the sub-continent, notwithstanding the infamous 'Black Hole of Calcutta' incident in 1756. Commercial benefits encouraged many to turn a blind eye to the less palatable aspects of British incursion in India. Eventually, however, native resistance to an increasingly domineering foreign power was inevitable, and the British public's positive sentiments towards India later changed, notably so after the Indian Mutiny of 1857. Nevertheless, India remained central to British Imperial consolidation and wealth generation throughout the nineteenth century, even as underlying tensions grew.

In the context of exotic and picturesque influences, the East Indies, and India in particular, as a source of artistic inspiration in its widest sense, were particularly prominent at the time Jane Austen was formulating her early novels and, by way of setting the scene, the following quotations tap into both the historical and literary themes explored in the book.

'Mr Daniell proposes to publish twelve views of Calcutta at twelve gold Mohurs the set, from complete plates and finished in watercolours.' (Extract from the *Calcutta Chronicle*, 17th July, 1786)

'He is Rear-Admiral of the White. He was in the Trafalgar action, and has been in the East Indies since; he has been stationed there, I believe, several years' (Jane Austen, *Persuasion*[8])

'In the East Indies the climate is hot, and the mosquitoes are troublesome .... his observations may have extended to the existence of nabobs, gold Mohrs and palanquins' (Jane Austen, *Sense and Sensibility*[9])

'Old English trees are felled to make way for the exotic plants of the hothouse. The history of the greenhouse is bound up with that of empire .... as a result of the increased cultivation of exotic plants brought back from the empire in the East and West Indies.' (Jonathan Bate[10], discussing the Dashwoods' fictional estate alterations in *Sense and Sensibility*)

'To send me carefully packed some fresh ripe walnuts or seeds, or an entire plant, if it can be transported; and any other curious or valuable seeds or plants, the rhubarb and ginger especially. Any curiosities, whether natural productions, manufactures, paintings, or what else may be acceptable to persons of taste in England. Animals only that may be useful, unless any that may be remarkably curious.'[11] (Instructions from Warren Hastings to George Bogle who he sent on a mission from India to Tibet in 1774.)

'The Indian movement in this country had its nerve-centre at a house near Moreton-in-Marsh in Gloucestershire called Sezincote. ... Here were gathered, as at a sort of Regency Bauhaus, all the prophets of the new enthusiasm'.[12] (Musgrave, commenting on the background to Brighton Pavilion, in *Royal Pavilion*)

'You must not inquire too far, Marianne – remember, I have no knowledge in the picturesque ...' (Edward Ferrars to Marianne Dashwood, *Sense and Sensibility*[13])

'The Tilneys were soon engaged in another [subject] on which she had nothing to say. They were viewing

the country with the eyes of persons accustomed to drawing, and decided on its capability of being formed into pictures, with all the eagerness of real taste. Here Catherine was quite lost... a lecture on the picturesque immediately followed, in which his instructions were so clear that she soon began to see beauty in everything admired by him ... He talked of fore-grounds, distances, and second distances – side-screens and perspectives – lights and shades; - and Catherine was so hopeful a scholar, that when they gained the top of Beechen Cliff, she voluntarily rejected the whole city of Bath, as unworthy to make part of a landscape.' (Extract from Austen's Northanger Abbey[14])

The concept of 'taste' was critical both to Austen and to Regency fashions and is evidenced by two extracts from the above quotes, namely '*or what else may be acceptable to persons of taste*' and '*decided on its capability of being formed into pictures with all the eagerness of real taste*'. This latter extract also links '*taste*' with views having the '*capability of being formed into pictures*' – the very essence of an associated concept, namely 'the picturesque', discussed in Chapter 5.

Austen's frequent references to India and to the picturesque were highly topical, as is readily evidenced through the impact of these influences on multiple aspects of Regency life in England. However, while the meanings of Austen's direct references to India and the picturesque may appear clear enough, understanding all of Austen's many contemporary allusions and their contexts is challenging and, at a distance of two hundred years, probably not entirely possible.

Recent research and analysis identify wide-ranging use by Austen of such contemporary allusions and indicate that she intended, indeed expected, her Regency readership to pick up on these and their thinly disguised social and moral messages. This was often achieved through satirical humour and

Jane Austen's Regency Context

occasionally outright mockery, a stylistic approach Austen had favoured and cultivated from the outset of her writing. However, this is only one facet of her outstanding literary skill, and it is a tribute to her works that they continue to operate and succeed so well, and on so many different levels, two centuries after her death; the almost certain loss of some of her more subtle contemporary allusions fails to blunt the novels' insights into enduring elements of the human condition and experience.

Austen's novels were, in some sense, the romantic comedies of their day, albeit infused with deeper meanings and messages, some of which – because we did not live and breathe her era - we may never fully appreciate. The body of literary criticism is a great help, but such analysis was very limited in her lifetime, largely because most of the novels were published very much towards the end of her life, with *Northanger Abbey* and *Persuasion* published posthumously, and *Sanditon* left unfinished when she died. The posthumous literary criticism in the nineteenth century has also dictated that her novels are often viewed through a Victorian prism, and in the context of Victorian values, themselves evolving significantly through that queen's long reign. In comparing Regency and Victorian values, one author comments that '*as the Victorian ideal of bourgeois domesticity took hold, as the English puritan instinct re-asserted itself ... the art of living became, somehow, equated with self-indulgence*'.[15] Barchas, for example, picks up this change in attitudes, noting that, '*unsurprisingly, the Victorian sensibility that buried the Hell-Fire legacy at West Wycombe (in the nineteenth century, Sir Francis* [Dashwood]'*s remaining statues were removed and his landscape judiciously edited) would insist upon the starched purity of an unworldly Jane Austen. Such censoring of Austen's popular allusions may have diminished her social satire.*'[16] This introduces themes explored later.

Early nineteenth-century 'Austen-contemporary' commentary, literary criticism, and analysis, is sparse and of limited use in identifying possible hidden or subtle references and allusions. Partly because of this, Jane Austen's writings, and particularly her novels, have continued to attract academic and literary attention with the aim of filling this gap. In trying to strip away later interpretations of her work, such research is focused largely on the meaning of her writing in its contemporary context, and parts of the exploration here lean heavily on recent research and the resulting publications. There have been several attempts to link Jane's own life experiences (and her likely knowledge of events and characters at the time), to specific names and narrative threads in the novels, with recent research continuing to make claims to hidden meanings and connections. Some such claims are made with conviction, backed by compelling evidence, with others put forward only tentatively. While some adopt an almost forensic approach there will, in summary, always remain insights and subtleties of expression within the novels which only a contemporary readership would have been able to fully know, sense, and appreciate.

New research incorporated in what follows not only adds to, and corroborates, certain proposed theories from other authors, but also introduces some fresh perspectives on Jane Austen's narrative sources and the way she incorporated these in creating her intricate writing. Such research increasingly reveals and emphasises that her novels, while structurally coherent, and with readily accessible storylines, also have multiple layers. The intention here is to excavate some of those layers by reference to selected aspects of contemporary events and social context.

The specific aspects explored are those linking India and the Cotswolds as well as cultural, aesthetic and more ethereal dimensions, including picturesque influences, with exotic overtones, prominent for example in fashion and the arts. The aim is to illustrate how these geographical and cultural aspects interact, both in historical reality and in Austen's writing. History and literature are therefore, not surprisingly, the principal sources of information and insights, and are employed and intended, as with Austen's novels, to reveal and convey an authentic sense of contemporary Regency society as experienced by a particular socio-economic readership.

History and literature feed into Austen's novels, which return the favour by significantly influencing our perceptions of the history and literature of the period. The extent to which these Regency perceptions are distorted, when seen through the medium of her novels, and with the passage of time, is ultimately for the reader to judge. However, Austen's writing is not only carefully crafted, but reflects her own meticulous observations, and I suggest therefore that any distortions are principally a result of our failure to appreciate the complexities and subtleties she deliberately and cleverly incorporates. In some small way, I hope that some of her coded messages are further deciphered in the exploration that follows.

With so many interconnections covered in the book, there are several narrative strands to be pursued, but a common and recurring theme is the significance of family names and relationships. A focus on two specific families in the next chapter provides an introduction to the complex and tangled web of Austen associations which link Jane, India, and the Cotswolds. The two family names are Leigh, her mother's maiden name, and Dashwood, the name chosen (for significant reasons asserted later) for key figures in *Sense and Sensibility*. The Dashwood name was infamous for late 18th century Hell-Fire Club associations and maintained a residual level of notoriety throughout Jane's life and the wider Regency period. The Leigh and Dashwood family names, alongside the name Austen itself, appear throughout, and in later chapters lead to a more detailed examination of Indian and Cotswold influences, involving several prominent late Georgian and Regency figures.

CHAPTER TWO
Leighs and Dashwoods – Lord Mayors of London & Silk Merchants

Through her mother Cassandra, Jane Austen was part of a family with an illustrious past, and this seems, not unnaturally, to have been the chief reason for her interest in genealogy, particularly that of historic aristocratic and gentry families. While Reverend George Austen, Jane's father, was from a family of woollen manufacturers from Kent and Sussex who had prospered several generations earlier, his wife, Cassandra (née Leigh), had connections with the aristocracy, including Mary Brydges (1666-1703), eldest child of James Brydges, Baron Chandos of Sudeley. Delving deeper into Jane Austen's family tree there are Greys, Staffords, Nevilles, Throckmortons, Fitzalans, Beauchamps, Beauforts and, going back further, King Edward III.[1] These links in her mother's ancestry, along with others outlined below, were not only a source of pride for her mother, but also a significant spur for Jane's interest in such matters, elements of which infuse her novels.

As outlined later, there were specific connections between the Dashwood family and both Jane's Leigh and Austen relatives, as well-evidenced by this and other literature. Naturally, therefore, Jane appears to have had a fascination with the Dashwoods' history, not least their high-profile and often infamous activities, which extended into and through her lifetime. As the chapter title implies, there were also several common factors in the histories of the Leigh and Dashwood families. To what extent the details were apparent to Jane is unclear, but there is certainly evidence - some explored later - that she exploited several background elements from their respective histories, and incorporated them, only thinly disguised in some cases, into her novels. Selected elements from the stories of the two families are therefore outlined, including the way in which they influenced Jane, as well as their links to India and the Cotswolds.

The Leighs

On 26th April 1764, Cassandra Leigh married Reverend George Austen, and on 16th December 1775 their seventh child, Jane Austen, was born at the Steventon Rectory in Hampshire, where George Austen held the living.

The Leighs were descended from Sir Thomas Leigh (c.1498-1571), who in turn was a great-great grandson of Sir Piers Leigh, wounded at the Battle of Agincourt in 1415. Thomas's half-brother William had been Gentleman Usher of the Chamber to Henry VIII. Sir Thomas was Jane Austen's five times great-grandfather. A successful career in the City of London led to Thomas becoming a freeman of the Mercers' Company, which specialised in importing and trading luxury fabrics including silks and velvets[2]. Having been made Lord Mayor of London in 1558, the year of Elizabeth I's accession to the throne, he was one of those chosen to escort her to St Paul's for her coronation and was knighted by her. He had links with Stoneleigh Abbey in Warwickshire, its history having specific connections which appear to have made their way into Jane Austen's novels. Following the Dissolution of the Monasteries, Henry VIII had gifted the abbey to his lifelong loyal friend Charles Brandon, Duke of Suffolk, the name immediately standing out as that chosen by Austen for the steadfast and loyal character, Colonel Brandon, in *Sense and Sensibility*. Subsequently, the abbey was bought in 1561 by Sir Rowland Hill who, like Sir Thomas Leigh, was an eminent city Mercer. On Sir Rowland Hill's death, it passed to his niece and heiress Alice Leigh (née Barker)who had married Sir Thomas Leigh in about 1536.

As well as arguably providing Jane with the name Brandon, the abbey itself also made a great impression on her. Still in the Leigh family through to the nineteenth-century, Jane and her mother travelled there in 1806 from Adlestrop during one of their Cotswold visits, shortly after the death of the last direct descendant of the Stoneleigh Abbey branch of the family. They accompanied Revd. Thomas Leigh, of Adlestrop, who was keen to make an early personal appearance at the abbey to enhance and promote his inheritance claims. Jane's family were optimistic of an indirect benefit from this inheritance, should he succeed, but also welcomed the opportunity to visit the magnificent building. Its grandeur had a profound effect on them, and for Jane it was possibly the inspiration and model for Pemberley in *Pride and Prejudice*, as well as its chapel matching very closely the one described by her in *Mansfield Park*.

Returning to the mid 16th century, Sir Thomas Leigh had purchased property at Longborough in Gloucestershire, and in 1553 also purchased the nearby manor of Adlestrop from the crown for the sum of £1,429[3]. Both are in the North Cotswolds, and within a few miles of these two villages are other settlements with important Austen links, developed in later chapters. Adlestrop Park and Adlestrop Rectory were both occupied by Jane's Leigh relatives when she visited and stayed at the rectory.

Adlestrop Park, early C19 print

Adlestrop Rectory

In the Adlestrop branch of the Leigh family, Cassandra's grandfather married Mary Brydges, a sister of the first Duke of Chandos, patron of the composer Handel. The Chandos marriage also provided the name Cassandra, chosen for both Jane's mother and sister, the second duchess's maiden name having been Cassandra Willoughby.

The name Willoughby is notably chosen by Austen as Colonel Brandon's rival for Marianne Dashwood's affections in *Sense and Sensibility*. Brandon and Willoughby are examples of frequent connections between the names Jane Austen assigns to characters in her novels and actual family names in her own heritage and experience, in this case from her Leigh ancestry. Perhaps also significantly, there is a further historic Brandon-Willoughby resonance, through the high profile 16th century marriage of the mature Charles Brandon to the much younger Catherine Willoughby. The associations of youth with the name Willoughby, and maturity with the name Brandon, strike a chord with the contrast between the youthful John Willoughby and the mature Colonel Brandon in *Sense and Sensibility*. These may just be coincidences, but it seems unlikely that Austen's choices of these two names, and character matches, emerged purely from her own imagination. They are further explored in the next chapter.

As well as being a possible source of material and names for her novels, the Leigh family connections provided Jane Austen with access to, and insights into, levels of society which would have been beyond the experience of most rural clergymen's daughters of the period. The tantalising prospect of some of this wealth and status becoming more closely attached to Jane's immediate family appears to have been a frequent topic of family interest and conversation, particularly on the death of the Leigh owner of Stoneleigh Abbey in 1806. Ultimately, however, this wealth and status passed entirely to a different branch of the Leigh family tree. Nevertheless, the historic narratives were a very real influence on Jane's self-perception and they find their way into her novels in a variety of forms, as noted by numerous commentators. Another example linked to the Adlestrop Leighs is Austen's use of the name Wentworth; as Victoria Huxley notes, *'the largest memorial tablet in Adlestrop Church is to Elizabeth*

Wentworth and recognises her benevolence to the Adlestrop Leighs'[4]. She had secretly married a lowly Lieutenant Wentworth in 1720, and '*the Wentworth's long loyalty to each other, despite family disapproval, remind Jane Austen's readers of Anne Elliott and her Captain Wentworth*'[5], two central characters in *Persuasion*. Another connection is that the Manor of Bourton-on-the-Hill, nearby, had been held by the first Lord Wentworth, and passed to his son, the second Lord Wentworth, in the sixteenth century. And in a link to the Dashwood family, in 1746 the second Baronet of West Wycombe, Sir Francis Dashwood, had '*purchased 43 lead statues with their stone pedestals, together with urns, flowerpots and garden rollers, from Lady Wentworth's sale at nearby Bradenham*'.[6]

The Leighs of Adlestrop, in the Cotswolds, while central to this book, represent just one strand of Jane Austen's extraordinary network of connections, which were important and influential in providing experiences she was able to exploit and adapt in her novels. Jane Austen's family was reasonably well travelled in England and Wales, and places she visited provided her with much of the social and spatial context employed for the settings in her novels, not least in physical exposure to the daily regimes and routines of the upper and middle classes in their habitual or fashionable environments. For example, despite her family's time at Bath not being Jane's happiest or most productive, the knowledge she acquired of the town and its structured social rituals enabled her to use it with confidence as a key setting for two of her novels. At the higher end of the social scale, her stays at her brother Edward's house and estate at Godmersham, and the visit to Stoneleigh Abbey, also provided invaluable context and insights.

The focus of her observations on those at her own social level, and aspirational levels above, is reflected in the central theme of at least two of her novels, featuring respectable and cultured, but far from wealthy, female characters aspiring to, and achieving, matches with partners from a higher social milieu. These fictional elisions, so skilfully portrayed in her books, between what were quite distinct strata of society, is arguably a reflection of Jane Austen's own experience as part of an immediate family of relatively modest means, but with family connections to higher social circles, and to which she had ready access. However, in reality bridging that gap was challenging and, as Claire Tomalin notes in her biography, social awkwardness was one of Austen's recurring themes, in some degree mirroring Jane's own discomfort in unfamiliar social situations. The words that Jane puts into the mouth of the shy, but perfectly respectable, Edward Ferrars in *Sense and Sensibility* have some resonance in this regard: *'I never wish to offend, but I am so foolishly shy, that I often seem negligent, when I am only kept back by my natural awkwardness. I have frequently thought that I must have been intendeded by nature to be fond of low company, I am so little at my ease among strangers of gentility!'*[7]

That Jane's cleverness, indeed genius, was not matched by her refinement, at least by the standards and conventions of the day, is a perception of some who knew her, notably cousin Phila Walter[8]. Tomalin also records her nephew James-Edward's comments that, *'she and her sister were generally thought to have taken to the garb of middle age earlier than their years or their looks required; and .... were scarcely sufficiently regardful of the fashionable, or the becoming. ..... After a ball at Lord Portsmouth's, Jane wrote, 'My hair was at least tidy, which was all my ambition' '*[9]. This apparent laissez-faire personal attitude to clothes and fashion tallies with the perceptive observations Austen makes in *Northanger Abbey* that *'it would be mortifying to the feelings of many ladies, could they be made to understand how little the heart of a man is affected by what is costly or new in their attire; how little it is biased by the texture of their muslin, and how unsusceptible of peculiar tenderness towards the spotted, the sprigged, the mull or the jackonet'*[10]. Overall, there is a sense that she was socially awkward outside a close family context and made some of those she met uncomfortable in her company. Tomalin comments that one *'unfriendly witness,*

Mary Mitford, ... likened her to a poker, perpendicular, precise and taciturn'[11]. She could be unpredictable, and therefore not easily pigeon-holed in such a highly structured society with its somewhat formulaic expected patterns of behaviour.

Her novels test these typically unwritten but well-understood society rules and etiquettes. While Jane herself often chose not to follow these conventions in the conduct of her own life, neither did she seek seriously or openly to confront convention in any concerted way. Instead, she relied on her critical powers of observation and perception of human behaviours in her novels to play out the consequences of those behaviours in their challenges to the constraints of contemporary social values and expectations. *Sense and Sensibility* is a good example of this, and the fictional Dashwood sisters' contrasting emotional persona and behaviours provide the pivotal dynamic, and indeed title, of the novel.

Jane's choice of the family name Dashwood in *Sense and Sensibility* invites exploration of the real, and high profile, Dashwoods, and her interest in them. As well as her various Dashwood connections via family and friends, explored later, the fact that the Dashwood Baronetcy of West Wycombe, created in 1707, was premier among the Baronetages of Great Britain, would no doubt have had great appeal given her interest in such matters. This interest would only have been enhanced by the fact that in 1738 Rachel Dashwood, the sister of the 2nd Baronet of West Wycombe had married Sir Robert Austen of Kent, one of Jane's distant relatives. There is also a letter[12] in the Dashwood Family Papers (referenced as 'Mr Austen's letter') from Milgate, near Maidstone, Kent, dated June 4th 1747 to Sir Francis Dashwood, 2nd Baronet of West Wycombe. The letter refers to the settlement of family affairs and management of an estate in which both parties appear to have had an interest and expresses *'hope that you & Lady Austen* [Sir Robert Austen's wife and sister of Sir Francis Dashwood] *will see the*

Joynture kept regularly payd.' It is evident that in the mid-18th century, just a few decades before Jane Austen's lifetime, there were close relationships, including intermarriage, between Austen family members based in Kent and the Dashwoods of West Wycombe.

The Dashwoods

As the chapter title suggests, the history of the Dashwoods has some parallels with that of the Leighs. The Dashwoods also provided a Lord Mayor of London and were similarly involved in the silk trade as one of their routes to wealth, resulting for both families in establishment of country houses and estates. The Dashwoods had originated in Dorset, and two of the family, Edmund (1588-1643) and Edward (who died c.1666/7) became Mayors of Dorchester, therefore being real, but much earlier, versions of Thomas Hardy's central character, Michael Henchard, in *The Mayor of Casterbridge*, Hardy's fictional name for Dorchester. Thomas Hardy, like Jane Austen, appears to have drawn some of his fictional names from historical reality, the name Henchard, for example, almost certainly having been derived by Hardy from an amalgam of the names Henning and Trenchard, two leading seventeenth century Dorchester families. As it happens, it was a Henning family member, Thomasine, who married Edmund Dashwood (1588-1643), Mayor of Dorchester in 1632.

By contrast with the fictional Michael Henchard's disastrous dealings in corn in Hardy's novel, the Dashwoods dealt profitably in sheep and wool, and had strong early colonial ties as merchants, recorded for example as having funded adventures to trade in Newfoundland and Virginia in the 1620s[13]. Some of their early 17th century trading out of Weymouth is evidenced in the following historical research extract:

Cargoes going through Weymouth: Francis Dashwood 11 Jan 1633 ship 'James' 11/- duty paid; 17th Jan 1633 ship 'Francis' 3s duty paid; 19th Feb 1633 ship 'Sarath' [Sarah?] 6s duty paid; Thomas Dashwood 8 Oct 1637 ship 'Nonsuch' & 18 Nov 1637 ship 'Francis' paid £6 duty; Edmund Dashwood 7 Oct 1637 ship 'Little John' £1.4s duty paid.[14]

The Dashwoods appear to have reused family names for their ships over the generations, with an entry in a later Sir Francis's account book for 1703 for example noting *'Ship Sarah & Cargoe Voyage to India'*.[15]

Having prospered as sheep and wool farmers, several of the family expanded their fortunes in the City of London. Francis Dashwood, having become an Alderman of the City of London in 1658, accompanied King Charles II a few years later, on horseback through the City, *'and was required to be "apparelled with velvet coat and gold chain"*.[16] After establishing themselves as prominent members of some of the great City livery companies, it is through their commercial and mercantile interests that the first oriental connections emerge, and in 1669 Francis Dashwood was part-owner of a 338-ton ship, the *Morning Star*, involved in the silk trade with Turkey, the silk being sold through the East India Company.

Francis and his two sons, Samuel and Francis, grew the business so rapidly that by 1678 they were the leading silk importers in the City of London, responsible for *'about one third of total silk sales made through the East India Company that year'*.[17] Samuel and his brother Francis were to become prominent members of the Company. Indeed, Samuel Dashwood, who was knighted in 1684, became its Vice-Governor in 1700, and in 1702 became Lord Mayor of London. As well as entertaining Queen Anne at the Guildhall, he staged a pageant which is recorded in the Court Minutes of the East India Company. The first float in the Mayor's procession was

'an Indian galleon crowded by Bacchanals wreathed with vines. On the deck of the grape-hung vessel sat

Bacchus himself, "properly drest". The second float was the chariot of Ariadne drawn by panthers. Then came St Martin, as a bishop in a temple, and next followed "the Vintage", an eight-arched structure with termini of satyrs and ornamented with vines. Within was a bar, with a beautiful person keeping it, with drawers {waiters} *and gentlemen sitting drinking round a tavern table. On seeing the Lord Mayor* {Samuel Dashwood} *the bar-keeper called to the drawers:*

> *Where are your eyes and ears?*
> *See there what honourable gent appears!*
> *Augusta's great Praetorian lord – but hold!*
> *Give me a goblet of true Oriental mould.'* [18]

Of specific interest in this description is the mix of references: to India and the Orient, to the Classical and mythological world, to religion, and to drinking and general bacchanalian activity. These elements are the very ones which characterise the later eighteenth century notoriety of Samuel Dashwood's nephew Francis Dashwood in relation to the Hell-Fire Club at West Wycombe, namely a propensity for enjoyment and celebration of a wide range of pleasures, not only those derived from aesthetic and intellectual interests, but those of the flesh as well.

At the same period, a more serious form of pageantry was being rolled out in India as a means of impressing a very different audience. Given the sub-continent's influence on most of our key characters, some early Indian context may be helpful at this point. The East India Company figurehead at the turn of the eighteenth century was Sir William Norris, Ambassador to India for William III initially, and then briefly, from 8th March 1702, for Queen Anne. In 1699, Norris had been sent to India on an ambassadorial mission, and in pursuing political and trading concessions, was attempting to assert his own authority as well as that of the Company. One of his geographical targets in India was the town of Panalla. Willson records that, *'after six weeks at Surat, Norris set forth gloriously for Panalla, many hundred miles away. In his train were sixty Europeans and 300 natives, the latter bearing costly presents ... It is needless to describe the slow and painful course along the vile roads of this egregious embassy. Norris would on no occasion abate anything of his ambassadorial pomp and dignity; he refused an audience with the Imperial Grand Vizier, whom he met on the way, because he was not permitted to approach with beating drums and sounding trumpets. Norris found Aurangzeb and his army drawn up before the Mahratta stronghold of Panalla. The order of the procession, on 28th April 1701, deserves to be given as an example of English Ambassadorial state in India in the hundredth year of the East India Company's existence. It was as follows :-*

Mr. Cristor, Commander of his Excellency's artillery on horseback.

Twelve carts, wherein were carried the twelve brass guns for presents.

Five hackeries, with the cloth etc. for presents.

One hundred cohurs and messures, carrying the glassware and looking-glasses, for presents.

Two fine Arabian horses, richly caparisoned, for presents.

Two ditto without caparisons, for presents.

Four English soldiers, on horseback, guarding the presents.

The Union flag.

The Red White and Blue flags.

Seven state horses, richly caparisoned, two with English furniture and five with Indian.

The King's and his Excellency's crests.

One state palanquin, with English furniture, of silver tissue brocaded.

Two other crests.

The music, with rich liveries on horseback.

Mr. Basset, Lieutenant of his Excellency's Foot-guards on horseback.

Ten servants, in rich liveries on horseback.

The King's and my Lord's Arms.

One kettledrum in livery on horseback.

Three trumpets in liveries on horseback.

Captain Symons, Commander of his Excellency's guard.

Twelve troopers every way armed and accoutred after the English mode.

Mr. Beverley, Lieutenant of his Excellency's Horseguards.

The King's and my Lord's Arms richly gilt and very large; the first being borne by sixteen men.

Mr. John Mill and Mr. Whittaker on horseback, in rich lace coats.

Mr. Hale, Master of the Horse, richly drest, carrying the Sword of State, pointed up.

His Excellency in a rich palanquin, Indian embroidered furniture.

Four pages, two on each side of his Excellency's palanquin richly drest.

Edward Norris Esq., Secretary to the Embassy, in a rich palanquin, carrying His Majesty's letter to the

Emperor, on each side, Mr. Wingate and Mr. Shettleworth, in rich laced coats on horseback.

Mr. Harlewyn, Treasurer, wearing a gold key, and Mr. Adiel Mill, Secretary to his Excellency, in a coach.'[19]

The original "Old East India Company" was being challenged by the "New Company", and the display described above was symptomatic of attempts to establish and evidence the New Company's presence and ambitions. The two eventually merged as the United East India Company in 1708. Sir Francis Dashwood's account books have entries for both the Old and United Companies.[20] Making an impression on the sub-continent was part and parcel of the dynamics of gaining political and trading agreements, ideally through negotiation and gifts but ultimately, if necessary, through force. In this case, Norris's grand gesture - more visually imposing than having any persuasive military significance - failed to impress, and when political and trade negotiations stalled, '*Aurangzeb told the haughty Norris he had an alternative: he "knew the same way back to England that he came". ... Sadly, Norris died on his voyage back to England later in 1702. The embassy had been a miserable failure, partly owing to Sir William Norris's temper and ignorance of the Oriental character, partly through his repudiation of advice, and partly also to the inherent difficulties of the mission*'.[21]

This contrasts markedly with the more successful subtle approach employed later in the eighteenth century by Warren Hastings as British India's first Governor General, notwithstanding criticisms at his famous impeachment trial. Charges against Hastings included accusations that he was far too close to Indian culture in its widest sense, including inducements bordering on direct bribery. As outlined later, Hastings' story is intimately bound up with that of Jane Austen's family.

Having taken a short diversion to provide some background to the early British involvement in India, with its fluid and volatile political and trading context, the specific Dashwood family story is now resumed. Evidence of the Dashwoods' direct trade with India is recorded when Sir Samuel made his first purchase of Bengal raw silk in 1685 and in 1700 their 375-ton frigate, the *Dashwood*, was despatched to the East Indies with £40,000 of gold bullion and goods[22]. In the Dashwood Family Papers in the Bodleian Library is a letter dated 22nd November 1700 from Marmaduke Rawdon, the Commander of the *Dashwood*, outlining Francis Dashwood's personal stake in this particular voyage:-

> *'Received of Sir Francis Dashwood the Sume of One hundred pds being his proportion of Sixteen hundred pounds Stock in the ship Dashwood Now bound for the East Indies and whereof I am Commander, and for which Said Sume of One hundred pounds and the produce & Increase thereof I promise to be accountable unto him the said Francis Dashwood his Executors Or Assigns, Losses, Bad Debts & pennalty of the Seas Excepted.'*[23]

The *Dashwood* is also referenced by Beckles Willson[74] and was still operating in 1703 when it made another voyage to India, referenced in a 'cash booke & Ledger' kept by Sir Francis.[25] It appears, not unnaturally, that ships plying their trade between England and the East Indies were often named after key traders, politicians or administrators. For example, one was named *Norris*, in honour of the ambassador whose vainglorious exploits were briefly outlined above. A steady supply of new names was required because of the very short life-expectancy of these ships, frequently encountering treacherous seas on their journeys nearly half way across the globe, and forced to round the Cape of Good Hope, long before the days of the Suez Canal short-cut. The voyages were dangerous, but the potential wealth they generated outweighed the risks, as the Dashwoods were well-aware.

As their wealth grew through commercial trading, it appears from a letter sent by Samuel to his brother Francis, dated 5th July 1690, that there was some friction between them regarding who had contributed more to the family business, with direct reference to the constraints of their different domestic circumstances. For example, Samuel comments on *'the Differences between your family & circumstances & mine & ye great charge I have to ... maintaine soe many children'*. He also gently criticises his brother for taking *'Sole management'* of parts of the business, as well as *'treating customers with Sack and Clarrett'*.[26]

The subsequent winding up of Francis and Samuel's joint commercial trading interests is alluded to in an undated memorandum[27] in the Dashwood Family Papers, with the brothers taking equal half shares:-

Its hereby declared and agreed by and between Sir Samuel Dashwood and Sir Francis Dashwood both of London, Knights, That the debts due and oweing by the Persons hereunder mentioned and all or any the Returns or Effects that shall be made and sent home to England for the same And alsoe all the Bales of Silk in Warehouses hereunder mentioned; do belong to and are for the Account of us the said Sir Samuel Dashwood and Sir Francis Dashwood Our heirs Executors and Assigns jointly, and in Equall halves.

As well as reference to the East India House in London, the list of *'Persons hereunder mentioned'* in this Dashwood memorandum includes one significant entry, namely *'Thomas Leigh and Company Merchants in Smirna'*, evidencing a direct commercial link between the Dashwood and Leigh families. As set out later, other commercial connections between the Dashwoods and certain friends of Jane Austen's family, again involving imports of goods from abroad, continued throughout the 18th century with specific links to the West Wycombe estate which was to become the main Dashwood family home.

The purchase of West Wycombe by the Dashwood brothers was executed in parallel with the winding up of their joint commercial ventures. As one of the later Dashwood baronets comments,

> *'With their mounting wealth, the Dashwood brothers now began to turn their attention to acquiring land and building grand country houses set in parks which they proceeded to lay out and embellish. So it was that in 1698 Sir Samuel and Francis bought West Wycombe in Buckinghamshire. .... Francis duly bought out his brother's share for £15,000 and proceeded to change the face of his new estate. He pulled down the [Earl of Carnavon's] Elizabethan house which stood near the village and built one of red brick half-way up the hill – the nucleus of the present house.'* [28]

It is evidenced in Sir Francis's account book for the years 1707 to 1710 that immediately after securing the West Wycombe estate for himself and rebuilding the mansion, he proceeded to purchase adjoining and nearby farms, woodland and other lands within the wider '*Mannour of Westwiccomb & Stoken Church in the County of Buckinghamshire*'. [29] This Dashwood acquisition of neighbouring property mirrors the fictional Dashwoods' activities in Jane Austen's *Sense and Sensibility* and is revisited later.

Created first baronet of West Wycombe in June 1707 in recognition of his known loyalty and affection for Queen Anne and her government, Sir Francis Dashwood died in 1724 and was succeeded by his son Francis, who would become by far the most famous, or perhaps more accurately infamous, of the Dashwood lineage. It is this Francis Dashwood, the second baronet, together with Sir John Dashwood-King, the fourth baronet, who feature prominently in later chapters. The name King was appended to Dashwood as a partial concession to a condition of the 1736/7 Will of Dr John King, Master of the Charterhouse, a wealthy relative of the Dashwoods, which stipulated that '*All persons benefited by my Will to change their name to King*'.[30] The possessions included in his Will reflect the 18th century fashion for oriental influences, as evidenced in '*An Inventory of the late Dr King's Household Goods, Linnen, Watches, Wearing Apparrell &c Taken at Charter House March 3 & 5 1738/9*'. Among the possessions itemised are the following - '*Japan Cloath Chest Ornamental*', '*Japan writing stand*', '*Japan cabinet*', '*Large Indian Japan cabinet*', '*Blue and White China Tea Pot*', '*Blue and White China Jars*', and '*2 Indian Handkerchiefs*'.[31] These oriental interests were not at all unique to the Dashwood-King family, but did have particular relevance to them because of their active involvement in trading with the East. Following on from the earlier engagement of the Dashwoods with the East India Company in the late 17th and early 18th centuries, continuing involvement of the Dashwood family in India is evidenced in a painting by Zoffany during Jane's lifetime which is discussed towards the end of Chapter 10.

Although there are many similarities between the Leigh and Dashwood family histories, there are also differences, certainly during the 18th and early 19th centuries. The Leigh family included many clerics and academics while, in stark contrast, the Dashwoods' most well-known 'religious' connotation was their lead role in the formation of the self-styled Order of the Monks of Medmenham, more commonly, and notoriously, known as the Hell-Fire Club. And while Francis Dashwood, the second baronet, was well-educated and culturally sophisticated, this was not the case with many other Dashwood family members. The Dashwoods' interests during Jane's life, at least on the male side, were more focused on politics and country pursuits, common enough for families of similar status. While Jane's immediate family background gave her specific insights into the clergy and the religious debates of the day, she was, partly through living much of her life in a rural Hampshire environment, at least aware of these other, largely male, common interests. Irene Collins notes that, '*In Sense and Sensibility Jane Austen complained that women's talk was habitually more boring than men's. Gentlemen, she thought, could always add a little variety to the constant repetition of local gossip by talking about "politics, inclosing land, and breaking horses".*'[32]

Jane Austen would have been aware of several links between her own family and the Dashwoods, including knowledge of their estate at West Wycombe, and Janine Barchas explores these in some detail, both in her journal article *Hell-Fire Jane* and her book *Matters of Fact in Jane Austen*. A summary of these and other possible connections is considered in more detail later, as are other activities of the Dashwoods, both at West Wycombe and at Bourton-on-the-Hill in the Cotswolds, including their relevance to Jane Austen's *Sense and Sensibility*.

The next chapter considers the extent to which Jane Austen transposed real life knowledge and experiences into her fictional writing. After that, subsequent chapters sketch out the contemporary Regency context, including Indian and Cotswold influences, and notably the 'picturesque' aesthetic reflected at various points in *Sense and Sensibility* and other Austen novels.

CHAPTER THREE
Fact into Fiction

The following two extracts, the first factual and the second fictional (taken from Austen's *Mansfield Park*), are linked by their references to the landscape gardener Humphry Repton. As well as serving as an initial example of Jane's incorporation of fact into her fiction, they also conveniently provide a direct link with the Dashwood family introduced in the previous chapter.

The first extract is from a letter dated October 28th 1799, from Humphry Repton to Sir John Dashwood-King, 4th Baronet of West Wycombe, requesting payment for landscape design works in 1796, 1798 & 1799.

'Sir, As I suppose I shall not have the pleasure of meeting you again at West Wycombe for some time, tho' it is an event to which I look forward at a future period, I hope you will allow me to trouble you with a memorandum .....

Your much obliged & obedient Humble Servant,

    H Repton

1796 - Jan.y 31 part of a day & expenses --- £5: 5: 0

1798 - Jan.y 21 & 22 Two days ------- 10: 10: 0

1799 - June 17th Visit expenses ---------------- 10: 10: 0'[1]

The second extract is from *Mansfield Park* :-

> '... "but depend upon it, Sotherton will have *every* improvement in time which his heart can desire."
> "I must try to do something with it," said Mr Rushworth, "but I do not know what. I hope I shall have some good friend to help me."
> "Your best friend upon such an occasion," said Miss Bertram, calmly, "would be Mr Repton, I imagine."
> "That is what I was thinking of. As he has done so well by Smith, I think I had better have him at once. His terms are five guineas a day."
> "Well, and if they were *ten*," cried Mrs Norris, I am sure *you* need not regard it ..... Such a place as Sotherton Court deserves everything that taste and money can do."'[2]

Before commenting further on the direct Repton link between the two extracts, key words to pick out from the *Mansfield Park* text above are 'improvement' and 'taste', which pepper Austen's novels, 'taste' for example being used three times in a single sentence in *Emma*[3]. Austen often uses these specific two words, which resonate with Regency cultural fashion, in a satirical or mocking manner. By referencing him explicitly in *Mansfield Park*, the highly fashionable and self-styled 'landscape gardener' Humphry Repton is made part of her satirical commentary on the pursuit of 'improvement'.

What is striking from the two extracts above is the exact match between the daily rates Repton actually charged Sir John Dashwood-King, and the fictional 'five guineas a day' Austen quotes in *Mansfield Park*. Although his fees appear to have been standard across most, if not all, of the properties he was consulted on, and were probably neither secret nor commercially sensitive, it is unlikely that Jane Austen would have accidentally come across this information without some personal interest. This was almost certainly provided by Repton's work at her relatives' homes at Adlestrop which enabled Jane Austen to see his impact at first hand. As well

Fact into Fiction

as other Leigh family commissions nearby, Repton was also involved in the ground-breaking Indian architectural and garden remodelling at Sezincote in the same Cotswold neighbourhood. It seems likely therefore that she would have gained insights into his work and his daily rates through knowledge of these Cotswolds commissions. It is therefore no surprise that she made direct reference to 'Mr Repton' in *Mansfield Park*. It is also possible that she acquired inside knowledge in connection with the Dashwoods of West Wycombe Park, who had, as evidenced above, also employed Repton. Either way, it is a perfect example of Austen's propensity for turning fact into fiction, hinting also at her obsessions with authenticity, topicality, and accuracy of observation. Indeed, Austen's work often draws inspiration directly from her personal observations and experiences, as well as exposure to literary sources, thereby providing a sound contemporary context and foundation on which she could so successfully overlay her invention and imagination.

In tracing the influences of India and the Cotswolds on Jane Austen and her writing, it seems clear that these personal experiences, observations, and her network of family, family friends, and their near neighbours in the North Cotswolds, are pivotal not only in the choice of names within her novels but also in their underlying narrative themes and, arguably, their moral messages. The name Dashwood and its use in Austen's novel *Sense and Sensibility* is the springboard for much of what follows. The landscape architect Humphry Repton is further linked with the Dashwoods and the Cotswolds as evidenced by the entry '*£43·1s:0d paid to H Repton Esq.*' in Sir John Dashwood-King's personal account book for 11th December 1795, while at his hunting lodge in Bourton-on-the-Hill.[4]

The Indian and Cotswolds contributions to the overall themes being pursued here are intrinsically connected with Warren Hastings, the first Governor General in British India. On his return from the sub-continent, Hastings employed Samuel Pepys Cockerell, later architect to the East India Company, for alterations, including Indian motifs, at

Daylesford, his Cotswold estate, with close relatives of Austen entrenched at the neighbouring village of Adlestrop less than a mile away. As outlined later, the family connections and intimacy went far deeper than this geographical proximity.

Jane visited her Adlestrop relatives in 1794, when she was just 18, and around this time was in the process of drafting *Elinor and Marianne* (an early version of *Sense and Sensibility*). She visited Adlestrop several times and, *'throughout her life, kept in constant touch with events there by letter'*.[5] Given the Dashwood, Leigh, Austen, and Repton connections already outlined in this North Cotswold community, a tight network of high-profile individuals is revealed, including Samuel Pepys Cockerell's family who, at this time, purchased nearby Sezincote, lying between Bourton-on-the-Hill and Longborough, the latter settlement, as we have seen, also having strong ties to Jane's Leigh family history.

Austen drew on such factual connections and contexts in constructing her fiction, and her choice of the Dashwood name is the focus of an article entitled *Hell-Fire Jane*, published in 2009 by the American academic Professor Janine Barchas, which positions the Dashwood origins of the infamous 18th century 'Hell-Fire Club' as central to a proper understanding of *Sense and Sensibility*. This 2009 article forms the basis of chapter 5 of her subsequent book, *Matters of Fact in Jane Austen* (2012), which explores and develops other connections between names chosen by Austen in her novels and their equivalent real-life individuals, with emphasis on their personalities and contemporary associations. Barchas explains how these may have influenced the way in which Austen's readers would have responded to such allusions. In her use of topical names and associations, Austen was obviously constrained by the extent to which knowledge of them was accessible to her, both specifically, via relatives and friends, and more generally from formal literature and more informal contemporary media, such as journals, newspapers and cartoons. For this reason, Barchas focuses much of her research effort on establishing which literary and other sources were available to Austen, for example by establishing which books were held in her relatives' libraries, and which journals they were likely to have subscribed to. She remarks that among these sources Austen had access to Collins' books covering the peerage, including *The Peerage of England*, asserting that she had something of an obsession with genealogy and prominent lineages. It is suggested that this explains Austen's use in her novels of so many family names associated with the aristocracy and high-status gentry. Barchas succinctly concludes that, '*Mixing fact into her fiction, Austen appeals to history for authority*.'[6]

Austen's choices of fictional names are, beyond reasonable doubt, often far from accidental, and there are numerous examples of her fictional names having associations with real figures and place names, often with seemingly deliberate contemporary connotations. With reference back to the quote at the head of this chapter, relating to the Dashwoods of West Wycombe, Austen, as well as choosing the name Dashwood for the central family in *Sense and Sensibility*, also picked the name Wickham (a homophone for Wycombe) as the anti-hero in *Pride and Prejudice*. The Dashwood and West Wycombe links between fact and fiction, and their significance in *Sense and Sensibility*, lead to a focus on other names in *Sense and Sensibility* as examples of how Austen 'appeals to history for authority'. The first two names, already touched on, are those of the rivals for Marianne Dashwood's affections, Willoughby and Brandon.

The name Willoughby is intriguing, and its choice arises from several possible sources. Given the strong and compelling evidence (see Chapter 10) that Austen tapped into the family history, circumstances, and notoriety of the Dashwoods of West Wycombe, it may be more than coincidence that these Dashwoods also had an estate in Willoughby, Lincolnshire. Also, among the Dashwood Family Papers is a brief letter[7] catalogued as concerning the enclosure of Dunston Heath in Lincolnshire and being from a

Lord Middleton to Francis Dashwood, 2nd Baronet of West Wycombe :-

> Sir
> *If you had intimated to my kynsman Charly Willoughby (who was with me last week) your small request, it should without the trouble of an epistle have had as if by now the immediate concurrence of*
>
> WolEaton Sir – Yr very obedient
> Jan: ye 14th & most humble servant
> 1749 Middleton

Although possibly just coincidental, this letter is from a Middleton to a Dashwood, with Willoughby referenced as a kinsman, these being the trio of names chosen by Jane Austen for three central characters in *Sense and Sensibility*. What we do know is that the names Dashwood and Willoughby had been used in combination by Jane Austen in about 1791/2, much earlier than their appearance in *Sense and Sensibility*. She had used them in the second of *A Collection of Letters*, dedicated to Miss Cooper, a childhood friend, sometime before Miss Cooper's marriage to Thomas Williams on 11 December 1792. In this fictitious and satirical letter, described as being *From a Young lady crossed in Love to her freind*[8], the writer, Sophia, bemoans the loss of her latest love, namely Willoughby, and questions why she has been more disappointed than with previous losses. *"Can it be that I have a greater affection for Willoughby than I had for his amiable predecessors?"* she asks, listing some of the many others. To distract her from her loss, her friends arrange for various visitors at Christmas, most notably the Dashwoods, Lady Bridget Dashwood and her sister-in-law Miss Jane Dashwood. Bridget is afforded dull connotations, and Jane bright and positive ones. Use of names appears again to be very deliberate. In another early work, an over-the-top parody of exaggerated aesthetics and sensibilities, Jane Austen makes a derogatory point about the name Bridget

Fact into Fiction

when her protagonist refers to a young lady who '*was just Seventeen – One of the best of ages; but alas! she was very plain & her name was Bridget ...... Nothing therefore could be expected from her.*'[9]

Sophia, the writer of the fictitious letter created by the young Jane Austen, talking of 'sweet' Jane Dashwood, says, '*Although I have been acquainted with this charming Woman above fifteen years, Yet I never before observed how lovely she is. She is now about 35, & in spite of sickness, Sorrow and Time is more blooming than I ever saw a Girl of 17.*'[10] Again, although perhaps only a coincidental link between fact and fiction, Jane and Cassandra Austen, who were inseparable in many ways, are perhaps partially mirrored by this fictitious pair of Bridget and Jane Dashwood, who also live together. The down to earth Bridget character very much mirrors Cassandra Austen's anchoring role in the close relationship with her sister Jane. This is a very early piece of Jane Austen literature, but it almost seems as if it may have been a template, or perhaps even a premonition, shaping Jane's outlook and future. In both these early writings she certainly seems to be aware of the age of 17 as having some special significance, perhaps as the age at which a contemporary female's potential and prospects were perceived to be at a pivotal point. She was about that age herself at the time of writing these early works and was perhaps projecting how she thought she may be at age 35.

So, in her *Collections of Letters*, the names of Dashwood and Willoughby were used by Jane Austen in combination as early as 1791/2, with Willoughby being a lost love who marries someone else, just as in the later novel *Sense and Sensibility*, into which Jane Austen transports these names.

Referencing an earlier possible source, Barchas[11] implies that Jane may have derived the name of Willoughby from the rake, Sir Clement Willoughby, in Frances Burney's *Evelina* (1778). This seems a likely typecasting link, particularly at the time of the 1791/2 fictional letter above, and in the context of Jane's admiration for Burney's writing, which is outlined further in Chapter 9.

Another possible source is Lord Willoughby, one of Jane's distant relatives, and Jane's ancestry also throws up a further possibility. As previously alluded to, the '*head of the Adlestrop branch* [of the Leighs] ... *made an extremely advantageous marriage to Mary Brydges, the sister of Lord Chandos*'.[12] The Chandos marriage introduced not only the name Cassandra – used frequently within Jane's family – but also the name Willoughby, the second duchess having been Cassandra Willoughby. Jane Austen would almost certainly have been aware of these family connections.

Yet another possibility for Jane's choice of the name Willoughby relates to her chosen name for his rival suitor in *Sense and Sensibility*, Colonel Brandon, as briefly referenced above. The juxtaposition of Willoughby (the young and romantic suitor) with Brandon (the relatively elderly and dependable competitor for Marianne Dashwood's affection) may have its origins in historical connections familiar to Austen and to her more knowledgeable readers. After the dissolution of the monasteries, Stoneleigh Abbey had been donated by Henry VIII to Charles Brandon (later 1st Duke of Suffolk), and his story is a colourful one. His father, William Brandon, had been Henry Tudor's standard bearer, cut down at Bosworth Field (1485) in Richard III's well documented, and fatal, charge. On becoming Henry VII as a result of the battle, the new king effectively adopted his standard bearer's son, Charles Brandon, bringing him into the royal household. In his book *Winter King*, Thomas Penn notes that Charles Brandon grew up in the royal household, had access to the stables, excelled at horsemanship, and by the age of seventeen jousted at the wedding of Arthur, Henry VII's eldest son, and Catherine of Arragon.[13]

Through this upbringing, Brandon became a lifelong friend of Henry VII's younger son, Henry, who acceded to the throne in 1509 as Henry VIII. Charles Brandon accompanied Henry VIII abroad, had a distinguished military career in France, and was a reliable, dependable, and stabilising figure in Henry's court, as described, for example, in Hilary Mantel's *Wolf Hall* and *Bring up the Bodies*. The gift of Stoneleigh Abbey was just one of the rewards for his loyal service to Henry. In his mature years Brandon, by now made Duke of Suffolk, 49 years old, and a powerful figure at court, married the 14-year-old Catherine Willoughby. This Brandon-Willoughby pairing, with its stark contrast in ages, quite possibly influenced Jane's choice of the names for Brandon and Willoughby, in *Sense and Sensibility*. As an aside, after Charles Brandon's death the widowed Catherine Willoughby was seriously considered as a possible 7th wife for Henry VIII, as outlined by David Baldwin in *Henry VIII's Last Love*.[14]

So, just as with the portrayal of Brandon's character in *Sense and Sensibility*, the real Brandon was a reliable figure with an honourable military career and with a more interesting personal background than his outward appearance and demeanour might indicate. The personal story Austen attaches to the fictional Colonel Brandon, and which enlivens and adds interest to his otherwise apparently bland and dour character – he is described as '*silent and grave*' when first introduced to the reader - is only gradually revealed as the novel unfolds. This slow revelation is entirely in keeping with the factual and fictional pair of Brandons with their reserved, self-effacing natures, inherent in this character type, and exactly what Austen was seemingly trying to portray. It is notable that the rather low-key, but important, foundation of the eventual relationship between Marianne Dashwood and Colonel Brandon – namely a respect on her part for his consideration (and quiet attentiveness) when she plays and sings at Barton Park is established almost as soon as Brandon appears in the novel: '*Colonel Brandon alone, of all the party, heard her without being in raptures. He paid her only the compliment of attention; and she felt a respect for him on the occasion which the others had reasonably forfeited by their shameless want of taste*'.[15] As noted earlier, Austen's use of the word 'taste' makes frequent appearances in her novels.

The above referenced Brandon-Willoughby connection is also picked up in *Jane Austen's Names* (2015) by Margaret Doody, who takes the parallels with the storyline of *Sense and Sensibility* a step further. Regarding Austen's choice of the name Brandon and having noted that Brandon was also the name of Charles I's executioner, Doody points out that Brandon married his ward, the heiress Katherine Willoughby, even though the initial intention was that she should marry his son. Doody compares this with the scenario in *Sense and Sensibility* in which Colonel Brandon's brother married his father's unfortunate ward, Eliza: '*In both cases a duty of guardianship was grievously abused.*'[16]

Colonel Brandon's character is complex, and while Austen gradually reveals more about his background, readers will form potentially very different attitudes towards him. A sympathetic reading would portray him as having endured a difficult life involving significant emotional turmoil and, having survived this and gained wisdom in the process, he provides a stabilising character in the novel, with consistent feelings towards Marianne. As a counterbalance to his rival Willoughby's more impulsive behaviour, this exemplifies Austen's use of binary, contrasting, or opposing, elements in her novels. Other readers may see Brandon in a less favourable light, with him being an unnecessarily passive victim of circumstance, and who, because of his weaknesses and dull character, will not - imaginatively projecting beyond the end of the novel - prove to be a fulfilling husband for Marianne. As one modern author and commentator puts it, '*the ending of Sense and Sensibility has always seemed discouraging. Passionate, vital, sensuous Marianne Dashwood hitched to worthy old Colonel Brandon – a resolution that makes absolute sense in terms of the steely pragmatism of Austen's take on the economics of matrimony, but which feels brutal in its refusal of romance*'.[17] Austen's attitudes to marriage, including the pragmatic aspects referred to here, and the sparse developments of post-marriage narratives in her novels, are explored in the next chapter.

Margaret Doody broadly agrees with the commentary quoted above. She believes Brandon is rather passive and constrained by his past: '*Young Brandon in the end bowed to his father's will and acquiesced in the financially motivated marital rape of Eliza by his elder brother. He gives up and goes away. He carries a sword but is not dangerous. True, he fights a duel with Willoughby, but it is inconsequential*'.[18] Doody's mention of Brandon's sword is part of her development of the theme of metals, their characteristics and use in cutting implements, which she asserts have great significance in *Sense and Sensibility*. With reference to the same novel, and in citing that the real fourth Earl Ferrers/Ferrars (1720-1760) fatally shot his steward and was hanged at Tyburn in his wedding suit, she claims that as a consequence, in Austen's choice of names, Ferrars is as shocking as Dashwood. Based on *fer* (iron), '*the iron element in Mrs. Ferrars is discernible. Little does she know that she can be worsted by* Steele – *a tempered, more enduring, and flexible form of iron*'.[19] Lucy Steele is indeed the winner in many of *Sense and Sensibility*'s 'battles' and conflicts.

Doody also points out the theme of 'cutting implements' in the novel. She cites Austen's description of Edward, distracted by explaining Lucy's marriage, taking '*up a pair of scissors ... spoiling both them and their sheath by cutting the latter to pieces*'.[20] Her other examples are Willoughby cutting off a lock of Marianne's hair, and Colonel Brandon wearing and wielding the most obvious steel weapon - a sword. Summarising, Doody notes that it is Lucy, however, who '*truly knows how to play with edged tools. Elinor gets only what Lucy does not want. Lucy, taking everything she wants from the Ferrars family, is indeed the force of unresisted Steele*'.[21]

Returning to the Dashwood connections, although the most obvious link is with *Sense and Sensibility*, if Jane Austen had something of a fixation with the family history of the

Dashwoods of West Wycombe, and delved deeply into it, does this spill over into any of her other novels? The one that immediately springs to mind is *Pride and Prejudice* because of the prominent character, Wickham. Like Willoughby in *Sense and Sensibility*, he has a weakness of character which almost ruins one of the key female heroines, although Austen doesn't quite allow it in either case. If the Dashwoods' supposedly dubious characteristics were the badge Austen was trying to pin on such characters as Willoughby and Wickham in her novels, then the name Wickham, when voiced, is an even more obvious allusion to West Wycombe and the Dashwoods, than is Willoughby. It is also potentially more than a coincidence that she gives Wickham the first name George, the name given by the fourth baronet of West Wycombe, Sir John Dashwood, to his eldest son, George (later the fifth baronet), born at Bourton-on-the-Hill in 1790. The fictional and youthful George Wickham in *Pride and Prejudice* (1813) is perhaps intended to flag to her readers an allusion to the young George (Dashwood of West) Wycombe.

And what of the name Charles Bingley, which Austen gave to one of her prominent characters in *Pride and Prejudice,* and to whom no negative characteristics attach? A figure of innocence in the novel, Bingley is untainted by any negative association with Wickham (or, by allusion, with West Wycombe and the Dashwoods). Is it just another coincidence that the 4th baronet Sir John Dashwood's mother-in-law, similarly entirely innocent of any negative Dashwood activities or traits, had the maiden name Bingley? There is also an entry in Sir John Dashwood's personal accounts of a payment in 1795 to 'Mrs Bingley's maid', this Mrs Bingley presumably also being an in-law relative.[22]

Again, there is no categorical proof of any intentional links here, and all these many perceived connections with the Dashwood family history, and particularly the names it throws up, may just be a series of coincidences. However, including those outlined later in Chapter 10, the multiplicity of these coincidences is remarkable and, on balance, having identified several new ones, I side with Janine Barchas and Margaret Doody in believing that Jane did not simply randomly make up these names. In summary, the circumstantial evidence indicates that many are a result of Austen choosing names which appealed to her from her voracious literary and genealogical interests, employing those names in her novels, where possible, as allusions to real people with specific connotations in the minds of her contemporary readership.

Jane Austen, as well as absorbing literary and 'media' information, would have learned much from direct observation and conversations at locations she visited. Her many letters demonstrate her acute interest in the activities of all those coming within her radar. This is particularly true of high-profile people, places, and events in the immediate vicinity of familiar locations. By incorporating and developing Barchas's research with specific and more detailed exploration of the Cotswold links, there is compelling evidence for Austen feeding such acquired knowledge into her writing. One example emerges from her documented stays with relatives at Adlestrop in the North Cotswolds, and this interconnects with some of the Cotswold themes in Victoria Huxley's *Jane Austen and Adlestrop* (2013), in which she notes that, '*the history of Adlestrop rectory and its grounds is uncannily like the long conversation .... in* Mansfield Park'. [23]

On the specific topic of Austen's choice and use of names to conjure up specific associations, Margaret Doody's *Jane Austen's Names* provides both corroboration of several of the linkages pursued here and a multitude of other connections, a few relevant ones being gratefully incorporated in the following chapters. A fourth female author, Paula Byrne, in her book, *The Real Jane Austen* (2013), also refers to connections between the novels and Jane's own experiences and observations.

These recent books by four female authors – Barchas (2012), Byrne (2013), Huxley (2013) and Doody (2015) – all put forward links, and often strong ones, between themes or names in the novels and Austen's own experiences, observations and reading. Claire Tomalin's excellent biography, *Jane Austen: A Life*, is a little more circumspect, asserting that, '*The truth is that Austen depended very little on fresh scenes and new acquaintances; her work was done in her head, when she began to see the possibility of a certain situation and set of characters, and her books are never transcripts of what she saw going on around her*'.[24] However, Tomalin does concede that Austen, '*used the odd particular point and incident – the amber crosses Charles* [her brother] *gave to her and Cass* [her sister] *become a topaz one given by Midshipman William Price to his sister in* Mansfield Park; *the Cobb at Lyme Regis suggests a dramatic scene;* [her brother] *Henry's experiences in the militia may have set her mind working on Wickham and his fellow officers ...*'.[25]

With regard to the crosses Tomalin mentions, there are some differences in use of terminology between amber and topaz. Tomalin uses 'amber', while Austen herself, in a letter to her sister Cassandra, dated 27th May 1801, notes that Charles, 'has been buying gold chains & Topaze Crosses for us'.[26] The terminology is used interchangeably, with Byrne, outlining this same link between fact and fiction in *The Real Jane Austen*, referring to '*a purchase of two gold chains and beautiful amber crosses, made out of topaz*'[27]. These are made the focus of her *Chapter 14 – The Topaz Crosses,* each of her book's 18 chapters highlighting factual associations and influences appearing in various guises in Austen's novels. Her *Chapter 2 - The East India Shawl*, for example, showcases what was a fashionable and highly valued item. There are literary references to such Indian shawls not only by Austen, but also by Thackeray in the opening passages of *Vanity Fair*, which are retrospectively set in this period.

Tomalin's assertion that Austen, '*did not draw from life, or write down the stories of her friends and family*'[28] is a contentious one. Although the more important point she is making, that Austen's invention is the main influence on her novels' brilliance, is undoubtedly true, I agree with Barchas,

Byrne, Doody and Huxley, that, as with nearly all novelists, Austen's output is necessarily informed at least in part by her own life experiences and observations. In this context, I later provide corroborating evidence for some of the links set out in these four authors' recent books, as well as fresh evidence of further connections.

There are several examples of Jane's own experiences being transposed into narrative elements in her novels, and which bolster the 'fact into fiction' theme of this chapter. The fictional Anne Elliot's dismay, in *Persuasion,* at having to move from her country house, Kellynch Hall, to Bath, is surely a mirror of Jane's almost exactly similar reaction to her family's move from rural Steventon to Bath. However, perhaps the most striking example of these parallels between fact and fiction involves a marriage proposal accepted and then, after much soul-searching, reversed overnight. Tomalin describes how a family friend, Harris Bigg, proposed to Jane Austen in December 1802 at his family's home, Manydown. Tomalin relates[29] that Harris proposed on the evening of 2nd December, and that Jane initially accepted his offer before dramatically changing her mind overnight. We will never know the reasons for her decision. The marriage would have provided Jane with social and financial security, but this was clearly not enough, and neither was there any great emotional match. With her free-spirited, even slightly rebellious, character Jane also probably feared the constraints that marriage would impose, particularly on her writing. Few would argue that it was a wrong decision.

In any event, her own, possibly equivocal and cornered, acceptance of a proposal of marriage one day, only to fret over it during the night, and renounce the acceptance the following morning, has some resonance with a scenario Jane employs in *Mansfield Park*, with Fanny Price and Henry Crawford substituted for herself and Harris Bigg. I suggest that Fanny is as close to an autobiographical image of herself as any in Jane's novels, and perhaps her decision to include in the novel a decisive rejection of any implied proposal acceptance, is a way of Austen dealing with the difficult associated personal feelings that may have lingered after her own such distressing experience.

Another 'fact into fiction' example is Austen's literary commandeering of the experience of her aunt Philadelphia Austen, who followed what was a far from unique marriage strategy for those with limited such prospects in England. This involved travelling to India and is therefore central to the themes in this book. Her Aunt Philadelphia's experience in feeling obliged to travel to India for what was seemingly an arranged marriage to Tysoe Hancock, a *'man she did not care for, making the basic bargain, her body and companionship for his money'*[30], was one that Jane subsequently adopted in her writing, as evidenced by the following passage from *Catharine, or The Bower*, (1792) about an orphan, Miss Wynne :-

The eldest daughter had been obliged to accept the offer of one of her cousins to equip her for the East Indies, and tho' infinitely against her inclinations had been necessitated to embrace the only possibility that was offered to her, of a Maintenance; Yet it was one, so opposite to all her ideas of Propriety , so contrary to her Wishes, so repugnant to her feelings, that she would almost have preferred Servitude to it, had choice been allowed her - . Her personal Attractions had gained her a husband as soon as she had arrived at Bengal, and she had now been married nearly a twelvemonth. Spendidly, yet unhappily married. United to a Man of double her own age, whose disposition was not amiable, and whose manners were unpleasing, though his Character was respectable. Kitty had heard twice from her friend since her marriage, but her Letters were always unsatisfactory, and though she did not openly avow her feelings, yet every line proved her to be Unhappy.

As Tomalin points out[31], Austen then uses dialogue, featuring two of the characters, Camilla and Catharine, to highlight conflicting attitudes to this practice of colonial marriages of convenience. Catharine comments, '*do you call it lucky, for a Girl of Genius to be sent in quest of a Husband to Bengal, to be married there to a Man of whose Disposition she has no opportunity of judging till her Judgement is of no use to her, who may be a Tyrant, or a Fool or both for what she knows to the Contrary. Do you call that fortunate?*' Camilla, portrayed as an unthoughtful rich girl, responds by saying, '*she is not the first Girl who has gone to the East Indies for a Husband, and I declare I should think it very good fun if I were as poor*'.

This technique of getting her literary characters to debate topical issues is one Jane Austen frequently employs, but her own attitude is often transparent, and in this instance she clearly thought such a colonial marriage far from 'fun', given the real-life example of her aunt. Few of Austen's adaptations of fact into her fiction are so direct, but Austen frequently draws from her own life experiences and those of family and friends, transposing these in variously disguised forms for her readers.

A final example of an apparent transposition of Jane's personal experience into her writing is the behaviour of Jane's brother, Edward, towards his close female family members, including Jane, her sister Cassandra, and their mother, after Jane's father had died. Despite his wealth, fortuitously acquired through his adoption by the childless Knight family, Edward displays a limited sense of responsibility in providing for his immediate female family members in their much less secure financial circumstances. This rather casual treatment of a mother and her two daughters by a male member of the same family directly mirrors the defining scene-setting passages at the beginning of *Sense and Sensibility*, which provide the novel's crucial contextual dynamics. The fictional John Dashwood has kind and generous initial intentions to provide for his half-sisters and their mother, when he has inherited substantial wealth, but these intentions evaporate and are never carried through. His fictional inheritance of considerable wealth through no merit of his own, and failure to provide even modestly for his less fortunate relatives closely mirrors what we know of Edward Austen. Her brother's dilatory behaviour in this regard may well have irked Jane and influenced her when finalising changes to the structural elements of *Sense and Sensibility*.

The narrative of a favoured son inheriting substantially, at the expense of other female family members, employed by Austen over two centuries ago, continues to resonate with at least one modern writer, Cory Taylor. She notes, with reference to her own family, '*I gathered there was no love lost between my mother and her sister-in-law. In a plot worthy of Jane Austen, Peter, as the only son, had inherited Beaconsfield outright, thus dispossessing his sisters of any claim to the place, other than a sentimental one. In this ... he was enthusiastically aided and abetted by Jan, who had taken the extra step of suggesting that my grandmother was no longer welcome in her own home*'[32]. Co-incidentally, even this last element chimes with Mrs Dashwood, Elinor and Marianne's mother, being eased out of Norland Park in *Sense and Sensibility*.

The complex and interrelated issues of marriage, wealth, status, and inheritance, together with legal constraints and moral obligations, were all relevant to, and affected, Jane's own life and family situation. As in most of Austen's novels, these issues are integral to *Sense and Sensibility*, in which the more wordly, or common sense, factors (such as wealth, inheritance, and legal constraints) are contrasted with the more romantic and spiritual factors (such as passion, morality, taste and sensibility). These contrasting realistic and idealistic contextual factors are often in a state of entangled tension in Regency England, and this is graphically exemplified and reflected in the dynamic, and often binary, structures and themes of Austen's novels. Sketching several of her favourite themes, as a way of preparing the ground for later chapters, is the aim of the next.

CHAPTER FOUR
Recurrent Themes in Austen's Novels

In sketching out context for Austen's novels, a few recurrent themes are particularly influential. These include marriage, the church, the military, country pursuits, and sibling relationships, as well as inheritance and property. Consideration of the latter mainly features country houses, but also covers aspects of their associated parks, gardens and landscapes, providing a prelude to exploration of 'the picturesque' in Chapter 5. The following thematic sketches maintain some focus on the Dashwoods and *Sense and Sensibility*, but other Austen novels are also selectively mined for material. The starting point for this exploration of contemporary context is the subject of marriage, a perennial one for Austen.

Marriage

Marriage is a central theme - often *the* central theme - in all of Jane Austen's finished novels, as well as many of her other works. Often portrayed in her novels from women's perspectives, the focus on marriage can come across as a personal obsession but was perhaps simply a reflection of contemporary social pressures and expectations as well as the opportunities which marriage afforded. These opportunities included gaining access to the increasing wealth accruing unequally to those benefiting from imperial expansion, the industrial and agricultural revolutions, and rapid growth in trade. Linked to this was an aspirational aspect, namely the enhancement of family status through strategic alliances. However, marriage strategies often simply targeted a secure personal future, and this links with two reasons why marriage was such an important aim for most women. Firstly, male domination of mainstream jobs and professions meant it was both difficult, and against social norms, for a woman to have an independent career or trade. For women to earn enough to live independently was very much the exception, and such independence was certainly not regarded as a natural life choice. Secondly, inheritance laws and customs dictated against women, the majority of inherited wealth passing through male family lines.

Despite this context, there were many who bypassed or resisted these reasons and pressures for marriage, notably Jane Austen herself. Her immediate family, although not particularly wealthy, was always able to support her, and the greater wealth of some of her wider family certainly meant that she would never face serious financial pressure to wed. Equally, despite her novels often featuring female characters securing financially and socially advantageous marriages, and although perhaps harbouring dreams of something similar for herself, there is no indication that Jane seriously attempted or sought any aspirational strategic alliances. Her writing seems to have been by far her main motivation in life rather than actively seeking either a romantic or a pragmatic attachment. Others were not so fortunately placed and marriage was a route to security, both financial and social.

For the middle and upper-classes the whole business of marriage was a structured process, with strict expected codes of behaviour and strategy. Securing a marriage was a serious matter and, for women, a time-pressured one, with female youth and attractiveness broadly perceived as lasting for a very short time between late-teens and late-twenties. However, while mutual attraction would always be a major factor, it was by no means the only one, frequently being sacrificed to the circumstances of the two parties. The manoeuvrings aimed at achieving an appropriate marriage are at the heart of most Austen storylines and *Sense and Sensibility* is no exception. Her novels frequently incorporate discussions by her characters balancing issues of age, attractiveness, personal characteristics, class and, not least, money, including very specific references to amounts of capital and income available to the potential marriage partners. Austen's own experiences and those of her wider family and friends provided her with direct, diverse, and sometimes colourful, source material. The balance between the 'observer' and 'participant' aspects of Jane's own life is addressed again later, but in respect of marriage, she is decidedly and proficiently an observer, and her novels make full use of these acute observations.

In the era and social context of Jane's novels, marriages would often be between couples living in a local neighbourhood or, if further apart geographically, between branches of loosely connected families, with marriages between cousins or distant cousins not uncommon. Our focus on the Dashwood family provides just such an example. John Dashwood, later 4th Baronet of West Wycombe, had married Mary Anne Broadhead in 1789, and in 1823 their son George Dashwood (later the 5th Baronet) married his cousin Elizabeth Broadhead. In stark contrast with this latter socially acceptable and close-knit family marriage, two other marriages of John and Mary Anne Dashwood's children, namely those of Mary (to Augustus Berkeley) and Edwin (to Emily Hare), flouted the usual protocols and, initially at least, caused considerable friction between the respective families, as outlined later.

Alongside the many marriages based on geographical proximity or family connections, less common scenarios included a very specific and speculative strategy referenced in the previous chapter. It was typically adopted by women whose conventional marriage prospects were compromised by a variety of circumstances, perhaps because of a precarious financial situation or because they had acquired some negative reputation in British society at a time when social gossip had great currency and influence. The decision they took involved braving the long and potentially perilous voyage to India, the West Indies, or other colonies, aiming to secure marriages more favourable than their reasonable expectations in Britain. Nelson, for example, is described as conveying a *'perky and plain daughter'* on one of his ships, the *Boreas, 'with the ill-concealed intention of finding a husband either on board or in the West Indies'*[1].

Whatever the marriage strategy, the goal was often improved financial security, social standing and respectability, reflecting other recurring themes in Austen's novels. Her fictional mothers, for example Mrs Bennet in *Pride and Prejudice*, are frequently portrayed as focusing on, and sometimes obsessed with, securing acceptable marriages for their daughters which would at least maintain the existing family social status, and ideally very much enhance it. Nevertheless, it is important not to underplay genuine romantic attachments and motivations, and Austen uses the interplay between romantic and pragmatic factors as one of her binary counterpoints. The compatability of aesthetic and intellectual capacities and interests (alluded to later, for example, in the context of 'the picturesque'), adds richness and complexity to the other factors, influencing what could be described, only slightly unfairly, as marriage negotiations and contracts; this is often effectively what they were in Austen's middle and upper-class Regency society.

Several of the various possibilities for women to secure their futures, and enhance their social and economic situations, through strategic marriages, are played out in Austen's novels. In *Mansfield Park*, the attitudes of Henry and Mary Crawford are representative of a particularly calculated approach to the whole marriage business, with the novel's heroine, Fanny Price, being the antidote to such cynical manoeuvring. It seems clear that Jane Austen drew elements of Fanny Price's character in her own mould, or at least her vision of herself, namely being highly intelligent, sensitive and perceptive, but something of an outsider. Despite her apparent personal ambiguity towards marriage, the happy ending for Fanny Price is perhaps a reflection of Jane's inner hopes. Although not autobiographical in any meaningful sense, the novel does incorporate Fanny Price's equivocal response to Henry Crawford's proposal of marriage only to dramatically clarify her refusal the next day, broadly mirroring Jane's own experience, as noted earlier. Both scenarios, fictional and real, again highlight Austen's binary tensions between 'sense' and 'sensibility', i.e. in this context whether to marry for pragmatic reasons (rejected in both cases here) or for more romantic ones (ultimately realised for Fanny Price if not for Jane herself). Perhaps Jane never really came to terms with the prospect of marriage in her own case, the frequent juxtaposition of pragmatic and romantic aspects of marriage in her novels possibly betraying spurious personal barriers to hide behind, or excuses for avoiding commitment.

Inextricably linked with attitudes to marriage were the issues of inheritance and family wealth. These factors fundamentally affected and constrained individuals' prospects in Austen's era, and their frequent appearance in her novels is merely a reflection of their contemporary importance. To the extent that they shape the structures of Austen's novels, this may be an accurate indication of how potential wealth and inheritance opportunities were close to a fixation in the outlook of many in the wider Regency era. For Jane Austen and her immediate family, their Leigh ancestry, with its tantalising inheritance potential, associated legal constraints and, ultimately, disappointments, appears to have been a significant and recurring concern. The complex issue of inheritance of Stoneleigh Abbey was a constant backdrop to the circumstances of the wider Leigh family, including Jane's mother, and Huxley asserts that the fragile mental condition of Jane's lordly cousin, and the rather vague conditions of the will, '*were part of family lore – a perpetual murmur during her upbringing*'[2]. She suggests this influenced Austen's structural themes in *Sense and Sensibility* and *Pride and Prejudice*, involving the way wealth was distributed in the detailed terms of family wills - another example of Austen drawing on her own experiences.

Austen has occasionally been criticised for her focus on specific pecuniary details, and the values of estates and incomes. She frequently characterises male marriage targets not only by their personal qualities, but also in terms of their statuses and wealth, frequently linked directly with property, notably country houses and estates. I suspect many readers of *Pride and Prejudice* would be hard pressed to divorce the marriage attractions of Mr Darcy himself from those of Pemberley, his country house and estate. The attraction of both was important. Indeed, the latter gets almost immediate approval from Elizabeth Bennet when she first sees it – love at first sight - while her affection for Darcy is, initially at least, qualified. It is only when she gets an independent commendation of his merits that he begins to match Pemberley in her ideal imagined future. Nevertheless, there is at least genuine human attraction on both their parts, whereas for Maria Bertram in *Mansfield Park* her marriage to Mr Rushworth (done in a 'Rush' and for financial 'worth'?) has no depth of mutual attraction.

It is an interesting feature of these contrasting cases that Elizabeth Bennet's 'ideal' marriage (satisfying both romantic and pragmatic aims) is never followed through by Austen in the novel, perhaps because the ideal partnership thereafter lacks the potential for excitement, whereas Maria's disastrous marriage is actively described, dissected, and dismantled by Austen, maybe because scandal excites her readers' interest, and is possibly also an addiction in her writing.

An example of a more rational calculation on the female's part is Charlotte Lucas's marriage to the odious but harmless Mr Collins in *Pride and Prejudice*. She explicitly acknowledges the compromise she is making and enters the marriage contract with her eyes wide open. It is a contract which suits both parties; we learn little more about it, and certainly no scandal. Both Mr Rushworth and Mr Collins are lampooned by Austen, but whereas Maria is portrayed (through her attraction to, and subsequent liaisons with, Henry Crawford) as never fully intending to keep her half of the marriage contract, by contrast Charlotte is fully resigned, and committed, to the sacrifices she is making in hers. The same could be said of Marianne in her ultimate acceptance of her compromise marriage to Colonel Brandon in *Sense and Sensibility*.

Margaret Drabble, in her Introduction to the 1974 Penguin Classics edition of *Lady Susan*, *The Watsons* and *Sanditon*, focuses considerable attention on the importance of marriage for females at the time Austen was writing. I quote two passages which further explore and emphasise why marriage was often an obsession. In the first, the avoidance of poverty is a priority :-

> *'And yet, of course, poverty is no virtue in Jane Austen's eyes, and the prospects of the Watson girls are in grim reality far from good. Poverty has turned the weaker of them into husband-hunters ... As Jane was well placed to realize, the plight of a poor old maid was not a happy one: a rich one, as Emma Woodhouse remarks, can make herself feared and respected, but a poor one is constantly subject to ridicule. Elizabeth's statement about marriage is very moving:*
>
>> You know we must marry. – I could do very well single for my own part. - A little company, and a pleasant ball now and then, would be enough for me, if one could be young forever, but my father cannot provide for us, and it is very bad to grow old and be poor and laughed at. - I have lost Purvis, it is true but very few people marry their first loves. I should not refuse a man because he was not Purvis.'[3]

In the second extract, Drabble describes the scene in *The Watsons*, '*when Tom arrives for the evening unannounced.*' :-

> *'His carriage is heard for miles in the silence of the country evening: the family wonders who on earth it*

could be, and are finally even more perplexed when they hear footsteps and conclude, "They were the footsteps of a man".

A man was indeed an intrusion of some importance ... engagements and marriages were then, unlike now, the events which determined the entire future of the female half of the race. A whole career and every prospect of happiness hung on finding the right (or at times, any) man. .... The period before marriage was the most decisive part of a woman's life, and the only period where choice played a considerable part."[4]

In this context, it is therefore no surprise that the period leading up to a marriage, and sometimes more than one marriage, is the principal temporal setting for most of Austen's novels. While the dynamics of existing marriages are briefly described, once new marriages are secured their stories thereafter rarely get much attention; it is the process of securing marriages that drives the narratives. For example, in *Sense and Sensibility* there are only cursory comments in the final few pages of the novel as to how the four new marriages turn out.

The central role that marriage plays in Austen's novels - and particularly its prospect and anticipation, rather than its actuality - appears to stem not only from the general pivotal role it played in the lives of women at that time, but also from Jane's own complex and satirical attitudes on the subject. It is sometimes difficult to sense whether her parodies are poking fun at the way many women viewed marriage prospects or are bitter reactions to the often unenviable decisions that women had to make in a male-dominated society and the expectations that this social environment demanded. Her own decisions on, and attitudes towards, marriage perhaps reflect both. What is clear is that at an early age she had identified it as fertile ground for her own brand of humour. Certainly, in her early writing Austen parodies some of the prevailing extreme sensibilities on the subject. In *Love and Freindship* she has one of her characters say, '*my natural sensibility had already been greatly affected by the sufferings of the unfortunate stranger and no sooner did I first behold him than I felt that in him the happiness or misery of my future life must depend*'.[5] As a further example of the young Jane's use of parody, the following passage is from *The Three Sisters* (an early short piece described, perhaps tongue in cheek, as a novel), in which Mary, who has two sisters, seeks advice from a friend, Fanny, about her response to a marriage proposal. Mary's sisters, Sophia and Georgiana, as well as the Dutton girls, are positioned as rivals in the marriage stakes :-

My Dear Fanny,

I am the happiest creature in the World, for I have just received an offer of marriage from Mr Watts. It is the first I have ever had & and I hardly know how to value it enough. How I will triumph over the Duttons! I do not intend to accept it, at least I beleive (sic) *not, but as I am not quite certain I gave him an equivocal answer & left him. And now my dear Fanny I want your Advice whether I should accept his offer or not, but that you may be able to judge of his merits & the situation of affairs I will give you an account of them. He is quite an old Man, about two & thirty, very plain,* so *plain that I cannot bear to look at him. He is extremely disagreable & I hate him more than anybody else in the world. He has a large fortune & will make great Settlements on me; but then he is very healthy. In short I do not know what to do. If I refuse him he as good as told me that he should offer himself to Sophia and if* she *refused him to Georgiana., & I could not bear to have either of them married before me. If I accept him I know I shall be miserable all the rest of my Life, for he is very ill tempered & peevish extremely jealous, & so stingy that there is no living in the house with him. He told me he should mention the affair to Mama, but I insisted upon it that he did not for very likely she would make me marry him whether I would or no; however probably he has before now, for he never does anything he is desired to do. I believe I shall have him. It will be such a triumph to be married before Sophy, Georgiana & the Duttons; And he promised to have a new Carriage on the occasion, but we almost quarrelled about the colour. For I insisted upon it being blue spotted with silver, & he declared it should be a plain Chocolate; & to provoke me more said it should be just as low as his old one. I wont have him I declare. He said he should come again tomorrow & take my final answer, so I beleive I must get him while I can. I know the Duttons will envy me & I shall be able to chaperone Sophy & Georgiana to all the Winter Balls. But then what will be the use of that when very likely he wont let me go myself for I know he hates dancing & has a great idea of Womens never going from home what he hates himself he has no idea of any other person's liking; & besides he talks a great deal of Women's always staying at home and such stuff. I beleive I shant have him; I would refuse him at once if I were certain that neither of my Sisters would accept him, & that if they did not, he would not offer to the Duttons. I cannot run such a risk, so, if he will promise to have the Carriage ordered as I like, I will have him, if not he may ride in it himself for me. I hope you like my determination; I can think of nothing better;*

And am your ever Affecte

MARY STANHOPE [6]

The reference to a carriage and the importance of its colour (however satirical its use here) is nevertheless another example of the Regency obsession with fashion and ways to display individual style and taste. In a coincidental aside, when Sir John Dashwood-King Bt. (of whom, much more later) sets out his intentions for his Will[7], as well as leaving his wife, Lady Dashwood, a variety of minor inheritances he also very particularly notes that she can have one, and only one, of his carriages, albeit of her own choice. Most of his estate, as was common, passed to his male heir, although he did make some provision for his other children including his daughters.

Cutting through the deliberate absurdity and satirical exaggeration outlined in the italicised passage above, the confused considerations serve to highlight the dilemmas and compromises involved for many women when there was so much focus on the importance of getting married, if not at any price, then at least by securing the best possible option. Satirical exaggeration is a strong feature of Austen's early writing (*Juvenilia*), which she moderates and presents more subtly in her mature novels, notably in *Emma* as outlined later in this section. While Jane may have mocked the way young females often felt obliged to weigh up these dilemmas and compromises when considering whether to accept a proposal of marriage, she was not herself entirely immune to the reality. Claire Tomalin, in her biography, *Jane Austen - A Life*, suggests that these same dilemmas and compromises applied to Jane herself when the possibility of marriage arose. As outlined earlier, the closest Jane got to marriage was the proposal by Harris Bigg in December 1802, which she initially accepted. In connection with her dramatic overnight change of heart, Tomalin outlines the turbulent thoughts that may well have gone through her head during that pivotal night[8]. These reflect the interaction and conflict between the worldly and romantic considerations which must have faced many women at the time.

If this was at least partly representative of a female viewpoint at the time, what about male attitudes? As a high-profile example of unfavourable male sensitivities and motivations in the early nineteenth century, the Reverend

Patrick Bronte, father of the Bronte sisters, having lost his first wife,

> *made three attempts to remarry. First, he approached Miss Elizabeth Firth of Kipping House, Thornton, an orphan in command of her own fortune who was twenty years younger than himself. Miss Firth declined the offer but remained gracious to Mr Bronte after her marriage in 1824 to the Revd Mr Franks (Vicar of Huddersfield). Mr Bronte was again ambitious when he approached Isabelle Dury, the Rector of Keighley's sister. Miss Dury said that she would never be so 'very silly' as to marry a man with no future and encumbered with six children. Then, in 1823-4 Mr Bronte wrote to an old flame, Mary Burder, with renewed attentions after an absence of fourteen years. During Mr Bronte's first curacy in Wethersfield, Essex, he had courted Miss Burder and written to her between 1808 and 1810, and she had accepted his proposal, but something happened to give her an impression of 'duplicity'. It is not surprising that Miss Burder still preferred to remain single ....*[9]

Although these rejections were mainly based on grounds of character and behaviour, factors of age and age difference clearly played an important role both for males and females, notwithstanding other social pressures. While a man's age was less of a barrier to marriage than a woman's, Austen makes it clear that for her female characters, who are generally strongly delineated, male age and attractiveness weighed heavily in the balance between romantic and pragmatic motivations. In *Sense and Sensibility*, Colonel Brandon's age and rather dour persona are pitted against the romantic young Willoughby. As Austen puts it, '*for what could a silent man of five-and-thirty hope, when opposed by a very lively one of five-and-twenty?*'.[10] Indeed, Austen develops this age theme in *Sense and Sensibility*. When discussing Colonel Brandon's age, Marianne objects to any hint of him being a possible match for her at age seventeen, saying, "*thirty five has nothing to do with matrimony*". "*Perhaps*" said Elinor, "*thirty five and seventeen had better not have any thing to do with matrimony together. But if there should by chance happen to be a woman who is single at seven and twenty I should not think Colonel Brandon's being thirty five any objection to his marrying HER*". "*A woman of seven and twenty*", said Marianne, after pausing a moment, "*can never hope to find or inspire affection again ...... In my eyes it would be no marriage at all. – To me it would seem only a commercial exchange, in which each wished to be benefited at the expense of the other*".[11]

Nevertheless, regardless of factors of age and attractions, economics could not easily be ignored. Indeed, Austen gives considerable attention to money and property, frequently citing specific amounts of wealth, with her characters also debating the different merits of property, capital and income. The calculating Mrs John Dashwood in *Sense and Sensibility*, for example, outlines in detail the capital and ongoing income that her poorer relatives can cope with, and warns of the dangers of commitments to paying out annuities. I believe to some extent this reflects Austen's own acute realisation about the security that money could provide. The relationship between money and marriage in Austen's world is, of course, exemplified by the oft-quoted opening sentence of *Pride and Prejudice* - '*It is a truth universally acknowledged, that a single man in possession of a good fortune, must be in want of a wife*'.[12] And the flipside of the coin in Austen's world is that such men are the prizes fought over by numerous aspiring female characters.

The reality was that wealth was predominantly held and controlled by men, and for those with considerable resources, or in a position to inherit such resources, the choice of partner was in many ways much less constrained. While social norms and expectations still played a part, there was greater freedom to select a partner for her personal attractions and characteristics, without financial pressures. Furthermore, for men there were not the same time pressures which gave women's quests for a partner such urgency (and sometimes desperation) associated with the perceived short time-window of female physical attractiveness. More pragmatically, age-related child bearing constraints also put women at a disadvantage where producing heirs was a male priority.

However, Austen's treatment of the relative strengths of male and female positions in securing marriage, are, as with many other aspects of her novels, never entirely straightforward. In her novel *Emma*, Austen cleverly subverts some of the usual expected dynamics between the male and female protagonists, also setting aside her normal satirical preferences. In describing Mr Knightley's proposal to Emma, the following passage from Ronald Blythe's excellent editorial notes in the Introduction to the 1966 Penguin edition of *Emma*, is a fitting one with which to conclude this commentary on marriage in Austen's novels. Referencing Mr Knightley's proposal to Emma and his words, "If I loved you less, I might be able to talk about it more", Blythe continues :-

> *'Irony, wit, burlesque and satire, all are shelved at this moment as the incandescent truth upon which all lasting human affection must depend lights and warms the day. "I have blamed you, and lectured you, and you have borne it as no other woman in England would have borne it ...". It is an odd declaration, implying a reversal of the old chivalric tradition when it was the man who had to undergo various tests of moral worth before he won his bride'.*

Citing R. Brimley Johnson's observation that "the vamps are all men" in Jane Austen and that he could not remember a single young man in her novels "who was not contemplating matrimony with more or less eagerness and enthusiasm", Blythe continues :-

> *'This .... partly explains the ambivalence of the Jane Austen male, who appears to pursue while he is actually being pursued. ..... None of the men in Emma doubts his worthiness to court and all the women display their worthiness to be courted. All except Emma herself, and she makes the mistake of thinking herself above this feminine role, or rather outside it. She is Miss Woodhouse. Mr Knightley neither needs nor wishes to marry Miss Woodhouse; he is concerned with 'my dearest Emma'. But he, too, has made an error. He has rejected the normal male courtship display as fripperies, with the result that Emma has never recognized him as a lover.'*[13]

In devising *Emma*, which appeared in 1816, Jane Austen wrote: '*I am going to take a heroine whom no-one but myself will much like*'.[14] It is therefore likely that Jane identifies at least to some extent with her heroine. Perhaps, like her Emma, Jane also makes the mistake of thinking herself above this feminine role, or rather outside it. Perhaps she also thinks of herself primarily as 'Miss Austen' and never really engages with the normal marriage manouverings.

Although she may well have used humour as a way of avoiding fully or openly expressing her feelings, no-one would suggest Jane Austen was without genuine emotion. She was, however, above all a woman of great sense. Her satire appears to have been aimed predominantly at those who lacked sufficient sense to counterbalance the more freeranging aspects of their personalities.

For her brother James, who was also a proficient writer, with something of the same satirical style and approach as Jane, Tomalin notes of his literary output that, '*the questions of how to marry money, and how to get a good Church living, were raised in several humorous pieces*'.[15] These appeared in

James Austen's own weekly magazine, *The Loiterer*, which was distributed and sold in a number of the largest towns and cities, including London, Birmingham, Bath, and Reading, as well as in Oxford, where he was writing. His humorous comments on acquiring a good Church living were also well-informed given the Austen family's substantial involvement with the Church. Consequently, for Jane Austen this subject was of heightened interest, and is the one next sketched.

The Church

Rather than commenting directly on the state of the Church in any of her writing, Austen delegates this task to her created characters, expressed through their religious attitudes. In her treatment of religion and the diverse portrayal of the many clerical characters in her novels, Austen pointedly and effectively highlights both the random nature in which the clergy were appointed and the associated lottery for parishioners. Some of her fictitious clergy are committed and conscientious, others simply in it for the social status and financial stability. As always, Austen is tapping into fertile ground for her readers, with contemporary perceptions about the clergy often imbued with a strong streak of cynicism. Her descriptions of the varied traits, attitudes, and morals of her fictional clergy probably chimed strongly with her readers' wide-ranging experiences of the clergy they themselves encountered.

Taking holy orders does not appear to have been particularly challenging for those with the right background and connections. It was often regarded as a default choice of career, particularly for younger sons. The key requirement was having access to a 'living' with a guaranteed annual income. There was great disparity, and little equity or logic, in the annual incomes available, but more importantly the power to appoint clergy to particular 'livings' was often held by the owners of the estates in which the settlement and church were located. In *Sense and Sensibility*, Elinor tells Edward Ferrars that,

> *'Colonel Brandon, who was here only ten minutes ago, has desired me to say, that, understanding you mean to take orders, he has great pleasure in offering you the living of Delaford, now just vacant, and only wishes it were more valuable. Allow me to congratulate you on having so respectable and well-judging a friend, and to join in his wish that the living – it is about two hundred a-year – were much more considerable ...'.*[16]

The suitability of the potential incumbent, let alone any proven ability, doesn't appear to have been particularly important, and the parishioners had little say in the matter. It is the arbitrary nature of the whole process of appointments which inevitably led to widespread disillusion and contributed to the upsurge in non-conformist branches of Christianity.

Austen did not hold back in criticising deficient clergy, for example those who were, like the sycophantic and pathetic caricature, Mr Collins, in *Pride and Prejudice*, chiefly concerned with status, and over-deferential to their sponsors. However, she retained enough belief in the calling to include it as a generally honourable occupation, and suitable for the partners of her novels' central female characters. Edmund in *Mansfield Park* is perhaps the best example, but even for the rather insipid Edward Ferrars in *Sense and Sensibility* the living at Delaford is positioned as at least being respectable. With her father and a brother being conscientious members of the clergy, the general respectability of the profession, regardless of variable individual competence and suitability, was to some extent hardwired into Austen's perspective. However, perhaps these positive family role models to which she was personally and directly exposed made her even more scathing about other shocking examples she may have encountered or read about, and which gave the clergy such a mixed contemporary reputation.

On the question of Jane's treatment of religion, and with reference to emerging alternative church movements, Blythe notes that in 1809 *'she dismissed the current evangelical arguments with, "They who are so far from Reason and Feeling, must be happiest." '* and adds that, *'Death rarely occurs in her novels and when it happens it is described with the minimum of sentimentality and sometimes with wit. "What a blessing it is when undue influence does not survive the grave!", says Mrs Weston'* [in *Emma*].[17]

The stability and continuity in Jane's orderly rural life, which her father's living at Steventon enabled, came to a sudden end with his retirement from the Church. The need for an agreeable writing environment in which she could flourish and create was crucial for Austen. Tomalin notes that, *'What she did depend on was particular working conditions which allowed her to abstract herself from the daily life going on around her; and these she lost just after her twenty-fifth birthday. What made her fall silent was another huge event in her "life of no event": another exile'*.[18] This exile was the family's move from her beloved rural Hampshire to Bath which, by all accounts and the evidence of her own letters, she had found extremely traumatic.

This personal trauma, in being forced to move to Bath, is reprised by Austen through her character Anne Elliot, in *Persuasion*. Anne bemoans the letting out of Kellynch Hall, her family's Somerset country house, and the enforced move to Bath :-

'Sir Walter would quit Kellynch Hall – and after a very few days more of doubt and indecision, the great question of whither he should go was settled, and the first outline of this important change made out.

There had been three alternatives, London, Bath, or another house in the country. All Anne's wishes had been for the latter. A small house in their own neighbourhood, where they might still have the pleasure of sometimes seeing the lawns and groves of

Kellynch, was the object of her ambition. But the usual fate of Anne attended her, in having something very opposite from her inclination fixed on. She disliked Bath, and did not think it agreed with her – and Bath was to be her home.' [19]

As alluded to earlier, this is surely further evidence of occasional autobiographical elements inserted by Austen into her novels. Jane Austen was upset by her family's move from Steventon to Bath, and her time there appears to have coincided with a reduction in her writing progress and output. It was the later return to her familiar Hampshire neighbourhood, and being settled at Chawton, less than 10 miles from Steventon, which gave her the motivation to complete and publish the novels, the early ones having existed in various stages of development for many years. Her strong determination to publish is reflected in the associated financial arrangements for *Sense and Sensibility*, which effectively left her underwriting any costs associated with potential failure to sell enough copies.

Revising and refining her draft texts to maintain their topicality was a key concern for Austen, as she targeted publication. With an eye to her readership and her awareness that she lived at a time of rapid change, her sensitivity to the need for her novels to be topical is illustrated by incorporation of references to Trafalgar, Waterloo and fashionable cottage orné architecture in *Sanditon*, the novel she was working on immediately before her death. There are further references to the Napoleonic Wars in *Persuasion*, published posthumously. These military references by Austen remind us that there was a brutal and lengthy war being waged on and off for a substantial part of her lifetime. However, for Jane, and for her characters, the military also had patriotic, exciting, and romantic associations. Its frequent appearance in the otherwise largely domestic context of her novels reflects Austen's acknowledgement of the major role of the military in the Regency period.

The military

The military equates to the one of the three 'estates' that had, long before Austen's time, reflected the skeleton structure of medieval society – those who pray, those who fight, and those who work. We hear little of the latter group, numerically the largest, in Austen's novels, and those who pray are associated with the generally sober and rather dull world of the Church and clergy. By contrast, the military field continued, as in the medieval past, to be associated with glamour and chivalry. Also, because the period during which Austen was writing coincided with the Napoleonic Wars, it had a heightened contemporary relevance. It is therefore no surprise that her novels incorporated several military characters and utilised the presence of the military more generally. In the same way that Austen delineates, and arguably exaggerates, differences in character between her various clerical figures, her military ones display greatly contrasting strengths and weaknesses.

Austen's military characters are often associated with dubious morals, with General and Captain Tilney in *Northanger Abbey* portrayed, for example, as slightly villainous. However, in terms of contrasts in military characters perhaps the most obvious example is in the generally positive portrayal of Colonel Brandon in *Sense and Sensibility* and the deficiencies of George Wickham in *Pride and Prejudice*. But even here the sensitively drawn character of Colonel Brandon has elements from his past which have slightly disturbing undercurrents, albeit later partially redeemed.

Some of Austen's military figures remain less prominent, such as Captain Weston, in *Emma*, who joined the local militia. His military life introduced him to Miss Churchill, of a great Yorkshire family, who fell in love with him. Another military figure in *Emma* is Colonel Campbell. With his wife, he brought up Jane Fairfax, the daughter of the Colonel's friend Lieutenant Fairfax, who had died in battle soon after Jane Fairfax was born. Although not major figures in the novel, Austen takes the opportunity to portray these two latter military figures as exhibiting honourable, even chivalric, military characteristics, one dying in battle doing his duty and the other doing the honourable thing in taking responsibility for bringing up his fallen colleague's offspring. This notably mirrors the historical military narrative outlined earlier, in which Henry VII, having led his troops at battle of Bosworth Field, took responsibility for the young Charles Brandon, the son of Henry's standard bearer who was killed in the battle. If, as suggested earlier, this well-documented historical episode inspired Austen's use of the name Brandon in *Sense and Sensibility*, it may well also have provided her with the chivalrous scenario just described in *Emma*.

Whatever the differing characteristics Austen employs in portraying the military, there is, at least for her female characters, always a sense of colour and excitement when the military were garrisoned nearby and could attend balls and other social events. The effect on females living close to garrisons and military manoeuvres is referenced at the very start of Thomas Hardy's novel *The Trumpet Major*. Written decades later but based on recollections of those living through the Napoleonic War period, its opening sentence sets the Regency scene for what follows: '*In the days of high-waisted and muslin-gowned women, when the vast amount of soldiering going on in the country was a cause of much trembling to the sex .....*'[20]

This excitement, as well as reflecting the potential for male company and liaisons, also included elements of genuine fear connected with the very real threat of Napoleon's ambitions, and possible invasion, which added to the military's significance and heroic status, even when this was not always merited. Indeed, in *The Trumpet Major* Hardy goes on to describe the reality that the quality and morals of the Napoleonic-era military was far from uniformly admirable. Likewise, in several episodes in her novels, Austen pointedly exposes the truth beneath the superficial attractions of a man 'in uniform', whether military or clergy.

Compared with her treatment of the clergy and the military, categorisations which retained vestigial elements of their original medieval social values, the contemporary Regency equivalent of the third medieval estate – those who work – was less susceptible to her critiques. By Austen's time, this element of medieval feudal structures was already fragmented, with the progress of the industrial revolution and the enclosure of land during her lifetime accelerating this breakdown, and 'those who work' was far too diverse a social or economic category to enable characterisations which her readers would immediately recognise or relate to. But in any event, most of Austen's potential readership were generally positioned, like Jane herself, somewhat distanced, if not physically at least socially, from the bulk of 'those who work'. For the most part her characters have the luxury of considerable leisure time, often in a rural environment, and for many of her male characters this leisure time was devoted to country pursuits.

Country pursuits

This is another sphere of activity of which Jane Austen would have had at least a rudimentary understanding, with direct exposure through her two rural Hampshire home environments and her visits to the rural North Cotswolds with its strong hunting traditions. If, as Janine Barchas asserts, Jane's knowledge of the real Sir John Dashwood provided inspiration for names and themes in *Sense and Sensibility*, it is worth noting that just like him, her own brother, the Rev. James Austen, kept a pack of harriers.[21]

As previously noted, it is allusions between fact and fiction that are used by Austen rather than direct narrative comparisons. The latter would have been far too crude a literary mechanism for Jane, for whom subtle approaches were the norm once she had developed her work into mature publishable novels, leaving behind her more transparent, raw, and experimental early writing. In addition to her theory that the connections and allusions to the real Dashwood family are central to an understanding of *Sense and Sensibility,* Barchas further suggests that the fictional Dashwood West country base at 'Barton' may be an allusion in name to the real Dashwood country base at Bourton-on-the-Hill, inviting exploration of other possible parallels and allusions.

One question is the extent to which the fictional Sir John Middleton's interests in country pursuits at Barton Park in *Sense and Sensibility* coincide with those of the real Sir John Dashwood-King at Bourton-on-the-Hill, where the evidence indicates Bourton House as his probable residence. As well as the similarity between the names of the fictional Barton and factual Bourton, and the 'Sir John' match of names, their respective obsessions with hunting represent an obvious possible allusion. As outlined in more detail later, Sir John Dashwood-King's hunting lodge at Bourton was ideally sited for the sport, with several established hunts in the area, as well as the Bourton Hunt which he initiated. There were a number of like-minded country gentlemen in the neighbourhood, with whom Sir John clearly forged close friendships, and even after he had left Bourton, Sir John kept up frequent social contact with these Cotswolds neighbours.[22] Likewise, Austen's fictional Sir John Middleton and his wife, *'were scarcely ever without some friends staying with them in the house, and they keep more company of every kind than any other family in the neighbourhood'.*[23]

Sir John Dashwood-King's well-recorded passion for hunting and country pursuits is matched by Austen's explicit description of her fictional Sir John Middleton's main preoccupation. *'Sir John was a sportsman, Lady Middleton a mother. He hunted and shot, and she humoured her children; and these were their only resources. Lady Middleton had the advantage of being able to spoil her children all the year round, while Sir John's independent employments* [hunting and shooting] *were in existence only half the time'.*[24] The character difference between Sir John and his wife, Lady Middleton, is also underlined by Austen commenting that, *'the Middletons lived in a style of equal hospitality and elegance. The former was for Sir John's gratification, the latter for that of his lady*'.[25] This contrast in characters and interests between the fictional Sir John Middleton and his wife Lady Middleton, which Jane Austen draws so explicitly, mirrors that between Sir John Dashwood-King and his wife Lady Dashwood. Also, the two 'Sir Johns' are of similar age at the beginning of the nineteenth century, '*about forty*'[26], and there are other striking similarities in their characters.

While both appear sociable and hospitable, from Austen's perspective neither of the two Sir Johns has any discernible strong cultural or intellectual interest to match their focus on country pursuits. Austen notes that when her creation, Sir John Middleton, wasn't involved in country pursuits, '*Continual engagements at home and abroad, however, supplied all the deficiencies of nature and education*'.[27] Similarly, in describing the real Sir John Dashwood-King, a future Dashwood baronet notes that he '*had few of the qualities or vices of his fun-loving and cultured half-uncle*'.[28] It is only fair to say in his defence that while this latter assessment of the fourth baronet may well be broadly accurate, there is evidence which provides favourable counterbalance, as set out in Chapter 10.

Austen notes that her Sir John Middleton's '*countenance was thoroughly good-humoured; and his manners were as friendly as the style of his letter ...... His kindness was not confined to words; for within an hour after he left them, a large basket full of garden stuff and fruit arrived from the Park, which was followed before the end of the day by a present of game*'.[29] This kindness and generosity is matched in real life by Sir John Dashwood-King who is noted in contemporary journals as being a very kind master to his servants, and whose diary accounts evidence his many charitable donations, again as outlined later in Chapter 10.

However, the dominant similarity was that each Sir John, one fictional and one real, in valuing country pursuits to the exclusion of most other interests, didn't much sense what was valued by others. In the following exchange in *Sense and Sensibility*, initially between Mrs Dashwood and Sir John Middleton, regarding Willoughby, Austen's dialogue is pointedly illuminating :-

> [Mrs Dashwood] *'And what sort of young man is he?'*
>
> [Sir John Middleton] *'As good a kind of fellow as ever lived, I assure you. A very decent shot, and there is not a bolder rider in England.'*
>
> *'And is **that** all you can say for him!' cried Marianne indignantly. 'But what are his manners on more intimate acquaintance? what his pursuits, his talents, and genius?'*
>
> *Sir John was rather puzzled.*
>
> *'Upon my soul,' said he, 'I do not know much about him as to all **that**. But he is a pleasant, good-humoured fellow, and has got the nicest little black bitch of a pointer I ever saw. Was she out with him today?*
>
> *But Marianne could no more satisfy him as to the colour of Mr Willoughby's pointer than he could describe to her the shades of his mind.*[30]

And likewise, while both Sir Johns are described as, outwardly at least, essentially kind and hospitable, their actions or words, whether consciously or otherwise intended, are often perceived by others as insensitive, or even cruel. In the real world, Mary Anne's damning Bourton-on-the-Hill letter (see Chapter 10) to her husband, Sir John Dashwood-King, provides an insight into his priorities and disregard of her feelings at a particular time in their marriage. Likewise, the following two extracts from *Sense and Sensibility* illustrate the fictional Sir John Middleton's insensitivity to other people's feelings.

The first extract is an exchange between Sir John and Marianne Dashwood :-

'Aye, I see now how it will be,' said Sir John, 'I see how it will be. You will be setting your cap at him now, and never think of poor Brandon.'

'That is an expression, Sir John,' said Marianne warmly, 'which I particularly dislike. I abhor every common-place phrase by which wit is intended; and "setting one's cap at a man", or "making a conquest", are the most odious of all. Their tendency is gross and illiberal; and if their construction could ever be deemed clever, time has long ago destroyed ingenuity.'

Sir John did not much understand this reproof; but he laughed as heartily as if he did, and then replied, -

'Aye, you will make conquests enough, I dare say, one way or other. Poor Brandon! He is quite smitten already, and he is very well worth setting your cap at, I can tell you, in spite of all this tumbling about and spraining of ankles'.[31]

The second extract relates to Sir John Middleton's insensitive treatment of the delicate relationship between Elinor Dashwood and Edward Ferrars :-

Elinor could not suppose that Sir John would be more nice in proclaiming his suspicions of her regard for Edward, than he had been with respect to Marianne; indeed it was rather his favourite joke of the two, as being somewhat newer and more conjectural: and since Edward's visit, they had never dined together without his drinking to her best affections with so much significancy, and so many nods and wink, as to excite general attention. The letter F--- had been likewise invariably brought forward, and found productive of such countless jokes, that its character as the wittiest letter in the alphabet had been long established with Elinor.

The Miss Steeles, as she expected, had now all the benefit of these jokes, and in the eldest of them they raised a curiosity to know the name of the gentleman alluded to, which, though often impertinently expressed, was perfectly of a piece with her general inquisitiveness into the concerns of their family. But Sir John did not sport long with the curiosity which he delighted to raise, for he had at least as much pleasure in telling the name, as Miss Steele had in hearing it.

'His name is Ferrars,' said he, in a very audible whisper; 'but pray do not tell it, for it's a great secret.'[32]

Finally, both the Sir Johns also wish to retain a level of male control over their domains. Sir John Middleton, '*in settling a family of females only in his cottage .. had all the satisfaction of a sportsman; for a sportsman, though he esteems only those of his own sex who are sportsmen likewise, is not often desirous of encouraging their taste by admitting them to a residence within his manor*'.[33] This very much mirrors the real Sir John Dashwood-King's reaction to his wife's suspected dalliances with the Prince of Wales, by banishing her to their home of Bourton-on-the-Hill – 'his manor' – where he had control, and where natural meetings with the Prince of Wales, or other male admirers, were far less likely than in London society, and also far easier to monitor. At the same time, he was happy to be lending his hounds to the Prince of Wales as a fellow huntsman, and '*helped to select horses for the Prince of Wales and for King George III*'.[34]

Whether or not Austen deliberately and specifically mirrors Sir John Dashwood-King in creating her Sir John Middleton, she would appear at least to be using the latter as a stereotype of the ubiquitous hunting and shooting country gentlemen she would have encountered, and who she gently, but pointedly, mocks in *Sense and Sensibility*. If intended as a stereotype of a country gentleman, perhaps Austen deliberately chose the name 'Middleton' as representing the middling and common type of the species. Middleton also happens to be the name of the long-standing tenant of the manor house at Chawton, to whom Jane makes reference in a letter to her brother Francis.[35] In addition, as noted earlier, there was mid-18th century correspondence between a very real Lord Middleton and Sir Francis Dashwood, with the name Willoughby also referenced in the same letter.

Siblings

Austen was a prolific letter writer. Although she wrote to Francis and her other brothers, these letters were very much outnumbered by those to her sister Cassandra, with whom she had her closest relationship. While of very different temperaments, they exchanged innumerable letters, many later destroyed by Cassandra. Perhaps mirroring this great letter-writing enthusiasm, and possibly also influenced by a style recently employed very successfully by Fanny Burney, Jane's early composition *Elinor and Marianne*, later transformed into *Sense and Sensibility*, was also crafted in epistolary form.

It is tempting to consider the close sisterly link in *Mansfield Park* between Fanny and Susan Price, despite difference in character, and their somewhat contrived reunion as part of the novel's happy ending, as perhaps a reflection of Jane's own relationship with her beloved sister Cassandra, with whom she had such an intimate relationship, similarly with marked differences in their natures. In two of Austen's best-known novels, *Pride and Prejudice* and *Sense and Sensibility*, sets of sisters figure prominently and are pivotal to the storylines. Often these narratives comprise juxtaposition of the inherent characters of the sisters, which often differ substantially, and there is a focus on the way these contrasting personality traits influence outcomes. By contrast, brothers are often less prominent in Austen's novels, Edward Ferrars' younger brother Robert in *Sense and Sensibility*, for example, effectively featuring only as a shadow, but again used to establish opposing character traits.

In *Northanger Abbey*, the main characters include three pairs of brothers and sisters (Catherine and James Morland, Isabella and John Thorpe, and Eleanor and Henry Tilney) who are used to portray contrasting sensibilities, and as one commentator notes[36] :-

> *'The different ways in which the Picturesque is associated with the Thorpes and the Tilneys emphasizes the great differences in character and sincerity in the opposing siblings ... This disparity is keenly demonstrated in the two separate excursions Catherine Morland is taken on ..... the inappropriate jaunt in the carriages with the Thorpes, and the more decorous, and more fulfilling, country walk with the Tilneys. John Thorpe ... plays on Catherine's gothic leanings by proposing to lead the party as far away as Blaise Castle, in Bristol:*
>
> "Blaize Castle!" cried Catherine. "What is that'?"
>
> "The finest place in England–worth going fifty miles at any time to see."
>
> "What, is it really a castle, an old castle?"
>
> "The oldest in the kingdom."
>
> "But is it like what one reads of?"
>
> "Exactly–the very same."
>
> "But now really–are there towers and long galleries?"
>
> "By dozens."
>
> *As Austen well knew, Blaise Castle is a fake, not unlike John Thorpe.*

The so-called 'castle' was a garden feature built in 1766 and typical of the time - a 'folly', its artificiality masquerading as something else and reflecting the excesses of the enthusiasm for the Picturesque.

The contrast with Henry Tilney is sharply drawn, and *'on their country walk, Austen tempers Henry Tilney's interest in the Picturesque to an appreciation of natural beauty .... as opposed to a cultivated one, that first emerged from the Grand Tour:*

> "They were viewing the country with the eyes of persons accustomed to drawing, and decided on its capability of being formed into pictures, with all the eagerness of real taste"

On Catherine expressing her ignorance and a desire to learn to draw, "a lecture on the picturesque immediately followed".

> "He talked of foregrounds, distances, and second distances–side-screens and perspectives–lights and shades"

Though intelligent and reasonable, Henry must not be immune to the emotional pull of the Picturesque, and Austen undercuts his sense with a little sensibility, by allotting to him the poetic romance of "a piece of rocky fragment and the withered oak".

The way the two men are differently associated with the Picturesque yields an accurate portraits of their characters – one clever with the capability for feeling, even romanticism, the other unfeeling, devoid of taste, and foolish.'

This is just one example of Austen's use of the Picturesque as more than just a contextual element in her novels. As a pivotal theme, it is considered in the following chapters.

In summarising the sketches above, Austen's novels made frequent use of a small set of occupations or spheres of activity, such as marriage, the church, the military, and country pursuits. And as always, she could be acerbic as well as perceptive in her treatment of each of these spheres and their inhabitants. They were worlds Jane herself experienced directly through her Austen and Leigh family background and through her environment, but she appears always to have been ill-fitting for any one of these lifestyles, or for the prescribed social norms for women with her background and standing. Consequently, she appears, as intimated earlier, to have lived her life principally as a brilliant and highly perceptive observer rather than a fully committed participant. This trait of a certain detachment is true of many successful writers. The 20th-century provocative and controversial novelist Angela Carter voiced strong opinions, retained her independence, and rather than being one to join any clubs or groups, has been described as '*sniping from the sidelines*'.[37] While Austen's approach was neither as politically charged nor as directly challenging as Carter's, a similar retention of detachment or distance allowed her the freedom and objectivity to dissect character strengths and weaknesses in minute detail. This is not to say that she was cold and unemotional, but as someone who appears to have felt awkward, perhaps self-conscious, in polite society, the contrasting flamboyance, exuberance and extrovert character of her cousin Eliza, with her Indian origins and exotic lifestyle, made a great impression on Jane. Eliza's colourful life story is outlined later.

CHAPTER FIVE
The Regency Picturesque

" ….. and she would have every book that tells her how to admire an old twisted tree. Should you not Marianne?"
(Edward Ferrars referring to 'the picturesque' in *Sense and Sensibility*)[1]

This chapter outlines the roots of 'the picturesque' in its British context, traces its development during Jane's lifetime and beyond, and explores the ways she incorporated it into her novels, particularly in terms of character delineation. This provides a benchmark against which to explore and assess, in following chapters, how this aesthetic idea was, almost literally, shipped out to India and how the resulting 'Indian picturesque' was in turn transported back to Britain, featuring characters with strong Cotswold, Austen, and Dashwood connnections.

In the late 18th and early 19th centuries the aesthetic concept of the picturesque was highly fashionable, influencing numerous facets of Regency life, and frequently found its way into Austen's novels. Irene Collins, in *Jane Austen and The Clergy*, for example, notes that Austen's '*clergy as a whole were noted for their interest in the Picturesque, which formed the background to the novels. Edward Ferrars* (in Sense & Sensibility)*, despite his protestations of ignorance on the subject, was fully conversant with its themes and terminology*'.[2] There are several other specific references to the picturesque in Austen's novels, notably in *Pride and Prejudice*, *Northanger Abbey* and *Mansfield Park*, often employed in connection with country residences and the landscapes, parks and gardens in which they sit.

An overview is offered by Mavis Batey, in a volume of *Garden History*, in which both Austen's writing and the Dilettanti Society, of which Sir Francis Dashwood was a leading figure, are conveniently referenced, and in which the concepts of contemporary 'sensibility' and 'taste' are introduced. She positions the Picturesque as 'a peculiarly British reaction to the Romantic attitudes sweeping Europe', the movement having been :-

'sparked off by William Gilpin, whose published Tours to out-of-the-way parts of Britain, were sought after by every person of taste eager to draw, collect prints, and take part in the Discovery of Britain in the late eighteenth century. .... Jane Austen's heroines growing up in the 1780s .... were all, like the author, "enamoured of Gilpin and the picturesque from an early age".

It was important that picturesque sensibility should be seen as part of the eighteenth century's commitment to the canons of taste, which Rousseau's ideas challenged. Taste came down from the top, whereas feeling was individual and spontaneous and to Dr Johnson, the champion of anti-sentimental commonsense, and to Jane Austen, was suspect. In 1794, Gilpin's practical ideas for encouraging a 'picture-imagination' when travelling was developed into abstract picturesque theory by the two Herefordshire squires Richard Payne Knight and Uvedale Price.

Payne Knight as a scholar and connoisseur, widely travelled, and a member [as was Sir Francis Dashwood] *of the Dilettanti Society, was well placed to demonstrate that picturesque sensibility was a manifestation of 'real taste', but he made concessions to the subjectivity the Rousseau age demanded. In this Knight followed his mentor the philosopher Archibald Alison, who in his Essay on the Nature and Principles of Taste, published in 1790, sought to establish the 'connexion between Taste and Sensibility'.'[3]*

With reference to Gilpin's 'Tours' and the encouragement for 'every person of taste' to follow his 'picturesque' lead, an extract from one of Austen's very early works, completed in June 1790, sees her characters explicitly following this lead and embarking on just such a 'Tour' :-

'She told me that having a considerable taste for the Beauties of Nature, her curiosity to behold the delightful scenes it exhibited in that part of the World had been so much raised by Gilpin's Tour to the Highlands, that she had prevailed on her Father to undertake a Tour of Scotland.'[4]

Stepping back from Austen's fiction into the real Regency world, an excellent and highly relevant example of such a 'Gilpin Tour' is fortuitously provided by a lengthy excursion around Wales undertaken in 1792 by one of our central figures, John Dashwood (shortly to become 4th Baronet of West Wycombe), embarking from his Cotswold hunting lodge at Bourton-on-the-Hill. He kept a detailed account of this 'Sentimental Tour', as it is described in the Dashwood Family papers held at the Bodleian Library, and some key extracts are given here. These include direct references to the 'picturesque', together with use of other contemporary aesthetic jargon (highlighted by my underlining) which has clearly influenced his particular choice of descriptive language :-

'The chief objects of the following Tour were the mountains & sea ports in Wales & occasionally days

Grouse Shooting on the Hills [he clearly couldn't entirely put aside his country pursuits, even 'on Tour']

Left Bourton on the 10th August Ann. 1792

At Salop I repaired my carriage which was broken .... in Bridgewater.

The road leading to Mallwydd is on the side of the Hill through which the Dovey runs & adds greatly to the <u>beauty of the scenery</u> – From Mallwydd to Dinas the Hills are more varied with broken ground & the <u>prospects</u> are more <u>picturesque</u>. .. Mallwydd Bridge .... consists of a single arch and of <u>singular beauty and elegance</u>.

The Camarthenshire Hills approach ...... Here I was shown the <u>dreadful</u> effects of a storm which happened about ten years ago ... <u>By the violence of it Rocks were torn</u> from their centres .... Horses, cattle and herds carried away on the torrent.

Bala is apparently <u>situate</u> beneath the level of the lake. The <u>prospect</u> from it is dreary & gives one an idea of total seclusion from the world.

August 18th   This day I arrived on the confines of more <u>romantic scenes</u> – between Dinas and Dolgelly <u>the Rocks are more rude</u> & the Hills higher – but the scenery is still <u>undetermined</u> – The whole is a sort of <u>confused greatness</u>.

Descending the Hill about two miles from Dolgelly we saw the Town in a very <u>picturesque point of view</u>. Its <u>irregularities</u> from that <u>situation</u> appeared to great advantage.

Barmouth is said to resemble Gibraltar tho' in miniature has a very <u>singular appearance</u>'.[5]

Within these extracts we see examples of John Dashwood's sensibility to the three categories of art asserted by the philosopher and politician Edmund Burke at the time, namely the 'Beautiful', the 'Sublime' and the 'Picturesque'. Each in its own way could be said to contribute to the emerging Romantic movement in art, which would develop further and flourish during much of the nineteenth century. There is a fourth artistic category prominent at this time, the 'exotic', particularly relevant to our Indian themes, but we would not expect John Dashwood to have used this category in the context of his Welsh (or indeed any) British journey. Notably, however, he does explicitly use the words 'romantic' and 'singular beauty' and, even in these short extracts, twice incorporates the word 'picturesque', which he is clearly primed for (whether consciously or unconsciously) by contemporary fashionable expectations. The 'irregularities' he notes were an essential component of the picturesque. Although the word 'sublime' is not explicitly quoted, the focus on 'Rocks', associated with violence and rudeness, and the description of the 'dreadful effects of a storm', as well as 'confused greatness', all conform very closely to the contemporary dramatic requirements of the 'sublime'.

This theme of distinct artistic approaches and Austen's satirical incorporation of these in her writing is reflected in a passage from *The English Seaside Resort, A Social History 1750-1914* :-

The author (wisely anonymous) of The Isle of Wight, a Poem in Three Cantos, published in 1782, extolled the virtue of the Undercliff by pointing out that it needed three artists to do it justice; Claude to capture the 'delicate sunshine' over 'cultivated fields, the scattered cots, and hanging coppices', Salvator for 'the horror of the rugged cliffs', and Poussin for 'the majesty of the impending mountains'. By the early nineteenth century the conventional vocabulary of these modes of perception had become a fount of recognizable clichés, and its extravagant abusers were mercilessly lampooned by Jane Austen in her unfinished novel Sanditon. For many visitors who had cultivated these fashionable sensibilities, the sea carried a very special emotional charge of its own.[6]

John Dashwood's 'Sentimental Tour' includes coastal locations and scenes, and in tune with contemporary and fashionable terminology his use of the words 'prospect', 'situation', and 'point of view' explicitly highlight the requirement at that time for the observer to seek out the optimum spot from which to make an aesthetic judgment.

John Dashwood's account of his 'Sentimental Tour', by including the phrase 'but the scenery is still undetermined', perfectly exemplifies another specific contemporary attitude, namely that nature, or whatever currently existed, had the potential to be improved, or 'determined' (i.e actively re-ordered), to conform more closely to some concept or model of artistic perfection. On a more limited canvas, the general urge for gardeners to impose order has, of course, been an enduring one through to the present. Sir Roy Strong, for example, involved in one element of the current Prince of Wales's garden at Highgrove, on a subsequent visit in 1993, commented '*It's a funny garden, the result of too many people being involved in it. There are still unresolved areas, and it lacks a coherent statement*'[7]. The fashion for imposing order was particularly acute during Austen's lifetime, and this is precisely what Repton and others were aiming at by intervening and altering what already existed. Repton's trademark commercial approach aimed to impress potential clients with his 'before' and 'after' images using overlays in his famous red books, to show what 'improvements' could be achieved. A very personal example involves images of his own garden before and after his suggested improvements, shown below[8].

The Regency Picturesque

Repton's garden before suggested 'improvements'

Repton's garden after suggested 'improvements'

Clearly, part of the intention of these before and after images was to obscure the ugly realities of daily life. Of note in the pre-improvement Repton image above, these ugly realities include a very particular and highly topical stereotype, namely the male figure (presumably begging) with a wooden leg and an eyepatch, typical of many hundreds of wounded or disabled soldiers and sailors returning from the Napoleonic wars to a country struggling with debts and unemployment; 'improvement', in the context of such artistic manipulation, could have a ruthless and selfish edge. Another feature of Repton's suggested improvements in this example further underlines such selfishness in the apparent annexation of common land, with a triangle of village green being absorbed into his own garden. This is reminiscent of the fictional John Dashwood's annexation of land (on a far larger scale) at East Kingham Farm in *Sense and Sensibility,* the relevant extract being considered shortly.

In a further link between Repton and the picturesque (i.e. like a picture), it is notable that although Repton described himself as a landscape gardener on his business cards, he later wrote '*it ought rather to be called picture gardening*'. [9]

Returning to John Dashwood's Tour of Wales, even if we were not informed of the era in which it was written, the use of very specific terminology, as highlighted above, would enable a good estimate of its 1792 date. It chimes with Gilpin's slightly earlier, and Austen's slightly later, similar choices of words and phrases to describe, and accord with, contemporary aesthetic sensibilities.

Incidentally, later in the same decade, Nelson and the Hamiltons made a similar tour of Wales, but with far more public interest, and with less attention to the merits of picturesque scenery. The focus in that case was on the enthusiasm which locals displayed on seeing the victorious admiral, the party being referred to in some newspapers as '*Lord Nelson's tourists*'. On their return, Lady Hamilton reported that, '*We had had a most charming Tour ... Oh how our Hero has been received*'.[10]

While Nelson's was clearly not a typical 'Tour', those such as John Dashwood's, and their associated descriptions, focusing on the quest for the picturesque, were widely adopted by individuals with pretensions to cultural appreciation and with the necessary means to travel around the country at leisure recording their experiences. These tours became so common, and of such a formulaic pattern, that they became a target for satire, often of a far less subtle tone than Jane Austen's. William Combe's lengthy poem *The Tour of Doctor Syntax in search of the picturesque*, later published as a book in 1812, is the apogee of this satire, with its title page including and emphasising this satirical style in its pictorial representation of overgrown ruins contrived to loosely form the word 'Picturesque'. This very contrivance was, of course, part of the satire.

Frontispiece of 'The Tour of Doctor Syntax in Search of the Picturesque'

The poem recounts the exploits of a fictional curate, Dr Syntax, seeking out picturesque landscapes but continually encountering mundane and frustrating realities, such as being chased by a bull and stumbling into a lake while distractedly trying to find the ideal position from which to sketch a suitably ruined castle. Historic ruins, especially castles and religious buildings, were important contributors to this idealised model of the picturesque; seeking them out was therefore an essential component of such Tours. Indeed, while on his 'Sentimental Tour' in 1792, John Dashwood's diary notes while passing through Shropshire include the passage, '*A mile from this is Bilworth Abby* [Buildwas Abbey] *– a Magnificent Ruin - & in some few miles still further are the vestiges of a Roman fortification*'.[11]

Returning to William Combe's poem one commentator notes that :-

> '*Ironically, while the picturesque emulated organic and natural forms it prescribed a landscape adapted and altered by human intervention. In a much-quoted passage Gilpin commented, without humour, that 'a mallet judiciously used' would considerably improve the picturesque qualities of the insufficiently ruined gable of Tintern Abbey. This pursuit of the picturesque, even at the expense of common sense, made it a ripe target for satirists.*
>
> *Jane Austen who, towards the end of her life, owned a copy of the 1812 edition of Combe's poem, frequently mocked the picturesque in her novels. In Pride and Prejudice Caroline Bingley and Louisa Hurst oust Elizabeth Bennet from a walk with Darcy by placing themselves in a way that monopolises a garden path. Darcy attempts to offset their rudeness by inviting Elizabeth to join them once again, only to receive the reply: 'You are charmingly group'd, and appear to uncommon advantage. The picturesque would be*

spoilt by admitting a fourth' (ch. 10). This plays upon a comment of Gilpin's relating to the grouping of cattle in which he considers three to be the optimum number for a picturesque composition. Elizabeth Bennet is mocking the picturesque and simultaneously slyly comparing Caroline and Louisa to cows.'[12]

In Chapter 18 of *Sense and Sensibility*, Edward Ferrars, having visited the village near Barton Cottage, engages with Marianne and Elinor in a discussion about the surrounding landscape. This touches directly on the picturesque, linking to the 'Sensibility' of the novel's title and also to Marianne, her character portrayed as having highly-developed such sensibility. The passage from the novel is as follows :-

'Edward returned to them with fresh admiration of the surrounding country; in his walk to the village, he had seen many parts of the valley to advantage; and the village itself, in a much higher situation than the cottage, afforded a general view of the whole, which had exceedingly pleased him. This was a subject which ensured Marianne's attention, and she was beginning to describe her own admiration of these scenes , and to question him more minutely on the objects that had particularly struck him, when Edward interrupted her by saying, "You must not inquire too far, Marianne – remember I have no knowledge of the picturesque, and I shall offend you by my ignorance and want of taste, if we come to particulars. I shall call hills steep, which ought to be bold! surfaces strange and uncouth, which ought to be irregular and rugged; and distant objects out of sight, which ought only to be indistinct through the soft medium of a hazy atmosphere. You must be satisfied with such admiration as I can honestly give. I call it a very fine country – the hills are steep, the woods seem full of fine timber, and the valley looks comfortable and snug – with rich meadows and several

neat farm-houses scattered here and there. It exactly answers my idea of a fine country, because it unites beauty with utility – and I dare say it is a picturesque one too, because you admire it; I can easily believe it to be full of rocks and promontories, grey moss and brushwood, but these are lost on me. I know nothing of the picturesque."

"I am afraid it is but too true," said Marianne; "but why should you boast of it?"

"I suspect," said Elinor, "that to avoid one kind of affectation, Edward here falls into another. Because he believes many people pretend to more admiration of the beauties of nature than they really feel, and is disgusted by such pretensions, he affects greater indifference and less discrimination in viewing them himself than he possesses. He is fastidious and will have an affectation of his own."

"It is very true," said Marianne, "that admiration of landscape scenery is become mere jargon. Everybody pretends to feel and tries to describe with the taste and elegance of him who first defined what picturesque beauty was. I detest jargon of every kind, and sometimes I have kept my feelings to myself, because I could find no language to describe them in but what was worn and hackneyed out of all sense and meaning."

"I am convinced," said Edward, "that you really feel all the delight in a fine prospect which you profess to feel. But, in return, your sister must allow me to feel no more than I profess. I like a fine prospect, but not on picturesque principles. I do not like crooked, twisted, blasted trees. I admire them much more if they are tall, straight, and flourishing. I do not like ruined, tattered cottages. I am not fond of nettles, or thistles, or heath blossoms. I have more pleasure in a

snug farm-house than a watch-tower – and a troop of tidy, happy villagers please me better than the finest banditti in the world."

Marianne looked with amazement at Edward, with compassion at her sister. Elinor only laughed.'[13]

Here the discussion of landscape, and the picturesque, is used in the context of sensibility, but Jane Austen, in devoting considerable attention to the general topic in her novels, evidences both a personal interest and recognition that it would be a subject with contemporary resonance for her readership. As such, it would therefore be an effective lever with which to signal her characters' tastes and sensibilities, and in doing so present part of their psychological make-ups.

Just such a technique is employed again in *Sense and Sensibility*, with the description of changes made by John Dashwood at Norland Park displaying his lack of sensibility. The following passage, in his own words, reveals to the reader something of Dashwood's character :-

"The enclosure of Norland Common, now carrying on, is a most serious drain [on his finances]. *And then I have made a little purchase within this half-year – East Kingham Farm, you must remember the place, where old Gibson used to live. The land was so very desirable for me in every respect, so immediately adjoining my own property, that I felt it my duty to buy it. I could not have answered it to my conscience to let it fall into any other hands. A man must pay for his convenience, and it has cost me a vast deal of money."*[14]

His purchase of additional land is intended by Austen to show lack of feeling, Dashwood clumsily disguising it under a rather disingenuous cloak of obligation or conscience. It is also, together with enclosure of Norland Common, used by Dashwood to plead a degree of poverty, because of the cost of the purchase. Both the enclosure and purchase of additional land are signals of a rapacious grasping attitude, as well as overturning the history inherent in those land ownerships. Together, they evidence a lack of respect for, and a dispassionate sweeping away of, the past.

The changes at Norland Park, the previous state of which was familiar to, and cherished by, Elinor and Marianne, are very specifically and deliberately described, again in Dashwood's own words, when talking to Elinor :-

" ... there is still a great deal to be done. There is not a stone laid of Fanny's greenhouse, and nothing but the plan of the flower-garden marked out." [Elinor then asks him where the greenhouse is to be.] *"Upon the knoll behind the house. The old walnut-trees are all come down to make room for it. It will be a very fine object from many parts of the park, and the flower-garden will slope down just before it, and be exceedingly pretty. We have cleared away all the old thorns that grew in patches over the brow."* [15]

Austen immediately tells us that, '*Elinor kept her concern and her censure to herself, and was very thankful that Marianne was not present to share the provocation.*' And as for Dashwood, '*Having now said enough to make his poverty clear, and to do away the necessity of buying a pair of earrings for each of his sisters, in his next visit at Gray's, his thoughts took a cheerfuller turn ...*' [16]

Again, this whole passage in the novel is used to underscore the respective characters of Dashwood, Elinor and Marianne. Dashwood is portrayed as selfish, ungenerous, unfeeling and insensitive, Marianne as having highly-developed, perhaps over-developed, 'sensibility', and Elinor holding it all together with her 'sense' and adherence to politeness. Compared with Elinor's restraint, Marianne is far more inclined to say what she feels even if she offends by doing so. Austen exposes, and is critical of, the risk that personal sensibility can turn into a rather selfish attitude which ignores other people's different sensibilities. Dashwood and Marianne are both portrayed as selfish, albeit in very different ways, while Elinor's behaviour and sense always accommodates other people's feelings.

Jane Austen's portrayal of Marianne's sensibilities is in tune with that of the Prince Regent himself, whom the author and historian Stella Tillyard comments *'was uninhibited and expressive in every way. A child of the age of sensibility, when feeling was taken as a sign of sincerity and tears were a quite acceptable accompaniment to joy or sadness, he was emotionally, physically and verbally unrestrained. Visitors were charmed by his unselfconscious affection'*.[17] This sincerity was not universal, sensibility at this time often being regarded, superficially at least, as a required personal characteristic, which it was fashionable to adopt and display in refined society, whether genuine or not. A contemporary reflection on whether such displays were authentic is the assessment by William Beckford of Lady Emma Hamilton (Nelson's lover), who performed her dramatic '*Attitudes*' at what was described as '*a monastic fete*' at Beckford's Fonthill Abbey. He was not impressed and thought '*she affected sensibility*' but '*was artful*'.[18] The Abbey setting was, appropriately, also very much in tune with the contemporary fashion for such gothic follies, which tended to mix some genuine history, or historical location, with new and unauthentic replica elements. This not only strikes a chord with Austen's fictional *Northanger Abbey* but, in combining an Abbey, gothic sensibilities, and a monastic fete (itself an unauthentic contradiction in terms), it also has a remarkable resonance with the events of Sir Francis Dashwood and his associates, the self-styled '*monks*', at Medmenham Abbey and later at the nearby Hell-Fire Caves, where their activities were anything but monastic. As outlined elsewhere, because of Austen's fascination for such things, these latter connections may well have contributed to her adoption of the name Dashwood for central characters in *Sense and Sensibility*, as well as allusions to their activities in at least one other novel.

To return to the specifics of the passage of Austen's novel quoted above, two academics – Jonathan Bate and Janine Barchas - have focused on this extract, providing similar analyses and commentary, descriptions of treatment of the landscape being taken as thinly disguised code for more profound aesthetic and religious messages.

In her Journal article, Barchas quotes the passage from *Sense and Sensibility,* already set out above, involving felling of old walnut trees, and comments that,

'Austen conveys far more than commonplace picturesque sentiment, as Fanny's felling of a grove of "old walnut trees" recalls Dashwood's diabolism. The walnut tree was, since medieval times, a symbol of Christ. The removal of the thorn bushes from the "brow" of the knoll augments Austen's choice of this symbolic species of tree with a detail that further invokes the crown of thorns upon Christ's brow. Fanny is lavishing great expenditure on an aesthetic blunder tantamount, Austen's symbolism insists, to the sacrilegious. With West Wycombe Park and its history of black masses as the novel's primary touchstone, Fanny Dashwood's arboreal sacrilege neatly echoes the doings of her moral twin and namesake, Francis Dashwood. In fact, the diabolism associated with the real Francis Dashwood may explain the presence of other religious allusions that run through Sense and Sensibility. For example, ... with the requisite number of denials from her betrayer, Marianne rises from the third day of her near-fatal illness, while in the netherworld below stairs, the fork-tongued Willoughby speaks to Elinor of "the devil" in one breath and "God" in the next. In such scenes, Austen may draw upon the known history of the Hell-Fire Club's mock-Catholic ceremonies, infusing Sense and Sensibility with a heightened religious quality.' [19]

Barchas highlights the 'King' element in the fictional name East Kingham Farm, pointing out the historical annexation of the name King to the name Dashwood. If she is on the right detective trail, then further support may be provided by the choice of the prefix 'East' in the name of the farm. In a phrase she uses in the same passage in her article, namely, *'The pouring of pious John King's fortune into the rakish coffers of his grandnephew John Dashwood'*, Barchas portrays a vivid contrast between the two landownings being amalgamated. If she is accurate in asserting that Austen, by inserting 'King' within the farm's name, was deliberately alluding to the *pious* (King) and *rakish* (Dashwood) opposites, which her more perceptive readers might pick up on, then I believe Austen's incorporation of the compass point *East* (Kingham Farm) may also be a deliberate opposite to *West* (Wycombe Park). Furthermore, there is the possible allusion that it was wealth accumulated from trade in the *East* Indies which had allowed the Dashwoods to purchase *West* Wycombe. It may also be deliberate that in weighing the opposites in the moral balance, there is a balanced and symmetrical four-syllable sound to each of West Wycombe Park and East Kingham Farm. Similar use of opposites by Austen is also noted by Margaret Doody, remarking that *'It is already Austen's custom in naming characters to set up patterns of binaries: northern versus southern, for example, or Anglo-Saxon versus Norman. In* Sense and Sensibility *she introduces a gallery of characters with questionable credentials and many lines of opposition: Tory and Whig, gentle and middle class'*.[20] Indeed, the title of the novel *Sense and Sensibility* is itself a binary form with opposing, or at least contrasting, characteristics.

As an aside, the addition of 'ham' to the name 'King' may have suggested itself to Austen because the village of Kingham in the Cotswolds is very close indeed to Adlestrop where Jane visited her relatives more than once around the very time she was revising and fine-tuning *Sense and Sensibility*. Also close by is Moreton-in-Marsh, perhaps providing the name for Miss

Morton in *Sense and Sensibility*, Doody noting that "Morton" derives from an ordinary locative, meaning '*settlement on a moor or on Marshy ground*'. [21] Yet another possible influence exerted by these real place names, all clustered within a small area of the North Cotswolds, near Jane Austen's relatives at Adlestrop, is provided by Warren Hastings' estate, Daylesford, with 'Delaford' being the name chosen by Jane for the church living that Edward Ferrars is offered by Colonel Brandon, once again in *Sense and Sensibility*.

Another local Cotswold location with close family connections for Austen is the village of Longborough, with its Leigh memorials in the church reflecting its long association with her mother's relatives. Longborough could be added to the list of suspects as inspiration for Jane's choices of names in her novels, this time in *Pride and Prejudice*, with the Bennets' home being at 'Longbourn', and a key character being 'Catherine de Bourgh'.

Returning to the annexation of East Kingham Farm in *Sense and Sensibility*, Jonathan Bate's text cites the following opening passage of the novel in order to draw out context and contrasts :

The family of Dashwood had been long settled in Sussex. Their estate was large, and their residence was at Norland Park, in the centre of their property, where, for many generations, they had lived in so respectable a manner, as to engage the general good opinion of their surrounding acquaintance.

Bate observes that,

'*This is Cobbett's resident native gentry, long settled through the generations. Respect emanates from the central point of the great house in an environing circle that embraces the community and the soil. .... The estate falls into the hands of Mr John Dashwood, who has only ever made occasional visits to Norland and has no feeling for the place. Having expelled his stepmother and half-sisters, he rides roughshod over the bond of reciprocal responsibility he owes to the local commoners and small farmers. He encloses and engrosses ...* '[22]

[Bate here quotes the passage from *Sense and Sensibility*, set out above, about enclosure and Dashwood's purchase of East Kingham Farm.]

In connection with indigenous trees at Norland being felled to be replaced with a greenhouse intended to house exotic plants, Bate notes that, '*the history of the greenhouse is bound up with that of empire*', being developed from its humble origins into a structure with more advanced climate control to house and cultivate the '*exotic plants brought back from the empire in the East and West Indies.*'[23]

Empire and associated trade represent another pervading contextual theme in Austen's Regency period and picking up on her possible East-West contrast, introduced above when discussing the name East Kingham Farm as a counterpoint to West Wycombe Park, this East-West dynamic may also mirror the contrasting perceptions of, and sentiments towards, the West Indies and East Indies during Austen's lifetime.

The East Indies influenced fashion in a variety of ways, on balance with positive associations, not only through the imported cultural innovations themselves, but also through providing the wealth to fund their infiltration into a home market ripe for such exoticism, and for which there was an almost insatiable contemporary appetite. We see these influences in such diverse fields as textiles (for example Indian calicos and muslins), art (notably representations of India by Tilley Kettle, William Hodges, and Thomas Daniell among others), architecture (including Mughal style, such as the Taj Mahal), food (as well as large imports of spices, the first Indian restaurant in London was opened at this time), and language (for example words such as avatar, dinghy, guru, pyjamas, shawl, and veranda). The overall sentiment in

Britain was positive enthusiasm for these new exotic influences, even if there was an undercurrent of envy for seemingly easy-made fortunes, intermingled with perceptions and accusations of widespread corruption. Warren Hastings' impeachment trial was based partly on such charges of corruption. However, the generality of public and state sentiment always plays a part in such judicial processes, and the overwhelming benefits of increased trade and other beneficial influences, to which Hastings' work in India had substantially contributed, were inevitably a factor in his eventual acquittal. In summary, if not yet seen as the jewel of the British Empire, India in the Regency period was nevertheless already a growing and vitally positive part of an embryonic imperial aspiration and vision.

By contrast, and despite there being some similarities (particularly in imports of exotic foods and spices, and generation of wealth), the West Indies had associations with much less positive sentiment. This sentiment was dominated by increasing unease and conscience about the slave trade, of which more shortly, but any positive aesthetic influences from the West Indies were also, in any event, much less significant. Whereas feelings about India (as with China) tapped into a respected culture with a long history, the West Indies offered no such equivalent respected civilisation or culture from which innovations could be enthusiastically adopted. One of Edmund Burke's speeches in 1783, with glowing and enthusiastic reference to Indian heritage and culture, ran as follows :-

> '*My next inquiry to that of the number* [the number of inhabitants of 'British' India, ... estimated to be about thirty million, more than four times the population of Britain] *is the quality and description of the inhabitants. This multitude of men does not consist of an abject and barbarous populace; much less of gangs of savages, like the Guarnaries and Chiquitos, who wander on the waste borders of the River of Amazons or the people of*

the Plate; but a people for ages, civilised and cultivated – cultivated by all the arts of polished life, whilst we were still in the woods. There have been (and still the skeletons remain) princes once of great dignity, authority and opulence. There are to be found an ancient and venerable priesthood, the depository of their laws, learning, and history, the guides of the people whilst living and their consolation in death; a nobility of great antiquity and renown; a multitude of cities, not exceeded in population and trade by those of the first class in Europe; merchants and bankers, individual houses of whom have once vied in capital with the Bank of England, whose credit had often supported a tottering state, and preserved their governments in the midst of war and desolation; millions of ingenious manufacturers and mechanics; millions of the most diligent, and not the least intelligent, tillers of the earth. Here are to be found almost all the religions professed by man – the Braminical, the Mussulman, the Eastern and Western Christian'.[24]

Burke himself had never been to India, but the the nineteenth century historian Thomas Babington Macaulay acknowledges that '*he had studied the history, the laws, and the usages of the East with an industry such as is seldom found united to so much genius and so much sensibility*'.[25] Burke's reverential comments reflected a general respectful perception about India among educated circles in England. Whereas India had these positive historical and cultural connotations, the West Indies carried darker associations. The lighter, colourful, and more refined East Indian influences are reflected in Jane Austen's own Indian shawl, iconically employed by Paula Byrne in *The Real Jane Austen* - a small example of the general acceptance of, and often enthusiasm for, Indian goods.

Foods and spices have been mentioned as being readily welcomed from both the West and East Indies, but even here there was a critical contrast between East and West. This related to the two main imported ingredients of a highly fashionable drink: sweetened tea. In the eighteenth century, both tea (from the East Indies) and sugar (predominantly from the West Indies) were luxury items and highly prized. However, whereas tea retained its positive status throughout Jane's lifetime, sugar at this time came to acquire negative and emblematic significance, directly related to the slave trade, one crucial element of the so-called triangular trade between Britain, Africa and the West Indies. The transatlantic slave trade flourished because a market existed for produce created using enslaved labour, namely rum, cotton, tobacco, coffee and particularly sugar.

The abolitionists understood that profits from the sugar they used in tea or cakes kept the slave trade running. If economic pressure could be put on slave-dependent industries, then this might hasten the end of the trade. An anti-sugar pamphlet by William Fox was published in 1791; it ran to 25 editions and sold 70,000 copies in four months. Spurred on by pamphlets and posters, by 1792 about 400,000 people in Britain were boycotting slave-grown sugar. Some people managed without, and others used sugar from the East Indies, where it was produced by free labour. Grocers reported sugar sales dropping by over a third in several parts of the country over just a few months. During a two-year period, the sale of sugar from India increased ten-fold (see Adam Hichschild: *Bury the Chains*). James Wright, a Quaker and merchant of Haverhill, Suffolk, advertised to his customers in the General Evening Post on March 6th, 1792, that he would no longer be selling West Indian sugar. He declared:

> ' ...... *Being Impressed with a sense of the unparalleled suffering of our fellow creatures, the African slaves in the West India Islands ..... with an apprehension, that while I am dealer in that article, which appears to be principal support of the slave trade, I am encouraging slavery, I take this method of informing my customer*

that I mean to discontinue selling the article of sugar when I have disposed of the stock I have on hand, till I can procure it through channels less contaminated, more unconnected with slavery, less polluted with human blood ....' [26]

The preference for sugar from the East Indies as a substitute for the slave-produced West Indies product is well recorded. An example, albeit after Jane's death, is the following advert:-

EAST INDIA SUGAR

By six families using East India instead of West India Sugar one Slave less is required: surely to release a fellow-creature from a state of cruel bondage and misery, by so small a sacrifice, is worthy the attention of all.

N. B. The labour of one Slave produces about Ten Cwt. Of Sugar annually.

J. Blackwell, Printer, Iris Office, Sheffield [27]

Other media were involved in keeping the issue in the public eye, including satirical cartoons by George Cruikshank and others. With the help of such media support, the various anti-slavery campaigns were eventually successful, but it took many years after the initial anti-slavery Act of 1807 before slavery throughout the British Empire was eventually abolished by Parliament in 1833. It remained a high-profile social issue throughout Jane's life, and Jane would have been aware that women played a leading role in the campaign to boycott sugar, which provided a tangible way to show support for the wider anti-slavery movement. Another cartoon, 'Anti-Saccharites' by James Gillray and published in 1792, when Jane was 16, graphically illustrates female involvement in the campaign.

Jane Austen's Regency Dashwoods

'Anti-Saccharites – or – John Bull and his family leaving off the use of sugar'
By James Gillray [National Portrait Gallery D12446]

In this image :-

The King, Queen, and six Princesses, three quarter length, are seated round a frugal tea-table. The King, in profile to the right, faces his daughters, holding his cup and saucer to his lips, and saying, with a staring eye, "delicious! delicious". The Queen sits in the centre behind the small tea-pot, holding her cup and saucer in bony fingers, and looking with a wide and cunning smile towards the Princesses, saying, "O my dear Creatures, do but Taste it! You can't think how nice it is without Sugar: - and then consider how much Work you'll save the poor Blackeemoors by leaving off the use of it! - and above all, remember how much expence it will save your poor Papa! - O its charming cooling Drink!" The Princess Royal sits at the end of the row, on the extreme right, with four sisters diminishing in age on her right, a sixth just indicated behind the Queen. They hold, but do not drink, cups of tea, with expressions varying from sulky discontent to defiant surprise. Below the title is etched: 'To the Masters & Mistresses of Families in Great Britain, this Noble Example of Economy, is respectfully submitted.' [28]

A recent commentary notes,

'As the main food purchasers, women played an important role in organising the sugar boycotts of the 1790s, after the bill for the abolition of the Slave Trade was defeated in Parliament in 1791. Over 300,000 people joined a boycott of sugar which had been grown on plantations that used the labour of enslaved people.' [29]

The role of women in these sugar boycotts may have contributed to Austen's interest in the slavery question, and the aspect involving sugar would have struck a very particular chord with Jane because it was *'the wine and sugar stores which constituted her part of the housekeeping'*.[30] The slavery issue is directly and critically addressed by Jane Austen in *Mansfield Park,* the climax of which is at a time (1806) when the abolition campaign was gaining ground, fuelled by growing awareness of, and disgust with, the slave trade. The title of the novel is the name of the fictional English country house owned by Sir Thomas Bertram, whose plantations in the West Indies finance the estate. The name *Mansfield Park* was probably chosen intentionally by Austen as a reference to Lord Mansfield (1705-1793) whose 18th century *'legal decisions put Britain on the path to abolishing the slave trade'*, as Norman Poser's biography of Lord Mansfield puts it.[31] The topic of slavery is handled in *Mansfield Park* in a way which reflects the prevailing tensions inherent in the issue at the time. The novel also weaves in various strong female characters who, although widely different in behaviour and attitude, portray increasing consciousness of changes to the traditional subservient role of women as the 19th century begins.

Having meandered somewhat off course, we return now to a concluding consideration of 'the picturesque', and its extensive use by Jane Austen in her novels. It is alluded to in five of her novels: *Pride and Prejudice*, *Mansfield Park*, *Northanger Abbey*, *Emma* and most notably in *Sense and Sensibility*, not surprisingly given the strong links between sensibilities and the picturesque movement.

Because it was such an important facet of aesthetic taste in the eighteenth and nineteenth centuries, Jonathan Bate makes 'The Picturesque Environment' the title and focus of chapter 5 of *The Song of the Earth*. As noted, given that Jane Austen's characters' considerations of the picturesque feature several times (often centre-stage) in her novels, it was clearly also of great personal interest to her. The reasons for this are various, some of which we may never know, but key drivers must surely have been the way in which it reflected contemporary aesthetic attitudes and a specific perspective on the relationship between nature and humanity.

In *Jane Austen and the Clergy* (1994), Irene Collins examines Jane Austen's own stylistic preferences for treatment of parks and gardens and finds these ambivalent. One constant reference point, however, is her general dislike of 'improvements' devised and executed with little or no sensitivity or respect for long-established forms. Such improvements were applied to property in general and not just to parks and gardens.

From the gentry houses of the earlier Tudor period, to the prodigy houses of Elizabethan England, and through to eighteenth century estate houses built on the back of imperial conquest and trade, property was an expression of wealth and often also of taste. In this context, and as a broad generalisation, Austen uses her brief descriptions of houses as indicators of wealth, and their settings (in terms of surrounding parks and landscaping) as indicators of taste. Another dimension, which applies both to the houses and their settings, is that of continuity and historical depth, with great reverence attaching to this quality in her novels. 'Improvements', when introduced into the novels, usually carry negative associations. This is evident, for example, in *Sense and Sensibility* as described earlier.

The architectural writer Nikolaus Pevsner in an article entitled *The Architectural Setting of Jane Austen's Novels*, contrasts Austen's vague descriptions of buildings in her novels with the following passage from Benjamin Disraeli's novel *Sybil* (1845).

'The building which was still called MARNEY ABBEY, though remote from the site of the ancient monastery, was an extensive structure raised at the latter end of the reign of James I, and in the stately and picturesque style of that age. Placed on a noble elevation in the centre of an extensive and well-wooded park, it presented a front with two projecting wings of equal dimensions with the centre, so that the form of the building was that of a quadrangle less one of its sides. Its ancient lattices had been removed, and the present windows, though convenient, accorded little with the structure; the old entrance door in the centre of the building, however, still remained, a wondrous specimen of fantastic carving: Ionic columns of black oak, with a profusion of fruits and flowers, and heads of stags, and sylvans. The whole of the building was crowned with a considerable pediment of what seemed at the first glance fanciful open work, but which, examined more nearly, offered in gigantic letters the motto of the house of Marney. The portal opened to a hall, such as is rarely found; with the dais, the screen, the gallery, and the buttery-hatch all perfect, and all of carved black oak ... The apartments were in general finished with all the cheerful ease and brilliancy of the modern mansion

of a noble, but the grand gallery of the seventeenth century was still preserved, and was used on great occasions as the chief reception-room. You ascended the principal staircase to reach it through a long corridor. It occupied the whole length of one of the wings; was one hundred feet long, and forty-five feet broad, its walls hung with a collection of choice pictures rich in history .....' [32]

Pevsner comments,

'If you want descriptions as circumstantial and as evocative as this, you must not go to Jane Austen's novels, ... - she is without exception vague, when it comes to describing buildings. Moreover, the lack of interest in anything but people which explains this vagueness applies to her letters as much as her novels. But in spite of this contrast between precision in dialogue and imprecision in the description of setting there is enough to be got out of the novels for anyone eager to know what life was lived by the narrow range of classes which Jane Austen knew well and which she wisely confined herself to. These classes are represented by the major house or mansion and the parsonage and by various houses or lodgings in London and a number of resorts.' [33]

While Austen does afford some fictional buildings in her novels some prominence – for example, Pemberley in *Pride and Prejudice* – Pevsner's point is generally valid. In relation to Austen's fictional buildings, her novel *Northanger Abbey* provides the most evocative example, with the Abbey conjuring up in Catherine Morland's mind just the sort of gothic romantic building she has read about in late 18th century novels. Having been invited to stay with the Tilneys at Northanger Abbey, Catherine muses that,

> *'she was to be their chosen visitor, she was to be for weeks under the same roof with the person whose society she most prized – and, in addition to all the rest, this roof was to be the roof of an abbey! – Her passion for ancient edifices was next in degree to her passion for Henry Tilney – and castles and abbeys made usually the charm of those reveries which his image did not fill. To see and explore either the ramparts and keep of the one, or the cloisters of the other, had been for many weeks a darling wish, though to be more than the visitor of an hour, had seemed too nearly impossible for desire. And yet, this was to happen. With all the chances against her of house, hall, place, park, court, and cottage, Northanger turned up an abbey, and she was to be its inhabitant. Its long, damp passages, its narrow cells and ruined chapel, were to be within her daily reach, and she could not entirely subdue the hope of some traditional legends, some awful memorials of an injured and ill-fated nun'*.[34]

At this point, we should perhaps recall Medmenham Abbey and its sinister associations in relation to the Dashwoods of West Wycombe and the Hell-Fire Club, as noted elsewhere. The fashion for gothic art, literature and buildings, evidenced in the portrayal and mindset of Austen's fictional Catherine Morland, is also reflected in the critical and satirical fascination it held for Jane herself.

Medmenham Abbey, beside the Thames, portrayed in 1801 as a picturesque ruin

To return to Pevsner's comments, he is making essentially the same point (discussed elsewhere) about Jane deliberately restricting the parameters of her writing to those which she knew; even when she did, rarely, stray into areas of limited knowledge, her commentaries are similarly limited. She had seen enough real buildings to assign her fictitious buildings at least competent basic descriptions but made no claims to detailed architectural knowledge. She did, however, have a deep interest in, and knowledge of, the picturesque. The concept of picturesque style appears again in the passage from Disraeli's novel, as cited by Pevsner above. Still current in 1845, the term 'picturesque' used by Disraeli in connection with a seventeenth century style of building is a retrospective attribution of an eighteenth and early nineteenth century concept, and understanding, of the word. The term picturesque, to the extent that it was used at all in the early seventeenth century, would not necessarily have accorded with Disraeli's meaning.

The Regency Picturesque

The definitive treatise on the picturesque which shaped its use and meaning in the late eighteenth and early nineteenth centuries was that of Sir Uvedale Price, and Bate quotes a seminal passage by him, contrasting the classically beautiful and the romantically picturesque:

A temple or palace of Grecian architecture in its perfect entire state, and with its surface and colour smooth and even, either in painting or reality is beautiful; in ruin it is picturesque. Observe the process by which time, the great author of such changes, converts a beautiful object into a picturesque one. First by means of weather stains, partial incrustations, mosses etc., it at the same time takes off from the uniformity of the surface, and of the colour; that is gives a degree of roughness and variety of tint. Next, the various accidents of weather loosen the stones themselves; they tumble in irregular masses ... Sedums, wall-flowers, and other vegetables that bear drought find nourishment in the decayed cement from which the stones have been detached : birds convey their food into the chinks, and yew, elder, and other berried plants project from the sides; while the ivy mantles over other parts and crowns the top.

Bate comments that, '*The paradox of the picturesque is clearly visible in Price's description of a ruin. The scene is composed on aesthetic principles, the emphasis being on pleasing variety gathered into unity by a crowning feature such as ivy. Viewed thus, it is like a picture, hence picturesque.*'[35] Bate also highlights the parallels with landscape paintings of the previous century featuring ruined temples and palaces as symbols of decay and human mortality. He then directly tackles the issue of trying to get a handle on any contemporary Regency meaning of 'the picturesque', noting that, '*Because of their obsession with the rules of taste, it ... had become trapped by its own prescriptive jargon*'.[36]

As outlined earlier, it is this 'jargon' which is explicitly referenced in the exchange between Edward Ferrars and Marianne Dashwood, and which terminology also appears in the real world in John Dashwood's description of his 'Sentimental Tour' in 1792.

The difference between Edward and Marianne's perceptions of value in landscape is explored by Bate, with Edward being portrayed as taking a pragmatic attitude to landscape, rejecting any suggestion that the necessity of rudimentary farmhouses and other marks of agricultural activity are 'vulgar or disgusting'. Marianne acknowledges Edward's criticism of picturesque jargon but insists that anyone with sensibility '*will respond to a wild landscape*', and '*looks with 'compassion' on her sister Elinor, who is destined to marry a man incapable of thrilling to the sight of rocks and promontories*'.[37]

This vogue for appreciating 'the sight of rocks and promontories', with elements of 'the sublime' and 'the picturesque' overlapping, is again exemplified by John Dashwood's focus on these landscape features in the diary of his Sentimental Tour, cited earlier. It also indicates precisely why the topographical artist Thomas Daniell (when establishing himself in the late eighteenth century), chose to paint just such features, for example his 'Cheddar Cliffs' (Cheddar Gorge, Somerset) and 'Brimham Crags' (Brimham Rocks, NorthYorkshire). Thomas Daniell is profiled in some detail later.

In trying to understand Jane Austen's somewhat complex relationship and attitudes to the picturesque, it is important to dig a little deeper into the relationship between the picturesque and nature. In relation to landscape gardening in the late eighteenth century, the picturesque was reflected in the attempts to create views which artificially merged the garden with the wider landscape by incorporating features such as the ha-ha.[38] This also gave the impression that everything in sight belonged to to the house, as noted for example by Huxley in commenting on Lancelot 'Capability'

Brown's impact on eighteenth-century landscaped park developments.[39]

The term 'Capability' attached to Lancelot Brown's name expresses his ability to identify the potential of a landscape, i.e. what improvements it might be capable of to emulate the aesthetic fashions of the day. It is no coincidence that this potential for so-called improvement is mirrored by Austen's passage in *Northanger Abbey* (completed in 1803) in which she writes that the Tilneys, *'were viewing the country with the eyes of persons accustomed to drawing, and decided on its capability of being formed into pictures, with all the eagerness of real taste'*.[40] In this period, termed by Asa Briggs *The Age of Improvement*, Austen's phrase therefore further evidences the asserted potential for human intervention to improve the natural state into idealised 'pictures'. It also highlights the contemporary link between appreciation of the 'picturesque' and 'taste', which Austen employs as a mechanism more than once in her novels in delineating the nature of individual characters, not only positively or negatively, but often ambiguously, perhaps reflecting her own mixed feelings on the subject. In any event, as a subject ripe for satire the picturesque was a perfect one for Austen to exploit.

Huxley also makes a link between fashion, 'improvements', Humphry Repton, and satire, commenting that, *'It was Humphry Repton who would take over Capability Brown's position as the nation's most eminent improver to the people of fashion and he also became pilloried and satirised'*.[41] There have been several commentaries about Austen's attitude to the work of improvers such as Repton, who she mentions explicitly in *Mansfield Park*. On the face of it she is critical of such artful attempts at the picturesque, preferring an approach to landscape which is arguably more honest and natural. However, there are no definitive Austen preferences we can be totally sure of, and these waters are further muddied when retrospective analyses, including my own, are attempted. The contrast between the views of Mary Crawford and Edmund, the latter portrayed very sympathetically, in

Mansfield Park gives an insight into Austen's own preferences. Edmund states that, "*I should not put myself into the hands of an improver. I would rather have an inferior degree of beauty, of my own choice, and acquired progressively*", whereas Mary Crawford asserts that, " ... *I should be most thankful to any Mr Repton who would undertake it, and give as much beauty as he could for my money*".[42]

This surely indicates Austen's preference for owners relying on their own taste in implementing change in an evolving and gradual way as opposed to employing an improver to deliver instant (and transiently fashionable) beauty, purchased as a commodity. Mary Crawford's phrase 'give as much beauty as he could for my money' is a damning and coruscating indictment by Austen of the lack of taste and sensibility shown by many whose only desire was to purchase beauty in line with the latest fashion. Ironically, such instant transformations were usually specifically intended by the purchasers as an expression of taste.

As already outlined, ruins played a central role in the picturesque, both in art and as magnets attracting middle class visitors to well known sites, as exemplified in the following contemporary print. This image also highlights parallels with elements of Jane Austen's narratives in *Northanger Abbey*, with the male figure 'educating' his female companion about the ruins.

Ruins of Roch Abbey, Yorkshire, c.1790

Some of the most obvious ruins were those of the many monasteries, abbeys and other religious houses destroyed as part of their Dissolution by Henry VIII, associated with his dramatic break from Rome and Roman Catholicism.

Austen's deep interest in history, and this particular element, is referenced by Doody in the following passage :-

'Jane Austen seems always to have been antipathetic to the Dissolution and what it meant. Her "prejudiced Historian" in 1791 makes a mock defense of Henry VIII:

The Crimes and Cruelties of this Prince, were too numerous to be mentioned, (as this history I trust has fully shewn;) and nothing can be said in his vindication, but [*except*] that his abolishing Religious Houses and leaving them to the ruinous depredations of time has been of infinite use to the landscape of England in general, which probably was a principal motive for his doing it, since otherwise why should a Man who was of no Religion himself be at so much trouble to abolish one which had for Ages been established in the Kingdom. ("History," Juvenilia, 181)

Austen's remark that Henry VIII "was of infinite use to the landscape of England" by ruining the abbeys is a satirical reflection – not a distortion – of Gilpin's complacent view.[43]

Gilpin is an apologist for the Dissolution, portraying the Religious Houses as being corrupt and indulgent (mirroring the arguments put to Henry VIII by Thomas Cromwell in suggesting and justifying their abolition). Put crudely, Gilpin takes a Whig-Protestant stance, with anti-Catholic undertones. Doody notes that, '*In her novels, Austen implicitly combats Gilpin's biases. Two novels have at their center privatized abbeys, and there are other references to lost religious sites.*'[44] If the name Dashwood in *Sense and Sensibility* is indeed a reference to the Dashwoods of West Wycombe and the Hell-Fire Club, then the Club's origins at the ruins of Medmenham Abbey provide exactly the negative allusions that Austen would favour in countering Gilpin's positive and romantic picturesque attitude to such ruins.

In summary, Irene Collins' comment that, '*Jane's attitude to landscape gardening was always engagingly ambivalent*'[45] is pertinent because landscape gardening philosophy in her time incorporated a strong element of the picturesque. To the extent that Austen's attitude is ambivalent and complex, this complexity is mirrored in different and subtly evolving interpretations of the meaning of 'picturesque' during her own lifetime. I believe Austen's treatment of the concept in the novels accurately portrays this complexity and the paradoxes of the picturesque. What can hardly be disputed is that the rich and diverse concept of the picturesque, which she repeatedly wove into her novels, had a significant influence on Jane Austen and her writing.

CHAPTER SIX
Regency Icons and Indian Influences

"To lie beside the margin of that stream [Kingham Brook near Daylesford, Gloucestershire], *and muse, was one of my favourite recreations; and there, one bright summer's day, when I was scarcely seven years old, I well remember that I first formed the determination to purchase back Daylesford."* - Warren Hastings[1]

As a young schoolboy, **Horatio Nelson,** having survived a dangerous situation, is quoted as saying, *"Fear ... I never saw fear. What is it? It never came near me"*, and when challenged as to why he stole pears from his schoolmaster's tree said that he *"only took them because every other boy was afraid".*[2]

These boyhood quotes reflect the characters of two nationally important historic figures, both of whom significantly shaped the context of Jane Austen's novels. As examples of Aristotle's maxim, *'give me a child until he is seven and I will show you the man'*, the quotes above provide insights into these two remarkable individuals, highlighting the emergence of their determination and motivations from an early age. In Hastings' case, his mindset at 7 years old, in having a clear aim without any real idea how to achieve it, is reflected again much later in his life in a conversation he had with Philip Francis (with whom, in 1780 in India, he was to fight a non-fatal duel with pistols). Hastings, with reference to Daniel Defoe's fictional *Robinson Crusoe* having built a monstrous boat at a distance from the sea, said, *'the same thing has happened to myself an hundred times in my life. I have built a boat without any further consideration, and when difficulties and consequences have been urged against it, have been ready to answer them by saying to myself* "Let me finish the boat first, and then I'll warrant, I shall find some method to launch it".'[3]

In relation to the determination framed in the opening quotation above, Macaulay notes that Hastings' scheme,

> '*was never abandoned. He would recover the estate which had belonged to his fathers. He would be Hastings of Daylesford. This purpose, formed in infancy and poverty, grew stronger as his intellect expanded and as his fortune rose. He pursued his plan with that calm but indomitable force of will which was the most striking peculiarity of his character. When,* [many years later, in India] *under a tropical sun, he ruled fifty million of Asiatics, his hopes, amidst all cares of war, finance, and legislation, still pointed to Daylesford ... and it was to Daylesford that he retired to die*'.[4]

Daylesford House – historic Cotswold seat of the Hastings Family

Nelson and Hastings both had character flaws but these, combined with counterbalancing strengths, contributed at least in part to their notable, and globally significant, achievements. Nelson was notoriously vain, frequently craving attention and recognition for his naval actions. This, combined with his lack of fear, drove him to take risks and adopt bold strategies which often delivered victories against all the odds. Indeed, this was recognised even at the time. After his acclaimed leadership at the two naval encounters at Aboukir Bay and Copenhagen, Lady Elizabeth Foster commented that, *'this truly great hero has his weaknesses, but his love of praise has led to such glorious actions to obtain it that one must forgive him'*.[5]

Hastings' weaknesses, including elements of false pride, self-righteousness, stubbornness, and political insensitivity, contributed to severe criticism, resulting in his famous seven-year impeachment trial. However, his strengths, including personal determination, an adventurous and inquisitive nature, and responsiveness to Indian sub-culture, ultimately led to wide recognition of his contribution to the emerging establishment of British India, which in turn influenced his acquittal. Macaulay wrote that, '*I think Hastings, though far from faultless, one of the greatest men England ever produced. He had pre-eminent talents for government, and great literary talents too; fine taste, a princely spirit, and heroic equanimity in the midst of adversity and danger*'.[6] Given their substantial national contributions, it is surprising that Nelson and Hastings both shared the unfortunate experience of failing in their pleas to parliament for grants of widows' pensions for their respective partners, Emma Hamilton and the second Mrs Hastings. A further, more striking, shared experience was that of each effectively having an 'adopted daughter', quite probably a natural child in both cases. The true relationships were to differing degrees concealed throughout the remainder of their respective lives, while at the same time substantial expense and care was being lavished by each of them on these young females.

It was natural that such heroic, and sometimes controversial, figures rose to prominence at this time, because turbulent events demanded strong characters and leaders. Through their contributions to colonial expansion and trade involving exotic influences, Nelson and Hastings are important to Austen's Regency context. More significantly, they also both had direct impacts on her writing through their respective links with her immediate family and close relatives.

The period leading up to, and spanning, Jane Austen's lifetime, as well as coinciding with colonial and trading expansion, featured military conflict, and radical industrial, agricultural, and social transformation, as well as violent revolution in France and the threat of something similar closer to home. Nelson, for example, while on shore leave in the 1790s, was deeply distressed by *'reports of discontent and political agitation in the country, particularly in Norfolk* [his home county]. *Members of radical societies were going from alehouse to alehouse disseminating revolutionary ideas and* "advising the poor people to pay no taxes, etc".'[7] Nelson asked a Justice of the Peace why a particular individual, clergyman Joseph Priestley, known to be a supporter of the French Revolution, and propagating its ideas in Norfolk, had not been arrested. The reply he got was that no JP would make himself unpopular by doing so, for fear of retribution should the mob rise up, which was clearly seen as a real possibility.

However, it is noticeable that these unsettling factors are largely absent from Jane's writing. Referring to Austen's deliberate choice of a narrow framework for the setting of her novels , and with reference to the suffering caused by radical social change, Asa Briggs comments that, '*Jane Austen could ignore all these hard facts just as she ignored the wars against Napoleon*'.[8] With regard to the period of the Napoleonic Wars, another commentator notes that as far as upper and middle class society was concerned,

> '*the great war made no impression. The country-house life of the period is depicted in Jane Austen's novels;*

no-one thought of asking any of her heroes why they contributed no service of any kind to their country's war effort. .... The upper class was able throughout the war to cultivate all the pleasures of the intellect, and of the senses. ... Its polished and brilliant surface was unruffled by the hurricane which howled for nearly a quarter of a century about the length and breadth of Europe ...'[9]

The 'senses' referred to are very much at the heart of much of Austen's writing, most conspicuously in *Sense and Sensibility*.

Austen was not alone in such alleged blindness to the social distress which resulted from the wars, and which extended during her lifetime and much deeper into the new century. Slightly later, in Gloucestershire, at a time when there were sporadic agricultural riots all over the county, Mary Gibson notes that at Bourton-on-the-Hill, the Revd. Samuel Warneford [a generous philanthropist]

'seemed to have been oblivious to what was going on around him. He wrote to a friend on the very day he returned from driving through farms and villages pillaged by the rioters: "It is delightful to see fellow labourers sedulously employed in promoting the glory of God and the good of man. What a blessing it is to see these simple fellows thus employed!" *He drove about his district in his one-horse shay dressed in the shabbiest of clothes* [despite his wealth], *unmolested by any of the hooligans who marched along the highways in their unruly bands'.* [10]

Warneford would soon have his complacency shaken, and the reality was that the early 19th century was a time of great dissatisfaction among large sections of the population, with economic, political, and social grievances persisting well after Jane Austen's death. In a letter of 28th April 1831, Rev. Patrick Bronte, father of the Bronte sisters, advocating temperate (rather than radical) parliamentary and electoral reform, noted that otherwise, *'the inveterate enemies ... will work on the popular feeling – already but much too excited – so as to cause, in all probability, general insurrectionary movements, and bring about a revolution. We see what has been lately done in France.'*[11]

This was not just scaremongering. In the same year, 1831, there were serious riots in Bristol, which forced the Bishop of Bristol to flee the city and seek refuge with his friend Revd. Samuel Wilson Warneford at Bourton-on-the-Hill, the Cotswold village with direct Dashwood connections explored in later chapters. To quell the riots, a troop of the 3rd Dragoon Guards and a squadron of the 14th Light Dragoons were sent to Bristol under the command of Lieutenant-Colonel Thomas Brereton. Interestingly, just such a scenario, involving use of the Light Dragoons to quell riots, is presaged (albeit with a satirical literary twist) by Jane Austen in *Northanger Abbey* several years earlier, as noted below.

The real threat of riots, and worse, had persisted for several decades, and social unrest in the wake of the French Revolution in 1789 occasionally turned into direct action. In June 1792, for example, there were riots in Mount Street, London, triggered by the building of a new watch-house to oversee inmates at the local workhouse for the poor. Tomalin notes that Jane Austen's cousin Eliza, *'was frightened by a mob fighting with mounted Guards in Mount Street in central London'*[12] and this event is also directly referenced in the Dashwood family papers. At the time, John Dashwood (who, the following year, was to become the 4th Baronet of West Wycombe) was staying at his London town house in Argyle Street. A letter sent to him from his agent, back at his Bourton-on-the-Hill home in the Cotswolds, asked, *'What do you think of the Mount Street riots of which we have just had a long account in the paper?'*[13] John Dashwood's response is not recorded, but no-one could have been unaware of a general and serious tension in society. A further reference to riots in the wider Regency period appears in John Dashwood's diaries. His entry for Tuesday 14th August 1821, after recording '*The Queen's Funeral*', notes '*Riot in London near Cumberland Gate – 2 men or more killed – several wounded*'.[14]

Asa Briggs is not quite fair or accurate in accusing Austen of totally ignoring some of the threats and fears of this turbulent period, but even when she does reference such matters, they are not dealt with entirely seriously. The following passage from *Northanger Abbey* - which among other themes is infused with, and pokes fun at, the fashion for melodramatic Gothic novels - shows Jane Austen playing tricks with her characters, setting up a staged and satirical misunderstanding between some sort of feared riot and '*something very shocking indeed*' which '*will soon come out in London*' :-

> *The general pause which succeeded his short disquisition on the state of the nation, was put an end to by Catherine, who, in rather a solemn tone of voice, uttered these words, 'I have heard that something very shocking indeed, will soon come out in London.'*
>
> *Miss Tilney, to whom this was chiefly addressed, was startled, and hastily replied, 'Indeed! – and of what nature?'*
>
> *'That I do not know, nor who is the author. I have only heard that it is to be more horrible than anything we have met with yet.'*
>
> *'Good heaven! – Where could you hear of such a thing?'*
>
> *'A particular friend of mine had an account of it in a letter from London yesterday. It is to be uncommonly dreadful. I shall expect murder and everything of that kind.'*
>
> *'You speak with astonishing composure! But I hope your friend's accounts have been exaggerated; - and if*

such a design is known beforehand, proper measures will undoubtedly be taken by government to prevent it coming to effect.'

'Government,' said Henry, endeavouring not to smile, 'neither desires nor dares to interfere in such matters. There must be murder; and government cares not how much.'

The ladies stared. He laughed, and added, 'Come, shall I make you understand each other, or leave you to puzzle out an explanation as you can? No – I will be noble. I will prove myself a man, no less by the generosity of my soul than the clearness of my head. I have no patience with such of my sex as disdain to let themselves sometimes down to the comprehension of yours. Perhaps the abilities of women are neither sound not (sic) acute – neither vigorous nor keen. Perhaps they may want observation, discernment, judgment, fire genius, and wit.'

'Miss Morland, do not mind what he says; - but have the goodness to satisfy me as to this dreadful riot.'

'Riot! – what riot?'

'My dear Eleanor, the riot is only in your own brain. The confusion there is scandalous. Miss Morland has been talking of nothing more than a new publication which is shortly to come out, in three duodecimo volumes, two hundred and seventy-six pages in each, with a frontispiece to the first, of two tombstones and a lantern – do you understand? – And you, Miss Morland – my stupid sister has mistaken all your clearest expressions. You talked of expected horrors in London – and instead of instantly conceiving, as any rational creature would have done, that such words could relate only to a circulating library, she immediately pictured to herself a mob of three thousand men assembling in St George's Fields; the

Bank attacked, the Tower threatened, the streets of London flowing with blood, a detachment of the 12th Light Dragoons, (the hopes of the nation,) called up from Northampton to quell the insurgents, and the gallant Capt. Frederick Tilney, in the moment of charging at the head of his troop, knocked off his horse by a brickbat from an upper window. Forgive her stupidity. The fears of the sister have added to the weakness of the woman; but she is by no means a simpleton in general.[15]

A related footnote to the Wordsworth Classic edition of Northanger Abbey reiterates the serious fear of riots outlined already, and adds a socio-political comment :-

The idea of riots in the London of the late 1790s and early 1800s - and Northanger Abbey was completed in 1803 - should not be thought of as entirely fanciful. In the decade and a half after the French Revolution of 1789, conservatives in England feared that outbreaks of civil disorder were imminent, and the government used the fear of riot and disorder to exact a series of repressive measures against radical writers and societies. At one level, Eleanor's ready misunderstanding of Catherine's remark expresses the liability to political alarm of the Tilneys' social class.[16]

Despite '*the polished and brilliant surface*' of their world '*being unruffled*' as quoted earlier, beneath that surface there was an undercurrent of genuine concern. The nervousness among this class about civil unrest is exemplified by a letter dated March 5th 1804, and marked '*most private*', from the Mayor of Buckingham to one of our central characters, Sir John Dashwood-King, in which the Mayor states that he is, '*anxious that a cavalry association be formed in the neighbourhood & Town of High Wycombe of such persons as <u>you</u> can confide in so that <u>you</u> could command them*'.[17]

The concept of 'neighbourhood', both in terms of geography and a network of key individuals, is a socially important one at this time, and is picked up again shortly. Its specific importance here is reflected in the primary reliance for law and order being founded on local neighbourhood authority and action.

In summary, the half-century 1790-1840 saw major upheavals and uncertainty for much of the population, and although Austen lived through the first half of this period, this is only lightly touched on in her novels. While these dramatic economic, social and military events form important contextual elements for her writing, the action in the novels, like the calm in the eye of a storm, is predominantly played out within structured social and domestic contexts, protocols, and relative tranquillity, around which external and unsettling dramas swirl and unfold. Literary reviews at the time and in the decades after her death touch on this aspect of her writing, varying from withering criticism of its prim superficiality (for example, from Charlotte Bronte and from an anonymous writer thought to be George Eliot) to the other extreme, namely of glowing admiration for its intimate, realistic, and accurate perceptions (for example from Walter Scott, Richard Whately, and the literary critic G H Lewes).

Charlotte Bronte, writing to Lewes in 1848, and having acquired Austen's masterpiece *Pride and Prejudice* at his suggestion, comments,

'I got the book and studied it. And what did I find? An accurate daguerreotyped portrait of a common-place face; a carefully fenced, highly cultivated garden, with neat borders and delicate flowers – but no glance of a bright vivid physiognomy – no open country – no fresh air – no blue hill – no bonny beck. I should hardly like to live with her ladies and gentlemen in their elegant but confined houses. These observations will probably irritate you, but I shall run the risk.'[18]

Regency Icons and Indian Influences

Lewes was an Austen admirer, and had suggested to Charlotte Bronte (after reading her *Jane Eyre* and having a criticism of one its element) that she might improve her writing by reading some of Jane Austen's work. Lewes, in *The Lady Novelists*, 1852 notes,

> '*First and foremost let Jane Austen be named, the greatest artist that has ever written, using the term to signify the most perfect mastery over the means to her end. There are heights and depths in human nature Miss Austen has never scaled nor fathomed, there are worlds of passionate existence into which she has never set foot; but although this is obvious to every reader, it is equally obvious that she risked no failures by attempting to delineate that which she had not seen. Her circle may be restricted, but it is complete. Her world is a perfect orb, and vital. ... To read one of her books is like an actual experience of life: you know the people as if you had lived with them, and you feel something of personal affection towards them.*'[19]

However, what some see as praiseworthy achievements others see as deficiencies. In 1853, an anonymous writer, thought to be George Eliot, noted that,

> '*Without brilliance of any kind – without imagination, depth of thought, or wide experience, Miss Austen, by simply describing what she knew and had seen, and making accurate portraits of very tiresome and uninteresting people, is recognised as a true artist, and will continue to be admired, when many authors more ambitious, and believing themselves filled with a much higher inspiration, will be neglected and forgotten. .... People will persist in admiring what they can appreciate and understand ... But Miss Austen's accurate scenes from dull life ... must be classed in the lower division. ... They show us too much of the*

littleness and trivialities of life, and limit themselves so scrupulously to the sayings and doings of dull, ignorant, and disagreeable people, that their very truthfulness makes us yawn.'[20]

Partial exceptions to these observations and criticisms of Austen's narrow domestic focus are to be found in the unfinished novel *Sanditon*, in which social changes resulting from modern developments of a coastal resort (the title no doubt chosen to reflect such a 'sandy town') are discussed, and in *Mansfield Park*, where key disturbing strands, relating to the slave trade, intrude more directly into the narrative. Slavery was only one aspect of a wider concern about the extent to which wealth was being rapidly acquired on the back of questionable behaviour and exploitation associated with Britain's geographic, military, commercial, and economic expansion. During Jane's lifetime, employment of slavery in the West Indies plantations was certainly one troubling undercurrent, but plundering of riches in India was another, this latter being one of the charges levied formally against Warren Hastings, and informally against many other adventurers returning from the sub-continent. *Mansfield Park* and *Sanditon* partially excepted, Austen's novels pose the question as to whether her deliberate caution – largely avoiding, and only obliquely referencing, the major social and political issues of the day - was merely self-constraint regarding content, a reflection of an inherently narrow personal outlook, genuine ignorance of the details of these issues, or simply a pragmatic appreciation of the profiles, preferences, and tastes of her likely readership.

In his Introduction to the 1966 Penguin edition of *Emma*, Ronald Blythe makes an interesting observation in the context of Jane's upbringing and family on the one hand, and on the other the admiration she had earned from many prominent people, not least the Prince Regent, and his librarian Stanier Clarke. Blythe comments that, '*The great world, such as it was, was hers, it seems for the asking. No wonder she rejected it for her large and gifted family, so large as to make it unnecessary to search beyond it for happiness, so gifted as to make people like Mr Clarke seem fools*'.[21] But arguably she did gradually expand her horizons, possibly simply as a result of growing in confidence in herself and her writing, or in developing stronger feelings on topical issues, with wider scope and confrontation of contentious issues evident in those novels which were conceived as she, and her writing, matured. *Mansfield Park* exhibits elements of this transition and *Sanditon* has a very different feel from Austen's earliest literary conceptions. Nevertheless, elements of satire and parody remained a common thread throughout her writing career, and the success of these satires and parodies relied at least in part on a detailed understanding and appreciation of the very subtle contemporary distinctions of class and associated behavioural expectations. In discussing this class system, Asa Briggs notes that,

> '*There were various ways of classifying and subdividing the different ranks and orders which together made up the community. Many of them were complicated, for the English social system emphasised minute social distinctions and nuances of status rather than broad collective groupings. It needed a novelist like Jane Austen to trace the delicate pattern*'.[22]

Whatever the perceptions of, and theories about, Austen's notable narrow focus, her own few comments appear to support the view that she deliberately restricted herself to the types of situation she had experienced first-hand, knew intimately, and felt confident that her readership would be able to relate to or respond to. In any event, while she had access to very good sources of information on many of the wider issues of the day she chose, for whatever reason, not to exploit these more explicitly in the novels. As previously noted, rather than openly taking sides on divisive issues, she often adopted the technique of allowing her characters to debate them instead, albeit with her own position usually clear enough. The 'argument', as Tomalin describes it, between the characters Catharine and Camilla in *Catharine, or the Bower*, in relation to the 'Indian marriage strategy', is a good example, where Jane's position in the argument is barely disguised.[23] Another example would be the discussions between her characters regarding religion, the role of the church, and the status, duties, and responsibilities of the clergy, notably in *Mansfield Park*.

Margaret Drabble, in her perceptive Introduction to the 1974 Penguin Classics edition of *Lady Susan, The Watsons* and *Sanditon*, makes similar observations. Citing an example of Austen's projection of attitudes onto her created characters, in relation to romanticism, Gothic sensibilities, and appreciation of landscape, including the picturesque, Drabble notes that Austen :-

> '*did not herself dislike the new romantic writers, any more than she disliked the Gothic novel which she satirizes in Northanger Abbey. She enjoyed Scott, as a poet and a novelist. She had herself a strong feeling for landscape, though when her heroines enthuse over it, as Fanny Price does in Mansfield Park, they tend to get laughed at by her heroes. Though she may be an enthusiast herself, she cannot strike the right note in her prose, and she recognises this. She leaves lyricism, wisely, to others, and contents herself with parodying their excess, an easier role*'.[24]

More generally, Jane Austen employs controversial contemporary issues as backdrops, thereby adding richness to the plots and, perhaps most importantly, keeping them topical. In one sense, it is as well she didn't attempt to paint on a wider canvas, outside her comfort zone, as James Stanier Clarke (the Prince Regent's librarian), for example, urged her to do, because her novels' tight structures, allied to accuracy of observation, and conviction, are their key strengths. Extracts from the most relevant letters between Jane Austen and James Stanier Clarke are reproduced here both to emphasise Jane's decisive rejection of departing from her chosen subject matter, and to show that during her own lifetime her writing was already having an impact at the highest levels of Regency society.

Letter from Jane Austen to James Stanier Clarke [Librarian to His Royal Highness the Prince Regent][25]

Wednesday 15th November 1815

Sir

I must take the liberty of asking You a question – Among the many flattering attentions which I recd. from you at Carlton House, on Monday last, was the Information of my being at liberty to dedicate any future Work to HRH the P.R. without the necessity of any Solicitation on my part. Such at least, I believed to be your words; but as I am very anxious to be quite certain of what was intended, I intreat you to have the goodness to inform me how such a Permission is to be understood, & whether it is incumbent on me to shew my sense of the Honour, by inscribing the Work now in the Press, to H.R.H. – I shd be equally concerned to appear either presumptious or Ungrateful. –

I am &c –

Response from James Stanier Clarke[26]

Thursday 16th November 1815
Carlton House

Dear Madam,
It is certainly not incumbent on you to dedicate your work now in the Press to His Royal Highness: but if you wish to do the Regent that honour either now or

at any future period, I am happy to send you that permission which need not require any more trouble or solicitation on your Part.

Your late Works, Madam, and in particular Mansfield Park reflect the highest honour on your Genius & your Principles; in every new work your mind seems to increase its energy and powers of discrimination. The Regent has read & admired all your publications.

Accept my sincere thanks for all the pleasure your Volumes have given me: in the perusal of them I felt a great inclination to write & say so. And I also dear Madam wished to be allowed to ask you, to delineate in some future Work the Habits of Life and Character and enthusiasm of a Clergyman – who should pass his time between the metropolis & the Country – who should be something like Beatties Minstrel

> *Silent when glad, affectionate tho' shy*
> *And now his look was most demurely sad*
> *& now he laughed aloud yet none knew why*

Neither Goldsmith – nor La Fontaine in his Tableau de Famille – have in my mind quite delineated an English Clergyman, at least of the present day – Fond of, & entirely engaged in Literature – no man's Enemy but his own. Pray dear Madam think of these things.

> *Believe me at all times*
> *With sincerity & respect*
> *Your faithful & obliged Servant*
> *J. S. Clarke*
> *Librarian*

P.S.

I am going for about three weeks to Mr Henry Streatfeilds, Chiddingstone Sevenoaks – but hope on my return to have the honour of seeing you again.

Letter from Jane Austen to James Stanier Clarke[27]

Monday 11th December 1815

Dear Sir

My Emma is now so near publication that I feel it right to assure You of my not having forgotten your kind recommendation of an early Copy for Cn H. - & that I have Mr Murray's promise of its being sent to HRH. under cover to You, three days previous to the Work being really out. –

I must make use of this opportunity to thank you dear Sir, for the very high praise you bestow on my other Novels – I am too vain to wish to convince you that you have praised them beyond their Merit. –

My greatest anxiety at present is that this 4th work shd not disgrace what was good in the others. But on this point I will do myself the justice to declare that whatever may be my wishes for its' success, I am very strongly haunted by the idea that to those Readers who have preferred P&P. it will appear inferior in Wit, & to those who have preferred MP. very inferior in good Sense. Such as it is however, I hope you will do me the favour of accepting a Copy. Mr M. will have directions for sending one. I am quite honoured by your thinking me capable of drawing such a Clergyman as you gave the sketch of in your note of Nov: 16. But I assure you I am <u>not</u>. The comic part of the Character I might be equal to, but not the Good, The Enthusiastic, the Literary. Such a Man's Conversation must at times be on subjects of Science & Philosophy of which I know nothing – or at least be occasionally abundant in quotations & allusions which a Woman, who like me, knows only her Mother-tongue & has read very little in that, would be totally without power of giving. – A Classical Education, or at any rate, a very extensive acquaintance with English Literature, Ancient &

Modern, appears to me quite Indispensable for the person who wd do any justice to your Clergyman – And I think I may boast myself to be, with all possible Vanity, the most unlearned, & uninformed Female who ever dared to be an Authoress.

Beleive me, dear Sir,
Your obligd & faithl Hum.
Servt.
J.A.

Letter from James Stanier Clarke[28]

Wednesday 27 March 1816
Pavilion

Dear Miss Austen,

I have to return you the Thanks of His Royal Highness the Prince Regent for the handsome Copy you sent him of your last excellent Novel – pray dear Madam soon write again and again. Lord St. Helens and many of the Nobility who have been staying here, paid you the just tribute of their Praise.

The Prince Regent has just left us for London; and having been pleased to appoint me Chaplain and Private English Secretary to the Prince of Cobourg, I remain here with His Serene Highness & a select Party until the Marriage. Perhaps when you appear in print you may chuse to dedicate your Volumes to Prince Leopold: any Historical Romance illustrative of the History of the august house of Cobourg, would just now be very interesting.

Believe me at all times
Dear Miss Austen
Your obliged friend
J. S. Clarke

<u>Letter from Jane Austen at Chawton to James Stanier Clarke</u>[29]

Monday 1 April 1816

My dear Sir

I am honoured by the Prince's thanks, & very much obliged to yourself for the kind manner in which You mention the Work. .....

You are very, very kind in your hints as to the sort of Composition which might recommend me at present, & I am fully sensible that an Historical Romance, founded on the House of Saxe Cobourg might be much more to the purpose of Profit or Popularity, than such pictures of domestic Life in Country Villages as I deal in – but I could no more write a Romance than an Epic Poem. – I could not sit seriously down to write a serious Romance under any other motive than to save my Life, & if it were indispensable for me to keep it up & never relax into laughing at myself or other people, I am sure I should be hung before I had finished the first Chapter. – No – I must keep to my own style & go on in my own Way. And though I may never succeed again in that, I am convinced that I should totally fail in any other. –

I remain my dear Sir
Your very much obliged & very sincere friend
J. Austen

These letters exhibit Jane Austen's wit and style. They also display a certain freedom of expression and self-confidence, probably attributable at least in part to her then being a published and acknowledged writer. I believe her rejection of the suggestions by Prince Regent's librarian indicate the strength of her clear and assertive determination to '*go on in my own Way*', despite the obvious political, and probably commercial, advantages of following quasi-Royal requests.

She was also acutely aware that her literary strengths lay mainly in satire and comedy, the surgical accuracy and subtlety of which could only be skilfully expressed within contexts she fully understood. She would not, for example, have had the necessary intimate knowledge of the House of Saxe-Coburg to successfully deliver Stanier Clarke's very specific suggested Historical Romance, and therefore wisely steered clear.

However, in terms of writing about a typical English Clergyman the issue would not, as noted, have been lack of insight. Indeed, the roles and characters of the English clergy were subjects close to Jane Austen's heart and the extensive inclusion of clergy, or aspiring clergy, in her novels evidences her strong preference for sticking to subjects she knows well from personal experience. Her father, brother and several other relatives belonged to the clergy and so she was able to write with some authority when including individual fictional clergy. Her rejection of James Stanier Clarke's suggestion to write about a typical English clergyman and the reasons she puts forward for this rejection are therefore at first sight at least a little disingenuous. However, perhaps the wide variety of clergy characters in her novels, with dramatically contrasting merits, is illuminating, indicating that if she were to attempt this suggested archetypal portrayal she could not be truthful to her own strong belief that no such typical creature existed. During the time of my research, Irene Collins, author of the excellent book *Jane Austen and the Clergy*, sadly died. The author of Collins' obituary in The Times newspaper picks up the very point being discussed, noting that Collins (1925-2015) had once described *'a slight feeling of regret that she [Austen] did not take seriously the suggestion once made to her that she should devote a novel to depicting the lifestyle of a contemporary clergyman'*.[30] For whatever reason, Austen was simply uncomfortable entertaining the idea. It is also known that she experienced similar personal discomfort when outside her familiar surroundings, and this characteristic also seems to be reflected in the restricted fictional environments she chooses.

Regency Icons and Indian Influences

The limited influence of global and colonial events on Jane Austen's novels has been noted by several commentators, and perceptions of her work are dominated by a clear and narrowly-drawn focus on a specific layer of English society, manners and culture, associated with the label *Regency*. Also, the novels' geographical settings are almost exclusively restricted to England. The combined effect of all this is that Austen's novels stand as icons of the Regency period in England, alongside the Prince Regent himself, Nelson and Wellington as national heroes of the Napoleonic Wars, and Nash and Repton as shapers of fashions in buildings and landscapes. Nevertheless, these quintessentially English icons of the Regency period were inevitably coloured by wider global overtones, and those of India in particular. The last of Stanier Clarke's letters above is written from the 'Pavilion', this being Brighton Pavilion at the time of its transformation into the ultimate, but carelessly unauthentic, example of the exotic and flamboyant oriental influences so fashionable during the Regency period.

Brighton Pavilion

India was also important as the setting for the initial military experiences of both Wellington and Nelson. While Wellington's campaigns in Europe during the Napoleonic Wars naturally dominate his reputation, his earlier significant military and civil governor roles in India were the foundation for his rise to prominence. His numerous military victories in India, alongside those in the subsequent Peninsular War, were notably inscribed on the Wellington Pillar at Sezincote House, the latter directly influencing the Indian styling of the Brighton Pavilion, as described later.

Likewise, Nelson's early naval experiences of India (1773-6) are overshadowed by his later Napoleonic Wars achievements. Nelson's first experience of battle occurred off the Indian coast on 19th February 1775 when, as a young midshipman, his ship, the frigate *Seahorse,* was unsuccessfully attacked by two of Hyder Ali's ketches as it transported a cargo of East India Company money to Bombay. Even during the later Napoleonic Wars, India was once again a focus of Nelson's attention, his crucial strategic victory at Aboukir Bay ('The Battle of the Nile') in 1798 leaving a French army stranded in Egypt without a supply line, frustrating and ultimately wrecking Napoleon's plans to send this force to India to challenge Britain's growing interests there. Given the length and dangers of the sea route round the Cape of Good Hope, the overland route between Europe and India was one that Warren Hastings, among others, had earlier identified as strategically important. The lengthy sea route was always a constraining factor in East Indian trade-expansion, giving rise to Hastings' vision for an Egyptian canal, not realised until nearly a century later, despite Napoleon having started work on a similar project, soon abandoned, in 1799. The French were well-aware of the importance of India, but repeatedly failed to emulate the British success in exploiting the opportunities it offered.

As an indication of the significance of the successful naval engagement at Aboukir Bay for trade with the east, the East India Company presented Nelson with what was then a substantial reward of £10,000. Also, *'as a guest of honour, The Admiral .... attended a dinner given by the East India Company at the London Tavern, Bishopsgate Street Within, a large hostelry renowned for the excellent meals provided in a dining-room that could accommodate 355 guests; on this occasion it was decorated with transparencies depicting scenes from the battle of Abu Qir Bay, a victory for which the East India merchants had reason to feel particularly grateful'.*[31]

The victory had sparked off national celebrations. In Nelson's home county of Norfolk, a contemporary journal entry for Thursday 29th November 1798 noted that *'the celebrations in honour of the county's "most valiant son" were particularly joyous. "Great rejoicings at Norwich today on the Lord Nelson's great & noble Victory over the French. ... An Ox roasted whole in the Market Place etc"* '.[32] The success of any naval engagement at this time was to some extent judged by the number of the enemy's ships captured, and the Battle of the Nile was no exception, nine of the thirteen French ships of the line being taken, and therefore fully justifying the contemporary description of *'a glorious victory'*, as Davidge Gould, captain of *HMS Audacious*, reported it.[33] One of these nine captured vessels, after less than a year in service, was a French Navy ship called *Franklin* (after the American sympathiser Benjamin Franklin, who coincidentally features later in connection with the Dashwoods and West Wycombe). Transformed into a British Royal Navy 84-gun third rate ship of the line, and renamed *HMS Canopus*, she was later captained by Frank Austen, none other than one of Jane Austen's brothers. Appropriately, and presumably deliberately, *HMS Canopus* took its new name from one of two long-lost sunken ancient Egyptian cities at the mouth of the Nile delta. [The ongoing underwater archaeological excavations of Canopus and its sister city Thonis were featured in an exhibition at the British Museum in 2016.] Nelson commented on *HMS Canopus* being a suitable ship for Frank Austen, whom he described as '*an excellent young man*', who '*cannot be better placed than in the Canopus, which was once a French Admiral's ship, struck by me*'.[34]

In October 1805, as Captain of the *Canopus*, Frank Austen was temporarily detached from Admiral Nelson's fleet for convoy duty in the Mediterranean and missed the Battle of Trafalgar, something he always regretted. However, he did command the same ship the following year in the Battle of San Domingo, leading the lee line of ships into battle. It was therefore presumably with some pride that Jane Austen included her brother's *Canopus* as one of the ships specifically named in her novel *Mansfield Park*. Also, it is surely no coincidence that Jane Austen, when introducing the central character of Captain Frederick Wentworth in *Persuasion*, notes that he was '*made commander in consequence of the action of St. Domingo*', mirroring her brother Frank Austen's prominent role in that battle, and honouring it in her novel through this thinly disguised reference. For Jane, the name Wentworth also had positive and honourable connotations associated with Adlestrop, and links with Bourton-on-the-Hill, described elsewhere. As it happens, associations between the Austen and Nelson families were to continue after Jane's death, when the widow of Nelson's brother married one of Jane Austen's nephews, George Thomas Knight.

As with Nelson himself, and in yet another link back to India, Frank Austen's first serious naval voyage had been to the East Indies. Having entered the Royal Navy Academy in 1786 at the age of 12, and having graduated in 1788, he joined *HMS Perseverance* which was sailing for the East Indies under Captain Isaac Smith and was promoted to midshipman in December 1789. He joined the 64-gun third-rate *Crown*, and then the 38-gun *Minerva* in November 1791, being promoted to lieutenant in December 1792, while still in the East Indies. In July 1808, the Honourable East India Company gave Frank Austen £420, with which to buy a silver piece of plate. This was a substantial gift (perhaps the equivalent of a year's salary) in thanks for his having safely convoyed seven of their East Indiamen (ships operated by the East India Company) from Saint Helena to Britain. Both Frank Austen and another of Jane's brothers, Charles, later became admirals.

These various links - and there are many others, outlined later - illustrate that although Jane Austen's life may not itself have included many personal dramas, nevertheless, through her immediate and wider family connections, she was very well-aware of many of the key iconic events and undercurrents of the dynamic and revolutionary Regency era, during which India was emerging as an increasingly important contributor to the period's culture. In her book *The Real Jane Austen – A Life in Small Things*, Paula Byrne chooses an East Indian shawl belonging to Jane as one of the key objects around which aspects of her life are illuminated, using the shawl as the pictorial icon for one chapter. In something of a coincidence, a scrap of newspaper used as a lining paper and uncovered under fragments of early nineteenth century wallpaper in a cottage in Bourton-on-the-Hill (the Cotswold location with significant Dashwood connections) dates from October 1815 and includes the following advertisement :-

"INDIA and BRITISH SHAWLS ---- The most complete and superb Collection of INDIA SHAWLS ever offered for Sale, may now be inspected at WAITHMAN and SON'S Shawl, Linen, and Muslin Warehouse, 104, Fleet-street, corner of New Bridge-street, comprising some of the most curious ever seen in this country. They are likewise at present introducing a variety of novel Designs in British Shawls, manufactured expressly for their house, combining richness, elegance, and durability, and which they flatter themselves will be found, upon inspection, unequalled for correctness of imitation, as well as moderate in price. ---- Ladies or Gentlemen having commissions from the Continent, will find this

assortment deserving their attention, many of them being particularly adapted to the Foreign Markets."

An article entitled, '*The Gracefulness of Indian Shawls in the Georgian Era*'[35], outlines the impact of Indian clothing materials and designs :-

'Indian influence on Regency dress included fine Indian muslin, used for dresses and cravats, and beautiful, expensive hand-loomed shawls. During the late 18th-early 19th century, an unprecedented number of Indian cloths, made of quality fabrics, were exported to Britain. These cloths were expressly made for the British market, with colors and chintz patterns toned down to appeal to the more restrained British taste.

While cheaper and inferior imitation paisley shawls were increasingly made in Great Britain (by 1821, shawls made in British locations like Spitalfields and Scotland would overtake the Indian exports in numbers sold), the authentic Indian shawl was highly prized for its quality, cost, and prestige. These shawls were so popular with those who could afford them that they were presented to friends and family members by merchants, soldiers, and visitors returning from the East Indies. Made of durable cloth, they were carefully handled and handed down from mother to daughter and aunt to niece over the years.'

In Thackeray's *Vanity Fair*, with the early action positioned in 1818, the following passage exemplifies the common custom of shawls being brought back by those serving in India as valuable and prized presents. It also highlights the use of Indian garments as a marker of contemporary fashion, and the perception of riches being associated with all those serving in India :-

'She [Amelia] *insisted upon Rebecca accepting ... a sweet sprigged muslin ... and she determined in her heart to ask her mother's permission to present her white cashmere shawl to her friend. Could she not spare it? – and had not her brother Joseph just brought her two from India?'* . Her brother was, *'Mr Joseph Sedley, of the East India Company's service'.* ' *"Isn't he very rich?" said Rebecca. "They say all Indian nabobs are enormously rich"* '.[36]

The footnote in this edition notes that Cashmere shawls were *'originally made of fine wool from goats indigenous to the region of Kashmir in Northern India'*. One of our key characters, Warren Hastings, specifically requested his emissary George Bogle to acquire for him at least one pair of these goats, and these were later brought back to his estate at Daylesford in the North Cotswolds.

Indian shawls therefore provide just one example of the increasing influence of imperial expansion on fashion and consumption of new goods and materials in Britain. And it was not just tangible goods, but concepts and designs, which were enriched by imperial sources; even existing artistic trends, such as the picturesque, and the romantic, were given expanded scope. The relationship between fashion at home and the progression of British trading expansion is exemplified not only in the two-way interaction of 'the picturesque' in the arts but also by trends in both clothing materials and designs. A good example of the latter is a combination of Indian motifs, which, when replicated and incorporated in designs for British cloths and other fashion items, became known as the Paisley design.

Regency-era shawls 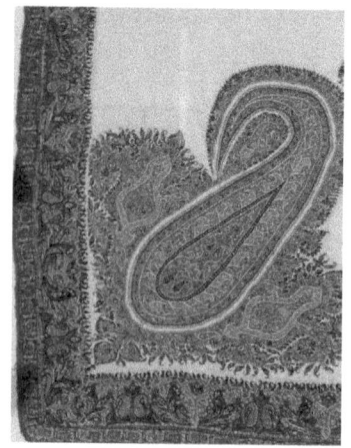   *Textile detail with 'Paisley' designs*

However, it is through the changing pattern of exports and imports of the clothing materials themselves that the dramatic shifts in trading power are most clearly evidenced.

Vinayah Purohit explores these themes, and a passage from his book highlights Jane Austen's references to Indian materials, contrasting these with references a generation later by Charles Dickens. The context is the changing situation for India at the end of the 18th and first half of the 19th centuries :-

> *'The pattern of external trade was revolutionised. From an exporter of manufactures, India became an importer of finished goods and an exporter of raw materials and food grains. ... In 1814 India still exported to Britain 4 lakh (i.e. 400,000) metres more cloth than she imported. In 1835, the imports from Britain were about 170 times the exports from India.'*

He then notes that this change was most marked in textiles, and points to comparisons between '*the novels of Jane Austen (fl. 1811-1817) and Charles Dickens (fl. 1836-61). Both in Austen and Dickens, there are references to the luxuries and exoticisms of India, like nabobs, gold mohrs, palanquins, gorgeous princes, hookahs and howdahs. But in Jane Austen, there is an awe cast by Indian materials. In Northanger Abbey, the hero impresses the heroine by his expert knowledge of "true Indian muslin". The hero proceeds to advice (sic) the heroine's elderly companion:*

But then you know, madam, muslin always turn to some account or other; Miss Morland will get enough out of it for a handkerchief, or a cap, or a cloak. Muslin can never said to be wasted. I have heard my sister say so forty times, when she has been extravagant in buying more than she wanted, or careless in cutting it to pieces.'[37]

In the 1780s and 1790s, muslin articles of clothing of various types appear in the invoices of Mrs Broadhead and her daughter Mary Anne (who married John Dashwood in 1789). The Indian source of other items of clothing material and jewellery are even more explicitly cited in other invoices for John Dashwood and Mary Anne, including 1 yard of Blue Bengall Calico, Drilling 14 dozen Indian peas [small semi-precious stones being made into beads], and 7 yards of Buff Bengall.[38]

The same extraordinary regard for Indian shawls and "anything else that is worth having" from India is to be found in *Mansfield Park*. Purohit contrasts this with Dickens' later novels, which although they still refer to exotic materials make it clear that, '*no longer do Indian textiles command the respect that they were once held in. ... As innumerable observers have noted, it was enough to announce in the House of Commons that some question relating to India was to be debated for the benches to be emptied.*' [39]

The final point made in this extract, concerning the dramatic change in perceptions about India as the nineteenth century unfolded, from exotic fascination to a degree of indifference, and even embarrassment and negativity, is directly mirrored by attitudes to the stylistic choice for a building which is central to the India-Cotswold connections explored in more detail later, namely the country house at Sezincote. Having been at the cutting edge of architectural invention in the period in which Austen's writing was flourishing, and visited with enthusiasm by the Prince Regent as it neared completion, its Indian styling fell out of fashion only a few decades after its initial makeover; when it was sold in the 1880s, its idiosyncratic style was deliberately omitted from the public sales particulars.

India, as well as affecting many aspects of Regency England, impacted on Jane Austen herself, not only through her two brothers' naval connections with the subcontinent, but also through links with Warren Hastings, the first Governor-General of British India. His connections and involvement with Jane's family, and particularly the Indian links with her aunt Philadelphia Austen, were highly significant in Jane's life (see Chapter 9). However, while Hastings incorporated only limited and subtle Indian external detailing into his Daylesford house, next to Jane's relatives at Adlestrop, using Samuel Pepys Cockerell as his architect, it was nearby Sezincote House which was the trailblazer. Comprehensively remodelled externally around 1805 as the only Indian-styled country house in Europe, it has been described as *'the first masterpiece in the Anglo-Indian or Moghul style which was such a delightful reflection of the movement toward Picturesque exotica in the early nineteenth century'*.[40] As well as influencing the slighter later dramatic and ostentatious oriental remodelling of Brighton Pavilion, it celebrated Wellington's victories in India (e.g. 'Amednagur' & 'Argaum' in 1803) and the Peninsular War (e.g. 'Ciudad Rodrigo' & 'Salamanca' in 1812), via its memorial Wellington Pillar, as noted earlier.

Wellington Pillar, Sezincote
[Courtesy of the Peake family]

Pillar detail highlighting both Indian and Peninsular War battles

The incorporation of Indian motifs in these two country houses in the Cotswolds was newsworthy at the time of Jane Austen's later visits to Adlestrop at the beginning of the 19th century. She would almost certainly have had some interest in, and awareness of, these local developments; the focus in her novels is often on what her characters were doing to their fictional houses, estates, parklands or gardens, indicating her acute observations of the latest trends and fashions in property and land 'improvements', which were a subject of great interest to the country gentry, clergy, and aristocracy at the time. In his *Age of Improvement*, Asa Briggs notes that,

> '*A first glance at the countryside would have revealed the presence not of farms but of 'estates', large and small, 'family seats' each with its hall or its manor house, its garden, its parkland, its 'acres'. ... The proprietors were of varying resources, background,*

and lineage. .... They often prided themselves, rightly, on the splendour of their homes – many of them newly built in the eighteenth century – and the beauty of their gardens, often newly planned. The site of the house was usually chosen on aesthetic grounds, 'to command the prospect' and to mingle delights of landscape with the refinements of taste'.[41]

It was a time when architectural styles, both in buildings and gardens, were going in and out of fashion at an unprecedented rate. Chinese, Egyptian and Indian stylistic influences, among others, were blended with familiar classical and gothic building models, in conjunction with variations on formal and informal garden and landscape settings. Critical analysis of the significance of Austen's treatment of such estate 'improvements' is given in Jonathan Bate's *The Song of the Earth*, and Janine Barchas's *Matters of Fact in Jane Austen*. Austen's own observations would have informed at least some of her knowledge of these aspects of the novels, not least in relation to Repton's direct involvement at Adlestrop and other local Cotswold properties, notably including Sezincote.

The Sezincote estate has neighbourhood connections with nearby Adlestrop, Daylesford, Longborough, Bourton-on-the-Hill, Batsford and Northwick Park. Each of these, and their associated country houses, has relevance to the themes being explored, and their proximity to each other in this compact North Cotswold neighbourhood facilitated a high degree of social interaction and sharing of local news and gossip. 'Neighbourhood' was an important contemporary social concept, as described by Irene Collins in *Jane Austen and the Clergy*, 1994. Indeed, her Chapter 7 is entitled 'The Clergy and the Neighbourhood' and Collins begins it by quoting, from *Sense and Sensibility*, Edward Ferrars' enquiry of the Dashwoods on his first visit to Barton – '*Have you an agreeable neighbourhood here?*'.

Collins notes that,

'The term 'neighbourhood' has had a variety of meanings over the centuries but – applied to person rather than to an area of land – it has usually implied a community of interest. Jane Austen habitually used it with reference to groups of families sufficiently equal in social standing and living near enough to each other to meet regularly for mutual entertainment and companionship – in other words, the social elite of each of the small residential areas which constituted rural England'.[42]

Linking the North Cotswolds area which Jane knew, with this concept of 'neighbourhood' and the Dashwood family living nearby at Bourton-on-the-Hill, we are told in *The Dashwoods of West Wycombe* that Sir John Dashwood-King *'hunted with private packs of fox hounds belonging to his neighbouring friends such as the Leighs* [Austen's relatives] *of Adlestrop Park, Sir Charles Cockerell at Sezincote and the Hon. George Annesley at Bletchington ...'*.[43] Also, in his later life, *'Periodically, Sir John set off to call on his hunting friends .... Lord Redesdale at Batsford Park, Sir Charles Cockerell at Sezincote, and Lord Northwich at Northwich Park'*.[44] ('Northwich' should read 'Northwick'.) So, for the Dashwoods, the concept of neighbourhood in their part of the North Cotswolds is well-evidenced, and explicitly included Jane's relatives at Adlestrop.

While such neighbourhoods and their associated domestic and social activities, including traditional country pursuits, provided a reassuring sense of continuity and stability, the Wellington Pillar at Sezincote was a local reminder of more unpredictable and violent activity abroad. Although most action in Jane Austen's novels focuses on specific fictional neighbourhoods, external events do obliquely influence many of the plots, and several of her individual characters have military backgrounds. Equally, there can be little doubt that the enduring popularity of Jane Austen's novels benefits from the general appeal of this period of English military and cultural history, and its romantic aura.

It is understandable that many readers focus predominantly on the romantic aspects of the novels. Even though much critical commentary argues that this completely misses the main thrust of her writing, which has deeper and more pointed contemporary moral messages, the more obvious romantic dimensions nevertheless tend to prevail. Given that Austen was heavily influenced by the writings of Fanny Burney, to whom we return later in the book, the following two extracts from the original preface to Burney's *Evelina* arguably shape much of Austen's own juggling of romanticism and realism :-

> *'Let me, therefore, prepare for disappointment those who, in the perusal of these sheets, entertain the gentle expectation of being transported to the fantastic regions of Romance, where Fiction is coloured by all the gay tints of luxurious Imagination, where Reason is an outcast and where the sublimity of the Marvellous rejects all aid from sober Probability. The heroine of these memoirs, young, artless, and inexperienced is No faultless Monster, that the world ne'er saw, but the offspring of Nature, and of Nature in her simplest attire.'*

> *'To draw characters from nature, though not from life, and to mark the manners of the times, is the attempted plan of the following letters.'*

Above all, we should recognise that Austen wrote topical novels for a limited, largely well-educated readership, and was a keen observer of the contemporary scene, with emphasis on fashion, both visual and behavioural, or to use Burney's words, *'to mark the manner of the times'*. As an example, Jane Austen lived in Bath for a significant part of her adult life, while the city was still highly fashionable, and Bath is explicitly and extensively cited in her novels, notably

Northanger Abbey and *Persuasion*. This explains not only her ability to talk with authority about the city and its activities at that time, but also meant that its fashionable and lively contemporary reputation ensured a familiar resonance with her readers. As with many successful art forms, Austen's keen observations and insights, based on accurate contemporary foundations, ensure that her novels are coherent, authentic, and resilient to the passage of time, while their many layers of detail and meaning can be appreciated on several different levels of understanding and interpretation.

Austen's anxiety that her novels should be topical is reflected in the fact that she appears to have been frustrated, and apologetic to her readership, when lengthy delays in publication risked making the texts appear out of date and old-fashioned. Her novel *Northanger Abbey* provides perhaps the best example of her concern. Finished in 1803, it was not eventually published until 1818, the year after her death. As David Blair notes in his Introduction to the Wordworth Classics edition of the novel, '*even by 1816, when Austen wrote her short "Advertisement by the Authoress" in anticipation of its publication, the novel had fallen prey to the passing of time and the accompanying changes to 'places, manners, books and opinions'.*'[45]

The "Advertisement" reads as follows :-

ADVERTISEMENT BY THE AUTHORESS TO NORTHANGER ABBEY

This little work was finished in the year 1803, and intended for immediate publication. It was disposed of to a bookseller, it was even advertised, and why the business proceeded no farther, the author has never been able to learn. That any bookseller should think it worth while to purchase what he did not think it worth while to publish seems extraordinary. But with this, neither the author nor the public have any other concern than as some observation is necessary upon those parts of the work which thirteen years have made comparatively obsolete. The public are entreated to bear in mind that thirteen years have passed since it was finished, many more since it was begun, and that during that period, places, manners, books, and opinions have undergone considerable changes.[46]

However, given the enduring popularity of *Northanger Abbey* and all her other novels, Jane need not have worried. Nevertheless, for her, accuracy of context in subject matter, time, and place were critical. She steadfastly refused to write about topics outside her experience and understanding, or in a style anything other than her own. That style could be characterised as informed, satirical, sharp-witted, observant, highly perceptive, humorous, and often irreverent. It was a style in tune with much of the Regency public psyche.

CHAPTER SEVEN
Passages to India

'... he has told you that in the East Indies the climate is hot, and the mosquitoes are troublesome ...'

'Perhaps his observations may have extended to the existence of nabobs, gold mohrs, and palanquins'.

[Quotes from *Sense and Sensibility*][1]

Nabob comes from the Hindi *naiwwab* or official. In England it came to signify someone returned from India with a fortune. A mohr was a gold coin worth 15 rupees or just under £2 and, to put this in contemporary context, Thomas Daniell was publishing a series of twelve printed views of Calcutta, costing twelve mohrs for the set.[2] One of these prints shows a palanquin, a closed carriage common in the East at this time.

The quotes above, about Colonel Brandon, the first by Marianne Dashwood, and the second by John Willoughby, appear in *Sense and Sensibility*, Austen's first published novel, indicating that Indian influences were familiar to her readers. Given Austen's sympathetic portrayal of Colonel Brandon, it appears that association with having spent time in India did not, for her, necessarily carry any negative connotations. Indeed, she may well have added these references to India as a further adventurous and exotic element of Brandon's mysterious background, his outward character being otherwise portrayed as rather colourless compared with the more obviously romantic figure of John Willoughby.

Both quotes are intended as sarcastic commentary by Marianne and Willoughby on Brandon's perceived dullness. They regard anything that Brandon says (even about the potentially exotic location of India) as providing no information, interest, or excitement other than commonplace facts about the subcontinent. As with other elements of Brandon's background, his reserved nature only allows the novel's other key figures glimpses of his life story, and likewise the reader is only gradually informed about his past as the narrative unfolds. If nothing else, the inclusion of these references indicates that Indian influences held a fascination for Austen and, as she would have been well-aware, for her readers as well. Reference to other characters having spent time in India or the East Indies are evidenced in other Austen novels, notably *Persuasion*, with its considerable naval focus.

In looking at the Leigh and Dashwood family histories in Chapter 2, trade with India in the 17th century was touched on, but it is through travel to India by some other key individuals in the latter part of the 18th century that more specific Austen connections emerge. The impact of many of these individuals arises from their personal experiences in India, in a variety of capacities, at a time when British influence and involvement in the subcontinent was still pioneering in nature, rather than the dominant force it was to become in the Victorian era. While their individual motives for venturing to India were as varied as their backgrounds, personalities, and abilities, the common factor for all of them was that the strength of these diverse motives clearly overcame their awareness of the considerable and very real risks and sacrifices involved. Not only were the voyages to and from the subcontinent lengthy, arduous, and inherently dangerous, but death rates once there were considerably higher than in England, largely because of infectious diseases and an unfamiliar climate. Despite this, India was increasingly enticing, with the prospect of exotic adventure as well as opportunities for personal advancement and rapid accumulation of wealth. For some, whether male or female,

Passages to India

there was also the advantage that any domestic negative reputations or difficult circumstances could be left behind, at least temporarily, and for women, as already noted, there could be the specific potential for an advantageous marriage.

To provide some introductory information about voyages to India, the following is a short table of ships transporting goods, and some of our characters, to and from India, often by way of China. Those termed 'East Indiaman' were large ships, on average about 1,000 tonnes, operated by the East India Company.

Name of ship	Type of ship	Key Passengers	Voyage Purpose/ Date	Comments
Dashwood	375 ton frigate	N/A	Oriental trading 1700	Early Dashwood family merchant vessel
London	East Indiaman	Warren Hastings	Voyage to Bengal, India 1750	Hastings was just seventeen
Bombay Castle	East Indiaman	Hastings' future first wife, Mary, and Philadelphia Austen (Jane's aunt)	Both voyaging to India in pursuit of a husband, 1751	Both female passengers were destined to have relationships with Warren Hastings
Duke of Grafton	East Indiaman	Hastings, Baron Carl & Baroness Anna Maria von Imhoff	Hastings second voyage to India, 1769	Anna Maria later became Hastings' second wife in 1777. Hastings called her Marian

Name of ship	Type of ship	Key Passengers	Voyage Purpose/Date	Comments
Aurora	Frigate	Henry Vansittart	Vansittart going to India to be the new governor of Bengal, 1769	Lost at sea, with no survivors. Vansittart was a friend of Hastings and the Dashwoods
Vansittart	East Indiaman	George Bogle	Voyage out to India, 1770. Bogle was an explorer, later sent on a mission to Tibet by Warren Hastings	The name Vansittart was probably chosen in the wake of the loss above
Seahorse	20 gun frigate	Horatio Nelson	Navy expedition to India, 1773-6	One of Nelson's early naval experiences
Ashburnham	East Indiaman	Philip Francis	Travelling to India, 1774	Warren Hastings and Philip Francis later fought a duel with pistols
Anson	East Indiaman	Judges of the Indian court	Travelling to India 1774	
Duke of Portland	East Indiaman	Edward Wheler	Travelling to India 1777	Chairman of the East India Company
Atlas	East Indiaman	Hastings' second wife	Returning from India, 1784	

Passages to India

Name of ship	Type of ship	Key Passengers	Voyage Purpose/ Date	Comments
Barrington	East Indiaman	Warren Hastings	Returning from India, 1785	Hastings brought back several animals including goats, cows and his favourite Arabian horse
Atlas	East Indiaman	Thomas and William Daniell	Travelling to India via China, 1785	The Daniells were topographical artists, with strong Dashwood links
Perseverance	British Navy ship	Frank Austen	Travelling to the East Indies, 1788/9	
Hope	East Indiaman	James Wathen, artist	Travelling to India, 1811	

The details of the ships used by Colonel John Cockerell and Sir Charles Cockerell (later settled at Sezincote) for their Indian voyages are currently undetermined, but their late 18th century experiences at sea would have been aboard similar vessels.

Journeys to and from the subcontinent aboard East Indiamen usually took about six or seven months. George Bogle's journey out to Calcutta on the *Vansittart* in 1770, for example, took from January 25th to August 19th. The ships run by the East India Company were a cross between a merchant vessel and a warship, and over time increased in size from about 500 tonnes, 90 crew, and 30 guns up to around 1400 tonnes and 48 guns, as noted by Anthony Wild. He adds that, *'they looked like warships and were run like warships; their officers usually came from the same families as those who served in the Royal Navy.'* Unlike Royal Navy ships, however, they carried paying passengers, and,

> *'until the 1830s, a passenger on an EastIndiaman could expect the most luxurious voyage of any by sea, but that was relative; first hand accounts paint a grim picture of danger and discomfort. ..... A passage, and the storage space to go with it were best negotiated personally with the commander, and passengers were advised to visit the vessel so that they knew what they were in for'.*[3]

So what sort of possessions would Jane's aunt Philadelphia Austen have had, travelling out to India in 1751 on board the *Bombay Castle*? Musical instruments were allowed for example, and Wild reports that,

> *'Ordinary passengers were allowed a table, a sofa or two chairs, a washstand, and bedding. The sofa generally incorporated two drawers underneath it, and the washstand could be shut down to form a table. Coffee-making equipment, a water filter, and a supply of tea, coffee, soap and sweets were considered necessities, while medicine chests with neatly arranged rows of medicine in glass bottles, portable soup (dehydrated concentrate), soda water and perfumes travelled in fine mahogany or teak boxes'.*[4]

Life on board was just as hierarchical and status-conscious as on land. The Daniells, for example, commenting on the society on board an East Indiaman, note that,

> *'it is not a commonwealth of liberty and equality, but a Chinese system of subordination, with all the minute*

distinctions of caste, and the watchful jealousy of precedence : it is no community of knowledge; and every individual is restricted to his own department, and interferes not with the duties of another : the steward in the cockpit rarely emerges from his submarine sphere to observe the heavens or the variations of the wind'.[5]

In *Persuasion*, Austen includes the following exchange regarding conditions on board naval vessels at the time, employing a favoured technique of allowing her characters to espouse opposing views :-

'If you had been a week later at Lisbon, last spring, Frederick, you would have been asked to give passage to Lady Mary Grierson and her daughters.'

'Should I? I am glad I was not a week later then.'

The Admiral abused him for his want of gallantry. He defended himself; though professing that he would never willingly admit any ladies on board a ship of his, excepting for a ball, or a visit, which a few hours might comprehend.

'But I know myself,' said he, 'this is from no want of gallantry towards them. It is rather from feeling how impossible it is, with all one's efforts, and all one's sacrifices, to make the accommodations on board, such as women ought to have. There can be no want of gallantry, Admiral, in rating the claims of women to every personal comfort **high** *– and this is what I do. I hate to hear of women on board, or to see them on board; and no ship, under my command, shall ever convey a family of ladies anywhere, if I can help it.'*

This brought his sister upon him.

'Oh Frederick! – But I cannot believe it of you. - All idle refinement! – Women may be as comfortable on board as in the best house in England. I believe I have lived as much on board as most women, and I know nothing superior to the accommodations of a man-of-war. I declare I have not a comfort or an indulgence about me, even at Kellynch Hall,' (with a kind bow to Anne) 'beyond what I always had in most of the ships I have lived in; and they have been five altogether.'[6]

This latter glowing fictional recommendation is somewhat at odds with accounts of voyages to and from India. Macaulay notes,

'No place is so propitious to the formation either of close friendships or of deadly enmities as an Indiaman. There are very few people who do not find a voyage which lasts several months insupportably dull. Anything is welcome which may break that long monotony, a sail, a shark, an albatross, a man overboard. Most passengers find some resource in eating twice as many meals as on land. But the great devices for killing the time are quarrelling and flirting'.[7]

In terms of conditions on board for women passengers voyaging to India, Wild notes that, *'It was quite usual for women to be forced to eat in their cabins (if they had one) because the language in the cuddy (main cabin) was so bad'*.[8] Being crammed together for many months inevitably resulted in arguments, usually between men, but

'women, too, were not above a good spat. Given the importance of preserving a white complexion in order to make a good catch in India [precisely what Jane's aunt Philadelphia was intent on doing, and leading to the vessels being known colloquially as 'the fishing fleet'], *it is not surprising to find that hatboxes were*

vital items of baggage, and that hats were worn whatever the weather. The Bengal Gazette wryly reported in July 1780 that, whether through accident or altercation, a group of eleven young ladies had arrived in Calcutta without an undamaged hat to show between them'.[9]

This focus on the effects of extremes of climate experienced in travelling to India is mirrored by Austen in a further extract of dialogue from *Persuasion* :-

'He is Rear-Admiral of the White. He was in the Trafalgar action, and has been in the East Indies since; he has been stationed there, I believe, several years.'

'Then I take it for granted,' observed Sir Walter, 'that his face is about as orange as the cuffs and capes of my livery.'[10]

Likewise, an observer of Nelson, walking about in London in 1805 some months before Trafalgar, noted that *'his features are sharp and his skin is now very much burnt from his having been long at sea'*.[11]

Worrying about skin complexion was, however, relatively peripheral to other concerns on lengthy voyages to the East Indies, not least encountering potentially treacherous seas. As already indicated, although passengers could surround themselves with personal belongings and furniture, such relative luxury could at best only distract from the very real risks of such voyages, which were fraught with a variety of dangers. While all our main characters survived their voyages, several East Indiamen vessels were lost at sea. The typical lifespan of one of these ships was only about 3 years. In addition, there were individual health risks, Hastings' second wife Marian, for example, suffering a miscarriage on her voyage back to England in 1784.[12] For some, their own survival was a close call, a young Horatio Nelson almost dying from malaria aboard *Seahorse* on the journey home. Another fringe character, who appears later in connection with West Wycombe and the Hell-Fire Club, namely Sir Henry Vansittart, Governor of Bengal in the mid eighteenth century, was less fortunate. He was lost at sea when the ship conveying him to India, the *Aurora*, sank in heavy weather on its voyage to Calcutta. After leaving Cape Town on 27th December 1769, the captain made the fatal decision to navigate the Mozambique Channel despite the bad weather.[13]

As an aside, many years later, during Jane Austen's lifetime, one of Sir Henry Vansittart's sons, Robert Vansittart, scored the first recorded cricket century in India, 102 for Old Etonians v. Rest of Calcutta in 1804.[14] The 'export' of cricket may seem trivial, but its introduction could be regarded as a metaphor for attempts by the British to impose structure and a common set of standards on what they saw as a disparate and chaotic environment. In the long term, its introduction, together with other 'exports', such as the railways, and hierarchical administrative civil service frameworks, had a significant impact on Indian culture, persisting long after direct British control and involvement ceased.

Returning to the long sea voyages, even when these were successfully completed crew members were constantly vulnerable. It was almost expected that a small number would lose their lives on any one passage, often falling from the rigging in stormy weather. Indeed, we know that in the case of the artists Thomas and William Daniell's passage in 1785 aboard the *Atlas*, rough conditions were encountered, and despite Captain Allen Cooper being an experienced sailor who had worked for the East India Company for 20 years, tragedy was only to be expected. Loss of a sailor on this particular outward voyage is described as follows :-

'On 25th June (1785) Cooper's log grimly records 'Lost Hugh Crockett Seaman overboard off the main top gall yard'. It was about eight in the morning, and the

Atlas was riding out a squall in the Indian Ocean, having rounded the Cape of Good Hope some days earlier. It was making rapid progress in the high winds, over 200 nautical miles in 24 hours, but it was precisely this speed that prevented it from pulling up in time to locate and rescue poor Crockett from what Cooper called the 'large and confused sea'. The event made a lasting impression on Thomas and William, who sketched the dramatic scene as if from the perspective of an expectant shark. This was not to be their only experience of a man overboard and unsurprisingly William returned to the subject matter later in his career. It was a rare voyage in which a sailor did not fall from the rigging or get swept from the deck and Cooper lost three men in this way on this run to China and back.[15]

Just as Austen achieved authenticity by transposing her acute powers of behavioural observation into her writing, the artist Thomas Daniell matched this with his visual observations, reflecting an almost obsessive attention to detail and accuracy. Even in a naval environment which he was experiencing for the first time, Daniell's precise observation later attracted complimentary comments from well-known naval art critic, E. Keble Chatterton. Commenting on a Daniell aquatint of an East Indiaman's quarter deck, which was published later, in 1810, he notes that :-

'It gives one an everyday, intimate aspect of the environment. The melodramatic bias is not absent, but there are indicated some features of sea-faring which all go to make more perfect the pattern of maritime knowledge. Right aft is seen the man at the wheel, ahead of him is a capstan, while just forward of the mainmast are some of the ship's livestock, and a couple of hands are lashing more securely the Indiaman's boats stowed on deck. The bellying staysail, the

heeling ship, the very atmosphere suggested, all seem so real that we can almost listen to the wind in the rigging. This is the kind of thing that makes a picture sometimes far more dependable for information than what we can ever discover in any ship-model'. [16]

Thomas Sutton remarks when citing this quote, that *'To be accurate without artistic sensibility is to be merely pedantic'*[17], but neither Thomas Daniell's images nor Jane Austen's writing could be charged with such mere pedantry – both combined accuracy of observation with genuine artistry.

Attention to detail in Thomas Daniell's paintings is a feature noted by several other commentators, notably Humphry Repton in relation to Daniell's Indian images and, much later, in the twentieth century, by the 11th Baronet of West Wycombe, Sir Francis Dashwood, who comments that :

'For the King's Room we had already determined to hang six glorious paintings of West Wycombe in 1781 by Thomas Daniell which were seldom seen as they were hanging in a spare bedroom. These were Daniell's most important commission before 1785 when he left for India, where he and his nephew William were to make their names through their paintings of Indian scenes. They are my favourite pictures of the house and we frequently study them to check features in the park. Russell Page, who helped us so much in the landscape garden, paid particular attention to them as they showed the original siting and species of shrubs and trees, and he encouraged Victoria and me to visit Kew Gardens to try to find similar species for replanting.'[18]

Thomas Daniell's precision can also be seen both in the level of detail in his design drawings for Sezincote and in his paintings of the finished house and gardens there. Daniell's images, both in India and in Britain, give historians valuable information precisely because they can be relied on for their accuracy. Wherever cross-checking of images against surviving fabric is possible, the matches are remarkable, so that when historic fabric and form has been lost or partially lost, his images are invaluable for conservation and restoration work. Although Daniell's focus was on scenery and views, he frequently incorporated human figures within these compositions. In this regard, Sutton comments on the similarities between Thomas Daniell and Canaletto. [19]

Although Canaletto and Daniell exhibited attention to detail in an era before photography enabled mechanically-accurate visual reproduction, and even though Daniell made extensive use of the camera obscura, both artists did more than merely record detail. *'Canaletto was an artist who combined accuracy with emotional appeal. His views of Venice tell us exactly how the parts he painted appeared at the time, and yet there is something about the light, the colour and those so necessary figures that no camera study could evoke.'*[20] Daniell very much followed in that mould.

Similarly, Austen's descriptions of contemporary manners and attitudes, and insights into the social pressures affecting behaviours, are invaluable not only because of their authenticity, but also because of their 'human element'. As artists in their respective contemporary fields, Thomas Daniell and Jane Austen therefore share some characteristics, most notably in being acute observers of the world around them. Perhaps in doing so they both remain just that, namely observers somewhat removed from full engagement in the action, letting their outputs speak for them. Austen allows her characters to debate and discuss issues rather than imposing opinions on the reader, and Daniell's work, while it panders to its viewers' picturesque expectations in its subject matter, rarely displays explicit social or political attitudes. Whether this shared characteristic as meticulous, and distanced, observers relates in any way to neither of them ever marrying, is an open question.

The importance of accuracy to both Austen and Daniell is also very closely associated with another joint intent, that of striving for topicality in their respective works. Austen shows this in her recorded concerns that the long gestation of some of her novels risked them appearing out of fashion, and Daniell occasionally updated original drawings to include later fashions so that they were as up to date as he could make them when eventually published. Sutton highlights a case of a drawing of a Malay village executed in the 1780s where *'the original drawing has been adapted to portray the prevailing fashion of the year of publication (1810)'*.[21]

Austen had much more reason to achieve accuracy, simply because her readers were themselves acutely aware of her very narrowly-drawn English geographical and social settings. By contrast, Daniell could have got away with much more artistic licence (as William Hodges had done with his earlier Indian scenes) given that many of his patrons, with little or no exposure to the East, were not familiar with the detail of Indian scenery or architecture. Nevertheless, the focus on accuracy and close observation was ingrained in both Daniell and Austen, sharpened by market awareness as to what subject matter would be well received.

In contrast to these similarities, a major difference between the two lies in their respective attitudes to risk and working conditions. Austen needed a safe, secure, and happy environment for her writing to flourish, and her forced relocation from Steventon to Bath resulted in a substantial period of disruption to this creativity. While Austen's strong preference was for a settled and familiar environment, Thomas Daniell took a huge gamble, and personal risks, in travelling out to India, not only financially but also in terms of safety and health. For example, he usually did his initial sketches on site, in what could be extremes of temperature and humidity, with unaccustomed disease an ever-present threat. Even though, as we shall see, he and his nephew William were usually accompanied by a substantial party of retainers, they also took risks travelling extensively around the sub-continent, including penetrating deep into its interior, at a time of persistent inter-tribal conflict and unpredictable reaction to British incursion. In January 1789, on their journey into the north of India, Sutton notes that,

> '*There was a scare on the 30th, when their camp was twice attacked by 'Mewattys', but they were fired on by the guards before they could do any damage. On the next day they had just camped at Aurungabad when they heard a "great firing in Scindia's Camp ...".*
> ... *These cold dispassionate entries* [in William Daniell's diary] *are typical of the Englishmen's faculty of understatement; they were in a country where constant fighting was taking place between rival Raj, and to a certain extent in danger of their lives. ..... Military operations did not prevent them from working ...*',[22]

The next chapter includes a brief account of some of their adventures in the East, and their search for picturesque inspiration.

CHAPTER EIGHT
Exploring the Indian Picturesque

"Preoccupying British aesthetes, tourists, garden designers, philosophers, writers, and artists from the 1790s until the 1820s, the picturesque shaped a powerful dialectic between artifice and nature, between land and landscape" - Under the Banyan Tree – Relocating the Picturesque in British India[1]

As artists determined in their pursuit of new subject matter – and particularly romantic, exotic and picturesque scenes in uncharted territory – the Daniells, working in India in the late 1780s and early 1790s, were also ground-breaking explorers, proceeding deep into the Indian interior, despite the dangers. For example, when they stated their intention to go into the Garwhal Mountains, their men refused to go on. However, 'volunteers' were found after cash was offered, and with fifty guards they embarked on a hazardous route which no Europeans had explored before.[2]

These intrepid explorations nevertheless retained aesthetic focus as their main motivation. While the notes of their journey are usually rather prosaic, their lyrical entry for one village they reached is quoted by Sutton[3] and describes ı

> " ... *the charms of the evening scenery of that enchanting, if not enchanted island ... The mild temperature of the atmosphere; the murmuring of passing streams; the visionary effect of the twilight; and ... the myriad swarms of fire-flies .. which*

illuminated every object, and diffused a magical radiance equally beautiful and surprising; it seemed in truth to be a land of romance, and the proper residence of those fanciful beings, the fairies and genii, that appear so often in Asiatic tales. But the delicious sensations produced by causes of such nature .... must be seen and felt to be conceived; purchased by toil and privations of every kind; and after all, they must be met with, and not sought; for pleasures that delight by surprise, vanish before anticipation."

Acknowledging the 'toil and privations' they endured, and their commercial as well as aesthetic focus, this particular experience went beyond the picturesque vistas they encountered and recorded on almost every day of their travels, and shows they were genuinely emotionally affected by the romantic and spiritual dimensions of their unique adventure. The East held a particular fascination for Europeans, and the Daniells' journeys exemplify one aesthetic element of this.

They regarded a central aim of their mission to be delivering accurate records of what they saw, and they also carefully selected the best positions from which to achieve picturesque compositions. In summarising the value of the Daniells' body of work in the East, Sutton comments that :-

'Not only are we given the architectural beauties of little-known countries at a time when architecture of this type was a subject of keen interest, but we have landscapes in the true 'romantic' styles. Each plate is carefully composed. The human element, however, is seldom absent, whether it be an encampment of Europeans, a group of Indian boats, a formal procession, or a farmer and his buffalo against the distant background of a hill-fort. It is this incorporation of human elements that has given rise to the noted similarity of grouping between Canaletto

and Thomas Daniell, and, undoubtedly, Thomas was acquainted with some of the works of the Venetian master'.[4]

Sutton stresses the value of the Daniells images as accurate historical and architectural records of buildings either lost or decayed - for example, the original form of the Temple in Rhotas Ghar is faithfully recorded in Daniell's *Oriental Scenery*. An extract from the Calcutta Monthly Magazine emphasises the authenticity of the images :

"The execution of these drawings is indeed masterly; there is every reason to confide in the fidelity of the representations; and the effect produced by this rich and splendid display of oriental scenery is truly striking. In looking at it, one may almost feel the warmth of an Indian sky, the water seems to be in actual motion and the animals, trees and plants are studies for the naturalist."

Sutton notes that, '*Oriental Scenery was a success. J.M.W. Turner, speaking of his projected Liber Studiorum, said he would 'like to have them (the plates) engraved like Mr. Daniell's'. In these views, it was said 'the East was as clearly reflected as the moon in a lake'.*[5]

The Daniells were supported in india by, among others, William Hickey, a flamboyant Calcutta lawyer. As noted in *An Illustrated Journey Round the World*, '*Hickey was no Warren Hastings (who had sponsored the artist William Hodges during his time in India), but his support must have been welcome to Thomas and William, whom he described as "two artists of splendid talents"* '. Hickey is quoted by Prior as follows,

"As I was always as great an encourager of merits as my humble means would allow, I not only subscribed myself but procured many other names to a work they

commenced upon of drawing and engraving in aqua tinta, twelve views of different parts of Calcutta".[6]

With a specific link to 'the Picturesque', Prior goes on to note that,

'Hickey's reference to aquatinting is significant. It was Thomas's adoption of this novel method of tonal printing that helped to sell the Calcutta views, even though learning the technique severely tried his patience and energy. ... It was prized above all for its ability to imitate the effect of watercolour painting, and its introduction to Britain coincided happily with the rise of the Picturesque aesthetic and the elevation of watercolour as a respectable pictorial medium. ... A good aquatint – and Thomas and William were to become masters of the art – was hard to distinguish from the original watercolour. But it was an extremely laborious and costly process, requiring continuing experimentation.'[7]

While the Indian influences which Thomas Daniell introduced back in Britain feed directly into the Austen, Dashwood and Cotswold connections, they also represent an important dimension of the wider Picturesque movement, so fashionable during Austen's lifetime. It was precisely this demand for Picturesque images that the Daniells sought to satisfy on their travels in the East, and India in particular. William Daniell's diary, written during their travels in India, evidences repeated reference to the picturesque, as the following extracts exemplify :-

'Soon after re-entering the great river [the Ganges] we passed Sultangunge on the westernbank, and near it a small island consisting of a rock of a conical form and considerable height. It bears many trees and shrubs, whether planted by nature or art I could not tell – by

both probably. ..... Although a picturesque object, it is a serious obstruction to the navigation of the river'.[8]

The Daniells sketched this picturesque landscape feature from several angles, and their phrase '*whether planted by nature or art*' hints at the picturesque concept that nature could be improved to fit an artistic ideal. Slightly later, on December 14th 1788, the Daniell diary records that, '*... Lackergee fort stands on a very high bank which is extremely picturesque*'.[9]

Having travelled from Agra to Sikandra, and set up camp near the tomb of Akbar, the most illustrious of the Mughal emperors, who had died in 1605, Prior notes that, '*His son Jahangir erected his tomb, the gateway to which Thomas* [Daniell] *spent the whole day drawing in the camera obscura*'.[10] William Daniell is quoted, writing that, '*It is one of the most magnificent buildings I have any where seen in the country. The gate leading to it is also grand and has a very picturesque appearance in many points of view*'[11] .... and finding the best point of view was part of the picturesque challenge.

Ruins were ideal picturesque subjects, and early in 1789 the diary entry for January 28th records that they, '*Set out very early & spent the whole day among the ruins of the palace of Akbar. We could spend a week or two very well among the ruins as they afford many most picturesque scenes*'.[12]

In 1792, the Daniells set off to explore southern India, and on May 29th William Daniell records in his diary,

'*Sent off our baggage &c., but recalled them as we began to ascend the hill at Trisengur. The scenes all the way up so uncommonly picturesque that we determined to spend another day here. ... Upon the whole Trisengur is the most compleat Hindoo town we have met with. Picturesque in the highest degree. At present but thinly inhabited .... The villagers tell us that we are the first Europeans that ever entered the pagoda on the hill*'.[13]

Even when they encountered difficulties and accidents they were always on the lookout for picturesque views but didn't always find them. On June 4th, Daniell's diary entry notes,

> 'Crossed several small streams of water about middle deep. Our cart by the carelessness of the driver got unfortunately into too deep water by which accident everything it contained (except a box of drawings, paper and books which happened to be uppermost) were wet. In one of the chests were all the small sketches we had made since we left Madras, which were injured very much. The road most part of the way very sandy and rather unfavourable for a wheel carriage. Not a picturesque view occurred'.[14]

The final sentence emphasises that, throughout their arduous travels, their focus was perpetually, and obsessively, on the search for 'the picturesque'. Although they failed in this one instance, the remote and largely unexplored areas of India they ventured into proved, as they had hoped, to be extremely fertile in throwing up picturesque scenes. In fact, as soon as the Daniells had arrived in the East, and particularly when they reached India and began to explore the interior, they knew that they would not be disappointed in their search for such imagery. Sutton notes that,

> 'Near Gangwaugh Colly, on the River Hooghly, they found the first of many Indian scenes, a typical riverside village with a small temple and a native boat. Having reached India, Daniell is justified in his poetic description of this Eden.
>
> "The banian puts forth its shoots, which strike the ground, and produce a rapid succession of younger trees. It is the asylum of animals ..... who subsist on its fruits, and are protected by its foliage. The peacock here unfolds its splendid plumage; doves nestle on the topmost boughs, and tribes of monkeys leap and

chatter among its branches. Beneath its shade, the herdsman watches his flock; the manufacturer plies his loom; the musician touches his pipe; whilst the Bramin, abstracted from all sublunary objects, performs his solitary though not silent devotions." '[15]

This focus on a native tree, 'the banian', and its multiple functions, is central to the Indian picturesque. One of the common contemporary features of the picturesque in Britain was the invasive vegetation - ferns, ivy, and other parasitic plants - spreading over and into the fabric of historic ruins. The banian, or banyan, tree with its organic, rambling and invasive habit, plays a similar role in the East, and particularly so in portrayals of India. It is such an iconic and emblematic element of the Indian picturesque that it is given star billing in Romita Ray's 2013 book, *Under the Banyan Tree – Relocating the Picturesque in British India.* This taps into multiple strands developed here, and Ray's book is therefore very helpful in encapsulating several specific themes. Relevant links are further signalled by the fact that the book's jacket cover illustration is a detail from one of Thomas Daniell's picturesque aquatints, '*Hindoo Temples at Agouree, on the River Soane, Bahar*', with Banyan trees framing the view of the temples. Also, on page i, is an image of William Daniell's design (featuring a banyan tree with an elephant beneath) for the Great Seal of the Royal Asia Society (1823).

Writing with hindsight in 1810, long after their 1786-1794 Indian journeys, Thomas Daniell made observations which reveal his thoughts on their artistic adventure, and the aesthetic essence of their mission. There is a clear sense in his words of an artistic duty and responsibility as part of a wider deployment of European knowledge and skills, including naturalists, philosophers, and 'students' of other branches of the sciences and arts. His words give the strong impression of a mindset sharing the zeal of the religious missionary and having just as clear a sense of purpose; these variously skilled explorers were very much 'men on a mission', acquiring and then spreading knowledge and appreciation of such newly explored territories. In this it taps back into the 18th century Enlightenment and, in its precision and 'delineation', as he puts it, it looks forward to the 19th century focus on rationalising, recording and categorising.

As Archer comments, the Daniells' book *A Picturesque Voyage to India by the Way of China*

'contained a highly significant introduction in which Thomas Daniell summed up in a masterly manner the attitude of the Picturesque Traveller engaged on a Picturesque Tour of India :

It was an honourable feature of the late century, that the passion for discovery, originally kindled by the thirst for gold, was exalted to higher and nobler aims than commercial speculations. Since this new era of civilisation, a liberal spirit of curiosity has prompted undertakings to which avarice lent no incentive, and fortune annexed no reward : associations have been formed, not for piracy, but humanity : science has had her adventurers, and philanthropy her achievements : the shores of Asia have been invaded by a race of students with no rapacity but for lettered relics; by naturalists, whose cruelty extends not to one human inhabitant : by philosophers, ambitious for the extirpation of error, and the diffusion of truth. It remains for the artist to claim his part in these guiltless spoliations, and to transport to Europe the picturesque beauties of those favoured regions .... delineation is the only medium by which a faithful description can be given of sensible images: the pencil is narrative to the eye; and however minute in its relations, can scarcely become tedious; its representations are not liable to the omissions of memory, or the misconceptions of fancy; whatever it communicates is a transcript of nature'.[16]

Exploring the Indian Picturesque

The artistic influence of Thomas Daniell and his nephew William Daniell, in revealing very accurately a particular perspective of India, directly affected the British public's perception of the sub-continent at the turn of the nineteenth century during Jane Austen's lifetime. Since then, the iconic vision of India created by the Daniells' prints has substantially declined but lingers on, and even today it is not uncommon for Indian restaurants in Britain to display Daniell images (often of the Taj Mahal).

As an example of the growing influence of India in the late 18th century, it is no surprise that the first Indian restaurant in Britain was opened in the Regency period by Dean Mahomet, an Indian born in Patna in 1759. He joined the East India Company Army at the age of 11 and rose to the rank of subadar (captain), before coming to Britain in 1784, where he later gave evidence in the impeachment proceedings against Warren Hastings. Having published the first book in English by an Indian author, he introduced an Indian treatment, champi (shampooing), or therapeutic massage, to Sir Basil Cochrane's vapour baths in London, and in 1810, he established the Hindoostane Coffee House at 34 George Street, Portman Square. Called a coffee house purely for the convenience of fashion, Mahomet offered a range of meat and vegetable dishes with Indian spices served with seasoned rice. In launching this new experience for consumers, he constructed bamboo-cane sofas and chairs and adorned the walls with a range of paintings including Indian landscapes. In 1821, having moved to Brighton, no doubt to capitalise on the new oriental-styled Brighton Pavilion, he opened Mahomet's Baths, patronised by Lord Castlereagh and Sir Robert Peel, and was later appointed 'Shampooing Surgeon' to George IV, before retiring in 1834. He died in 1851. His diverse involvement with the East India Company, Warren Hastings, George IV (previously the Prince Regent), Brighton's emerging exotic and fashionable image, and more general Indian cultural imports, neatly dovetails with many of the themes and individuals of interest here.

Returning to Romita Ray's book, focusing on the Picturesque in British India, figure 1 on page 5 features a watercolour (over graphite) by Thomas Daniell, *'Ruins on Pir Pahar near Monghyr, Bihar'* (1790). This depicts Thomas and William Daniell themselves, travelling by horse-drawn carriage, within a typically picturesque composition. The similarities of artistic treatment with standard picturesque prints featuring ruins in England are striking, such as the image of 'tourists' seeking out the picturesque by exploring the ruins of Knaresborough Castle.

The ruins of Knaresborough Castle, North Yorkshire

As it happens, Knaresborough was a venue that Thomas Daniell knew well, having visited the town in the period before travelling to India, and having produced images of Mother Shipton's Cave, a local Knaresborough attraction, as well as images of the nearby 'Brimham Crags', now known as Brimham Rocks, a timeless and picturesque location in Nidderdale.

Another, much later, literary and visual link between Nidderdale and India is sketched by Rudyard Kipling in his collection, *Soldiers Three*, set largely in India, the country of Kipling's birth. One of the three soldiers is a Yorkshireman, Learoyd. The other two soldiers are called Mulvaney and Ortheris. The entry for *On Greenhow Hill* in the 'Kipling Companion' by Norman Page[17], reads as follows :-

'The Yorkshireman Learoyd tells of an early love before he left England. Climbing a wall in the Yorkshire Dales, he falls and breaks his arm and is taken to a nearby house and nursed by 'Liza Rountree, with whom he falls in love. Under her influence he joins the Primitive Methodists, but he finds that the minister is his rival in love. In a dramatic scene in a lead-mine, he is tempted to murder the other man, who is physically puny but proves unexpectedly courageous. In the event neither of them wins 'Liza, for she goes into a decline and soon dies. In despair Learoyd enlists, seeing her for the last time just before going away. The recruiting sergeant advises him to forget her – 'And,' comments Learoyd, 'I've been forgettin' her ever since.' The frame-story, set in India, shows the three soldiers, who are encamped 'on a bare ridge of the Himalayas', lying in wait for a native deserter who, at the end of the story, is shot by Ortheris. The English and Indian settings are linked by Learoyd's realization that one of the Himalyan foothills reminds him of Greenhow Hill near Pateley Bridge, where the episode of his youth occurred.'

The above 'dramatic scene in a lead-mine' is reminiscent of the similarly dramatic hayloft fight in Thomas Hardy's *The Mayor of Casterbridge*, with its similar contrast in the physical strengths of the two protagonists, and with the seemingly weaker man in that case also showing great resilience. In this extract, Learoyd's enlisting and travelling to

India to escape and forget resonates with our Indian themes and Austen connections, very closely mirroring the motivation for Colonel Brandon's service in India in *Sense and Sensibility*. Furthermore, the use of *'Liza* as the name of the love interest, is reminiscent of Colonel Brandon's troubled "Eliza" connections in the same Austen novel.

Resuming consideration of the picturesque, its aesthetics are often founded in land and landscape, both in man's active and neglectful treatment of them. As Ray notes, W T Mitchell urges us to *'think of landscape as a "verb" rather than a "noun"'*.[18] Indeed, landscaping as a conscious activity was becoming ever more fashionable at this time in Britain. Humphry Repton aligned himself with the picturesque in a very distinct and commercially effective way in his famous red books, using revealing flaps which directly juxtaposed existing landscapes with proposed alterations to exploit their picturesque potential. The picturesque gained such influence that Edmund Burke considered it, as noted earlier, to be a third artistic category to be added to the 'beautiful' and the 'sublime'.

Notably, in this context of varying aesthetic categorisation and preferences, Repton's suggested improvements at Sezincote in the Cotswolds – so central to our Indian and picturesque themes – sit alongside other key portrayals of this unique building and estate, with Thomas Daniell, for example, employing accuracy allied to a gentle and essentially picturesque style, and John Martin (perhaps the most well-known "sublime" artist of the period) displaying a far more stark and elemental rendering of the subject.

The concept of the picturesque allowing, or even requiring, active human intervention is developed by Ray, describing it as *'a term that literally meant "like a picture" and whose application to gardens and landscape painting in Britain underscored the desire to improve nature, to recreate it as one imagined nature to be or expected it to look like'*.[19] As already noted, the burgeoning of the picturesque movement coincides with the period of Jane Austen's novel-writing, and it is therefore no surprise that she incorporated this 'dialectic between artifice and nature' in her novels as a highly topical subject with which to illuminate the aesthetic aspects of her narratives. This topicality also applied to the appetite for travel writing prevalent during Austen's lifetime. For the Daniells, combining the picturesque with travel in India was a winning formula, both for sales of prints to ex-patriots in India and for sales to the home market in Britain when they returned. So, *'while the picturesque formed a continuum with the landscape traditions of the past, it was very much an aesthetic of the moment in tune with the contemporary taste for travel writing in which it was embedded as the visual framework of choice'.* [20]

The Daniells fed this dual appetite for travel writing and associated imagery by combining written journals of their travels with their artistic output. The contemporary fascination for all things oriental incorporated both Islamic and Indian influences, and as one commentator notes[21] this was reflected in buildings in England

> *'that had been designed in the eighteenth and early nineteenth centuries – among them a Turkish mosque and two Alhambras at Kew, S. P. Cockerell's Sezincote (1804-5) and John Nash's Royal Pavilion, Brighton (1815-23)'.* These *'relied on the easy delights and connotations of Picturesque theory, which included remoteness as a value in itself. As such they could be designed from artists' images* [and] *travellers' impressions ... no painstaking or firsthand examinations of the originals was required'.*

While Thomas and William Daniell certainly did have firsthand experience, and indeed Thomas directly employed this at Sezincote, John Nash had never been to India and for his remodelling of the Brighton Pavilion he relied on the Daniells' images, borrowing a copy of their publication *Oriental Scenery* from the Prince Regent's Carlton House to do so. The Revd.

Hobart Caunter subsequently exploited this further, notably through the *Oriental Annual*, a series of publications from 1834 to 1840, which incorporated the Daniells' engravings within Caunter's own rather fanciful text of imagined journeys in India (which he had never made), largely based on the Daniells' descriptions of their own travels.

Photography had not yet entered the scene, and travelling artists still relied on sketchbooks, pencils, paintbrushes, camera obscura, and easels. '*By the time British artists began flocking to India, the picturesque had been well primed to travel .. [and] .. the very evolution of the picturesque followed the course of British rule as it spread across the Indian subcontinent in the late eighteenth century...*'.[22] This spread of influence was largely driven by commercial interests. Exploitation of land enabled trade in a variety of goods, including '*a steady supply of black pepper, cotton, raw silk, indigo, opium, saltpeter, coffee, jute, and tea bound for European ports. It also generated millions for those shrewd enough to invest in diamonds from the Golconda mines*'[23] in Southern India. As outlined below, even botanical curiosity in the many new exotic plants discovered in India, although originally purely scientific in nature, was quickly recognised as having great commercial potential, building on the well-established trade in spices.

The ethics and conduct of those involved in this trade and wealth creation were frequently questioned. Jewels, and particularly diamonds, from the East Indies were an obvious potential source for rapid accumulation of wealth. The background to their acquisition equally had potential for controversy, the most obvious and high-profile example being the circumstances in which the famous Koh-i-noor diamond came into the possession of Queen Victoria a few decades later. While it would be unfair to accuse the Queen of knowingly handling stolen goods, the legitimacy of its removal from India has never been entirely clear. There are parallels here with other colonial acquisitions such as the Elgin Marbles, removed from the Parthenon in Athens, and the subject of much debate,

Exploring the Indian Picturesque

and media comment, at the time and ever since. The central theme here, of imperial exploitation bordering on theft, is reflected in nineteenth century literature by Wilkie Collins' novel *The Moonstone*, a precious Indian diamond, whose name came from its association with Chandra, the Hindu god of the moon. Originally it had been set in the forehead of a sacred statue of the god at Somnath, and later at Benares. It was reputedly protected by hereditary guardians on the orders of Vishnu, waxing and waning in brilliance along with the light of the moon.

Not surprisingly, there was considerable criticism at home of the perceived pillaging of such treasures, in part driven by envy. There was also wider suspicion about how personal wealth was being accumulated in other more subtle ways by those operating in a loosely controlled commercial environment. While there were clearly macro-economic benefits accruing to Britain from its involvement with India, accusations of corruption at an individual level were not only to be expected but were also well-founded in many cases. Administrators had ample opportunity to supplement their official East India Company salaries through private local commercial arrangements, with few effective legal constraints.

The individual most publicly affected by accusations of corruption, self-enrichment, and abuse of office, was Warren Hastings, Governor General of British India in the late eighteenth century, who faced a lengthy impeachment trial, and with whom Jane Austen and her immediate family had such close and intimate ties. These ties, and his trial, are covered in Chapter 9. The evidence against him was always flimsy and, even before the trial, the politically motivated nature of his impeachment was lampooned in a James Gillray cartoon of 1786. This arguably shows Hastings in an exaggeratedly favourable light, with the politicians (Edmund Burke, Fox, and North) trying to 'ambush' him (by way of impeachment) portrayed in an equally exaggerated negative manner. The satire is targeted mainly at the politicians; all the accroutements attached to Hastings and his camel (particularly the money and jewels benefiting the treasury and the land in India he had acquired for Britain) advertise positive, if still morally questionable, economic and imperial impacts, highlighting the political absurdity of the impeachment. However, it is rare that anyone featuring in such cartoons is completely exempt from ridicule, and the exaggerated nature of any positive spin put on Hastings' portrayal simply perpetuates the satire.

'The Political Banditti assailing the Saviour of India'
By James Gillray, 1786 [National Portrait Gallery D1360]

Gillray uses obvious visual signals to identify Hastings in this image, including the camel, and the Indian apparel of the rider. One significant item of clothing is the turban. Ray notes, *'like the diamond, the turban also invoked visions of oriental excess, of despotism, cruelty, and greed'*.[24]

Two images incorporating turbans, and which relate to the Dashwoods, illustrate the point. The image below is of a diorama within the Hell-Fire Caves at West Wycombe, portraying a meeting of some of the Hell-Fire Club members and their female guests, based on contemporary eighteenth century evidence and costumes.

Diorama in the Hell-Fire Caves at West Wycombe

The second is the painting of Sir Francis Dashwood, 2nd Baronet of West Wycombe (see image on the book cover), who is not only central to the narratives elsewhere in this book, but whose notoriety fitted closely with the sort of behavioural excesses associated with this iconic headdress.

Visual signals and associations were powerful mechanisms in late eighteenth-century British society, with its focus on fashion, wealth and status. Indeed, visual representations generally counted for a great deal, and this was particularly so in relation to India. While questionable commercial aspects of imperial expansion affected perceptions at home, at least as important and influential was the way in which the subcontinent was conveyed and portrayed aesthetically. The artists were not really controlled by any of the normal mechanisms of East India Company governance in India and they were free to express themselves, albeit that their choices of expression had more than a casual eye to commercial realities. They were often not sponsored in any formal sense and had to put up significant capital outlay to fund their travels. For the Daniells, some of this capital accrued from sales of their aquatints in Calcutta, enabling their journeys 'up country' into the Indian interior.

The parties the Daniells travelled with varied enormously both in numbers and in the mix of European and local personnel. To what extent they directly paid for the support of those accompanying them is not clear, and some of the expeditions were probably undertaken opportunistically on the back of already-planned military reconnaissance exercises or private exploratory excursions by other Europeans. On one excursion to a remote hill area, *'they were to have the company as far as Hardwar of four of the officers stationed at Anupshahr, including Capt. John Guthrie, and commanded by Colonel Brisco, and with a "proper escort".'*[25] Later, when they visited Southern India, William Daniell gives the following list of their entourage :-

'2 Palankeens with 11 Bearers to each; 4 Bearers for Bottle Khannah safe; 2 Do. Bangies; 2 Coolies for ye Drawing Tables; 2 Do. for a Cot; 1 Do. Fowls &c; a second Dubash (who proved to be a great knave. He ran away from us on the Eveng. Of 24 Ap. from Sundapilly); a Matee; a Cook; 2 Peons; a Lascar; a Portuguese & a Mussulman Boy; 2 Horses; 2 Sises; a Cart & 4 Bullocks; 3 Bullocks for the Tent &c; 4 Bullock Men; Our Coolies & Bullocks rather intractable, a common case on the outset.'[26]

Within reason, they were free to make their own travel plans (provided they could acquire the necessary logistical support), and although they took great personal and financial risks, the benefit of a flexible itinerary was that they had considerable artistic freedom and stylistic choice. Their choice of subject-matter also inherently allowed considerable scope for their talents, but while this flexibility meant that compositions were carefully chosen, accuracy of presentation, including individual elements, such as the vegetation and, particularly, buildings was never deliberately compromised.

The fact that these picturesque compositions often featured architecture alien to British models, far from being a barrier, was very much part of their attraction to a home audience primed for novelty and idiosyncracy. In particular, follies in gardens and country estates had long been a means of innovative, imaginative, and occasionally symbolic expression, such as Thomas Tresham's Triangular Lodge in Northamptonshire, with its bold and pointedly religious symbolism, dating from the 16th century. However, by the 18th century, follies had typically taken on a lighter, often whimsical, character. Ray comments that, *'follies were primarily architectural distortions whose playful forms had ceased to have any ties "to locality and meaningful place" by the end of the eighteenth century'*, citing *'Sir William Chambers's Chinese-inspired tower or "pagoda" for the Royal Botanic Gardens at Kew and a host of other Chinese looking picturesque ornaments that dotted English Gardens'*.[27]

Defying rational geographical and climatic constraints, European styles were to some extent interchangeable at this time. For example, the 18th century fashion for incorporating eyecatcher buildings, often reflecting Roman and Greek classicism, into English landscapes, itself an anachronism, was (in a further removal from their origins) adopted by Marie Antionette in the late 18th century in her so called 'English Gardens' at Versailles.

The 'English Gardens' at Versailles, France

The Music Temple at West Wycombe Park, Buckinghamshire

Thomas Daniell had personal experience of just such garden features, or follies, from his time at West Wycombe Park (see image above), where he was engaged by Sir Francis Dashwood in 1781 to produce a set of six paintings of the house and estate, notably including several of the garden features which carried such notorious connotations and symbolism. These, and the background to Daniell's appointment for this commission, are explored in the next chapter, with the Dashwood link also taking us back once more to Jane Austen's use of the Dashwood family name in *Sense and Sensibility*.

Landscapes and gardens, prominently represented in Austen's novels, provided stages on which individuals could display their wealth and taste, often with the intent of outdoing their peers. The Royal Botanical Gardens at Kew was housing increasing numbers of new plant specimens, and there was particular kudos in being able to incorporate the latest exotic plants introduced from around the world, particularly when the fruits of these could be further displayed and consumed at the dining table. Pineapples are a good example of this and, satisfying the appetite for architectural follies, this exotic fruit was in turn adopted as a more permanent emblem at the Pineapple House, Dunmore, Scotland. Pineapple forms were also used more subtly as architectural ornamentation, such as ornate finials, in line with the fashion in built form for new and idiosyncratic motifs.

The discovery of new fauna and flora as a key aim of global exploration is evidenced in the East at this time involving characters already introduced. When Warren Hastings, based in Calcutta, sent George Bogle – who had travelled out to India on board the *Vansittart* in 1770 - on a mission to Tibet in 1774, he issued him with some private instructions which included the following :-

To send me one or more pair of animals called tus [goats] which produce the shawl wool. If by a Dooley, chairs, or any other contrivance they can be secured from the fatigues and hazards of the way, the expense is to be no objection.

To send one or more pair of the cattle which bear what are called cowtails [yaks]

To send me carefully packed some fresh ripe walnuts or seeds, or an entire plant, if it can be transported; and any other curious or valuable seeds or plants, the rhubarb and ginger especially.

Any curiosities, whether natural productions, manufactures, paintings, or what else may be acceptable to persons of taste in England. Animals only that may be useful, unless any that may be remarkably curious.[28]

As with other areas of the globe, the botanical opportunities in India were formally recognised in 1786, when Colonel Robert Kydd, an East India Company engineer and keen horticulturalist, obtained Warren Hastings' permission to establish a botanical garden in Calcutta. This became a centre for experimenting with exotic plants, resulting in links with Kew Gardens. The Calcutta Botanic Garden increasingly became a laboratory for testing plants' commercial viability. The Garden, in Kydd's conception, was

'*not for the purpose of collecting rare plants (although they also have their uses) as things of mere curiosity or furnishing articles for the gratification of luxury, but for establishing a stock for disseminating such articles as may prove beneficial to the inhabitants, as well as to the natives of Great Britain, and which ultimately may tend to the extension of the national commerce and riches*'.[29]

Commercial interests were never far away from the more aesthetic and cultural aspects of Britain's emerging empire.

However, it is the banyan, a far more common Indian plant, with little commercial value, which provides us with links back to Jane Austen's knowledge and interest in the picturesque. The plant was noted by Austen's picturesque protagonist and guru, William Gilpin, who in turn was picking up John Milton's seventeenth century references. As noted earlier, the banyan features in many of the Daniells' images, and its sprawling form is the main element of William Daniell's design for the Great Seal of the Royal Asiatic Society (1823). The Greek Theophrastus (372-288 BC), describing the banyan, noted that in India it was referred to as the 'fig-tree'. John Milton picked up on this and other "fig-tree" references, utilising the banyan as the tree beneath which Adam and Eve sheltered 'in their moment of shame in his *Paradise Lost* (1667) :-

> *So counsell'd he, and both together went*
> *Into the thickest Wood, there soon to chose*
> *The Figtree, not that kind for Fruit renown'd*
> *But such as at this day to Indians known*
> *In Malabar or Decan spreds her Arms'*[30]

Milton's reference to the "Figtree" is resurrected in Gilpin's musings but being

> '*part landscape gardener, part architect, and part hermit, Gilpin's "Bramin" is a solitary figure who artfully rearranges the tree into a picturesque amusement to pass the time. Organizing natural elements into scenic views was key to designing a picturesque garden*'.[31]

Gilpin was using the figure of a "Bramin" as the Indian equivalent of the hermits, druids and bards so often used in eighteenth-century British picturesque poems and paintings. Once again, the relationship between artifice and nature surfaces, with human intervention being an acceptable, or even essential, element of the picturesque.

So Gilpin's literary theory of the British picturesque is transported to, or perhaps more accurately, imposed on, the natural picturesque qualities of the Indian landscape. We also know, from her brother Henry's evidence, that Jane Austen was "enamoured of Gilpin on the Picturesque at a very early age". She would no doubt have followed his writings keenly, including his musings on the Indian picturesque, and although never directly linking the two, several passages in Austen's *Sense and Sensibility* relate to picturesque landscapes and to India.

The significance of the banyan tree in the Indian picturesque, and the Daniells' extensive use of it in their art, lies in the reverence it had for the indigenous population. The practice of building temples next to banyan trees is a tradition which persists in India to this day. In this context, Ray provides an analysis of one of Thomas Daniell's coloured aquatints *Hindoo Temples at Agouree, on the River Soane, Bahar* in his *Oriental Scenery* (1795-1807), concluding that *'not only does Daniell situate the currency of the picturesque in the leafy spillage of the banyan, he also inserts it within the matrix of Hindu ritual and worship'*.[32]

These links between picturesque landscapes and religion again chime with strong themes in Jane Austen's novels of the same period, in which the religious attitudes and outlooks of her characters are used as signals of their inner natures, and their attitudes to their treatment of landscape are gauged in various ways against picturesque 'rules' or ideals. The only difference is that while Austen's portrayals of contemporary attitudes to religion (projected, both favourably and unfavourably, through her fictional characters) are reasonably transparent, the way she treats attitudes to the picturesque is far more opaque and arguably inconsistent (perhaps deliberately), in the way it is portrayed in her novels. Nevertheless, both aesthetic and religious 'taste' were matters of great interest and importance to Austen, and to her contemporary readership, explaining their prominent and frequent appearances in the novels. Thomas Daniell's combining of aesthetics and religion in the above image is mirrored in Austen's use of the text in *Sense and Sensibility* describing in aesthetic terms the removal of thorns from the brow of a hill (portrayed as an act of desecration of landscape) combined with a clear associated religious reference to Christ's crown of thorns at his crucifixion.

Gradually, as the nineteenth century progressed, the influence of the Indian picturesque faded along with its European counterpart. It was always a two-way street, and the picturesque views from Thomas and William Daniell's influential *Oriental Scenery* (1795-1807), as well as Charles Ramus Forrest's *A Picturesque Tour Along the River Ganges and Jumna, in India* (1824), and Captain Thomas Williamson's *Oriental Field Sports* (1808), were transferred as decoration onto Staffordshire blue-and-white earthenware and even fashionable wallpaper.

Staffordshire 'Blue and White' plate with image from the Daniells' 'Oriental Scenery'

As Ray comments,

> '*If the picturesque had traveled to India, it now made its way back to Britain and Europe, to domestic spaces where the exotic was resurrected in the midst of everyday rituals like drinking tea. Drawing the taste for the picturesque into the sensory realms of eating and drinking, Staffordshire pottery embodies the*

very interface at which consumers partook of the picturesque on their plates and inside their teacups.' [33]

These 'domestic spaces' and 'sensory realms of eating and drinking' are just those which infused Jane Austen's world and novels. Staffordshire pottery increasingly featured new Chinese or Indian motifs as the eighteenth century ended and the nineteenth began, just at the time *Northanger Abbey* was being written, Austen completing it in 1803. Indeed, in *Northanger Abbey*, we encounter the following passage which picks up the links outlined above including the fashion for tea and for Staffordshire pottery from which to drink it. Austen's text also highlights the pace of changes in fashion at the time, and validates Asa Briggs' term, an *Age of Improvement* (reflecting continual rapid change and advancement), as an accurate one :-

'The elegance of the breakfast set forced itself on Catherine's notice when they were seated at table, and luckily, it had been the General's choice. He was enchanted by her approbation of his taste, confessed it to be neat and simple, thought it right to encourage the manufacture of his country; and for his part, to his uncritical palate, the tea was as well flavoured from the clay of Staffordshire, as from that of Dresden or Seve. But this was quite an old set, purchased two years ago. The manufacture was much improved since that time; he had seen some beautiful specimens when last in town, and had he not been perfectly without vanity of that kind, might have been tempted to order a new set.'[34]

In her excellent book, Ray concludes by asserting that we must,

'reconsider the Indian Picturesque as an extension of a system of ideas and practices developed in the

homeland in its fullest scope', and that, '*at the heart of its portability and mutability was the desire to travel and explore*'.[35]

In this context, the Indian adventures of Thomas and William Daniell were simply a dramatic extrapolation of Thomas's much earlier exploration and graphic recording of picturesque subjects in England, such as Cheddar Gorge and Brimham Rocks. After their return from India, and the labour-intensive processing of their large but unfinished Indian portfolio, William was on the move again, stamping his artistic mark through images based on extensive travel across Britain. Most notably, he embarked on a lengthy tour around the coast, commencing in 1813, and culminating in his collection of aquatints in *A Voyage Round Great Britain,* published by Longman in eight volumes between 1814 and 1825. One of the images, Plate 21, is of Barmouth, Merionethshire, also visited and remarked upon by John Dashwood as part of his 'Sentimental Tour' of Wales a quarter of a century earlier.

CHAPTER NINE
Out of India

In the context of the Indian picturesque, and British involvement in the subcontinent during Jane Austen's lifetime, our narrative is fuelled by two specific Indian adventures and the resulting impacts when those individuals returned to England. Both have their origins in the period before Jane Austen's birth, with consequences extending into, and throughout, her lifetime. Each features a small group of characters and their connections with Jane Austen, India, and the Cotswolds.

The Warren Hastings Connections

The first group of characters includes Warren Hastings, Fanny Burney, Jane Austen's aunt Philadelphia Austen, Philadelphia's daughter 'Eliza', and Eliza's son, Hastings de Feuillide. Also drawn in are Warren Hastings' son George, and Jane Austen's parents, these latter connections cementing the close relationships between Hastings and the Austen family which continued through much of Jane's life.

Warren Hastings was a major figure in British history, and a controversial one. His substantial contribution to the colonial development of the Indian subcontinent is generally regarded by later commentators, with the benefit of historical hindsight, as very positive, and provided a key foundation for the rapid development of British influence in India, envied by other European powers. Nevertheless, his impact raised contemporary questions about interactions with indigenous peoples and cultures, and how these could be managed at a time when Britain's global influence was spreading rapidly, and in culturally very diverse arenas. Although eventually acquitted, Hastings' lengthy trial after returning to England reflected both political and moral concerns over his behaviour in India.

Warren Hastings was born on December 6th, 1732, the maiden name of his mother having been Hester Warren. When asked about his father, Penyston Hastings, Bernstein records that Hastings replied, *'There was not much in my father's history that would be worth repeating except that when he became old enough he entered holy orders, and went to one of the West India Islands where he died'*[1] in 1744. Penyston had squandered the small trust funds of his two children to pay his own debts. However, Hasting's uncle was able to send him to Westminster School, where *'his best friend was a boy named Elijah Impey, whose destiny would interlock with his in India'*[2]. Many years later, during Hastings' period as Governor-General of Bengal, Sir Elijah Impey was the chief justice of its Supreme Court.

When his uncle died in 1749, Hastings became the ward of a relative, Joseph Creswicke, who had contacts enabling Hastings to be appointed as an East India Company writer (or clerk). It appears he paid for Hastings' kit and passage to India, sailing in 1750 at the age of 17, on the EastIndiaman *London*. It is worth noting at this point that the Creswicke family has strong Cotswold connections, centred on Moreton-in-Marsh, near to the Hastings' historic family estate at Daylesford, as well as the neighbouring Dashwoods' hunting lodge at Bourton-on-the-Hill, and the Cockerell's house at Sezincote, with its Humphry Repton and Thomas Daniell design inputs.

Any detailed consideration of Hastings' extraordinary career in India is outside our scope and is only referenced where it links to other characters and themes of interest. The most important connection lies in India being the setting for the development of Warren Hastings' close relationship with Jane Austen's aunt, Philadelphia Austen. Philadelphia and Warren had each separately been brought up in England predominantly by relatives rather than by their respective parents and, consequently, faced considerable pressure to find their own way in the world. For Philadelphia, this pressure was caused by her lack of a dowry and the associated limited prospects for a favourable marriage. The solution she chose, travelling out to India, was not an uncommon one in the second half of the 18th century and one which, given Jane's close family relationship with her aunt, was almost certainly what led Austen to use this as a theme in her unfinished novel, *Catharine,* as outlined earlier. Written when Jane was a teenager, the novel portrays a young woman with limited prospects sailing to India in search of a husband. In some such situations the 'search' was pre-arranged rather than speculative. There is circumstantial evidence that Philadelphia Austen's marriage in India may likewise have been arranged prior to her leaving England, and perhaps she would not have ventured there without certain promises having been made. The go-between in this case seems to have been Francis Austen, Philadelphia's uncle (and Jane Austen's great uncle), who had been principally responsible for Philadelphia's upbringing. He was a solicitor, with one of his clients being Tysoe Saul Hancock, an East India Company surgeon. Hancock, as with many others in India, grasped the opportunity to supplement his official salary with other commercial activities, sending Francis Austen Indian gems to sell in England on his behalf.

Against this backdrop, Philadelphia sailed from England in 1751 aboard the *Bombay Castle*. Among the other 10 women sailing with her, one was to become Warren Hastings first wife and another was Margaret Maskelyne, the future wife of Clive of India. Marriage was the purpose for all three women, and within six months of arriving in India in 1752, Philadelphia had achieved her aim, marrying Tysoe Saul Hancock in February 1753. Regardless of whether

Philadelphia was part of some marriage arrangement, her circumstances and the fact that Hancock was almost twice her age very closely mirror the theme in Jane Austen's *Catharine*. Surely, Jane's inspiration was this colourful story involving her own aunt.

At much the same time, and having arrived in India in 1751, a year earlier than Philadelphia, Warren Hastings married Mary Allot Buchanan, the widow of John Buchanan, one of the British officers who had died in the infamous Black Hole of Calcutta incident. Hastings kept in touch with his old guardian, Mr Creswicke, back in the Cotswolds, and in one letter to him from India regarding his first wife Mary, Hastings says that he, *'experienced every good quality in my wife which I always wished for in a woman'*. [3] Mary had been a fellow passenger of Philadelphia aboard the *Bombay Castle* on the long voyage to India, and they would undoubtedly have become acquainted during the voyage. In any event, Warren and Mary had two children, a son George born in 1758, of whom more shortly, and a daughter called Elizabeth in 1759, who unfortunately survived only for a matter of weeks. This was tragically followed by Mary's own death later that year.

Meanwhile, in the south of the country, Philadelphia's marriage to Tysoe Hancock afforded her security in terms of both financial and social status, and Tysoe appears to have been delighted with his marriage to this young and attractive woman, who he treated very well. For the first few years of their marriage, however, they failed to produce any children. This changed a short while after they moved north to Calcutta, in Bengal, in 1759, where they befriended the very recently widowed Warren Hastings.

Warren Hastings
By Joshua Reynolds, 1766-8
[National Portrait Gallery D4445]

Hastings and Hancock became engaged in trading and business ventures together and, in parallel with this, Hastings and Philadelphia became extremely close friends. When Philadelphia became pregnant in early 1761 and gave birth to a daughter later that year, there were questions and rumours about the paternity. Perhaps notably, this child's name,

Elizabeth, was the same as that of Hastings' own daughter who had died only two years earlier. Tomalin remarks that, '*Lord Clive asserted that Mrs Hancock "abandoned herself to Mr Hastings", warning his own wife not to keep company with her*'[4], but whatever the truth, Tysoe Hancock never treated the child (christened Elizabeth, but initially known as Betsy, and later Eliza) as anything other than his own daughter. Hasting's treatment of Eliza, however, certainly evidences his considerable commitment to her well-being and financial security, seemingly far exceeding that expected of the supposed platonic relationship between himself and Eliza's mother, Philadelphia.

Whether or not Eliza was his child, the friendship between Warren and Philadelphia was a very close one, and perhaps intimate. What is certain is that in 1761, with his wife having died two years earlier, Hastings entrusted his infant son, George, to the care, back in England, of none other than Philadelphia's brother, George Austen, a duty later shared with George's new wife Cassandra Leigh. George and Cassandra would have 8 children of their own, the seventh being Jane Austen, born 11 years later in 1775. The infant George Hastings was apparently, and rather bizarrely, a companion on George and Cassandra Austen's brief honeymoon in 1764. Unfortunately, the six-year old boy died (possibly of diphtheria) shortly after this, although it was only when Tysoe, Philadelphia, Eliza and Warren Hastings, along with their Indian servants, returned to England in 1765 that Hastings discovered this devastating news of the loss of his son, to add to that of his wife and daughter six years earlier.

In 1768, Tysoe Hancock returned to India, leaving Philadelphia and Eliza in England. Hastings also returned to India. Philadelphia continued correspondence with Hastings, her letters being willingly forwarded by Tysoe, who did however put his foot down when she suggested returning to India on hearing that Hastings had met a new woman. He also refused Philadelphia's proposal to allow Eliza to return, commenting on how 'lewd' the place now was, and perhaps tellingly adding the comment that, '*You yourself know how impossible it is for a young girl to avoid being attracted to a young handsome man whose address is agreeable to her*'.[5]

Tysoe Hancock died in 1775, but left Philadelphia and Eliza very little money. In a continuation of the close relationships between the parties, Hastings was the executor of Tysoe's will. Recognising Philadelphia's renewed difficult circumstances for the second time in her life, Hastings gave her £10,000 of his own money, an enormous sum in those days, enabling her, still a fairly young widow, to pursue a comfortable and active life. She decided to make the most of this opportunity, and once again decided to leave England, this time moving to Paris with Eliza. Their associations with Warren Hastings, and Eliza's status as a reasonably rich heiress, enabled her in 1781 to secure a romantic marriage with the Comte de Feuillide. Eliza moved back to England in 1786 for the birth of her son, who she named Hastings, outwardly at least in honour of her godfather Warren Hastings and the substantial assistance that he had afforded to her and her mother, but once again perhaps an indication of a much closer relationship between Eliza's mother Philadelphia and Hastings.

Back in England, Philadelphia and Eliza frequently visited the Austens at Steventon. The lively and attractive Eliza made a great impression on her cousins, particularly the young Jane Austen. Sadly, Philadelphia died in 1792, and Eliza's husband, the Comte de Feuillide, who was loyal to the monarchy in France, was arrested for conspiracy against the Republic, and guillotined in 1794. Subsequently, in a further link to Jane Austen's immediate family, the widowed Eliza was courted by her cousin, Henry Austen, Jane's brother, and they married in December 1797. Eliza's only son, Hastings de Feuillide, tragically died in 1801 and Eliza herself died in 1813 with Jane Austen at her bedside. The two cousins had been close ever since Eliza's return from France in 1786 when Jane was about eleven. In summary, relationships between the Austen family and Warren Hastings were extremely close and, from an early age, their underlying Indian context formed an exciting part of Jane's exposure to the wider world.

Whatever Eliza's relationship was to Warren Hastings, quite possibly his natural daughter, she appears to have held a deep fascination for her cousin Jane Austen. Eliza would no doubt have shared with Jane many experiences, stories and adventures from her eventful life, adding elements of worldly glamour and excitement to Austen's otherwise sedate rural Hampshire environment. One apparent early influence on Jane was Eliza's extrovert character, including her love of drama and theatrics. After her return to England in 1786, and visiting Jane's family at Steventon at Christmas 1787, Eliza involved the family in an impromptu dramatic performance in the great barn. Huxley believes that Jane, then twelve years old, projected something of Eliza's character in her later portrayal of *Mansfield Park*'s character Mary Crawford enthusiastically promoting the idea of the amateur dramatic production in the novel. The similarities between Eliza and the fictional Mary Crawford are notable: both played the harp, and both were drawn to the high life in town rather than the more sedate rural life which Jane herself experienced. Mary Crawford's aversion to the Church, and the clergy as a profession, may also be Jane Austen's reflection of Eliza's attitude.[6]

Eliza's Indian background, and its intriguing and possibly scandalous connections to Warren Hastings, opened Jane's eyes to an exotic and romantic world which she also incorporates tangentially in her writing. Eliza is used in *Sense and Sensibility* as the name of Colonel Brandon's former love interest as well as for the daughter she bears his elder brother, who Willoughby seduces. Given that Austen also deliberately highlights Colonel Brandon's service in India, Austen surely derives the fictional name Eliza from her cousin. There are certainly similarities in background in the sense of mysterious or questionable parentage or upbringing, as well as links with India; this may well be another example of Austen transforming real experience into fictional portrayal, seemingly taking inspiration from the Indian background of her cousin Eliza in creating her fictional Eliza in *Sense and Sensibility*.

The close relationships between Jane, Eliza, Warren Hastings, Jane's parents, and her aunt Philadelphia, gave Jane's visits to the Cotswolds, and frequent news from there in family correspondence, added significance, with Hastings' Daylesford estate lying adjacent to Jane's relatives at Adlestrop. Indeed, Jane appears to have had a reasonably detailed knowledge of the activities of Warren Hastings and his wife, and the daily routines at his Daylesford estate in the decades after their return from India, judging by extracts from two letters she wrote to her sister Cassandra. The first, in December 1800,[7] contains a passage referring to a pregnancy and imminent birth, which appears to be a cause of slight concern. Jane notes, '*But like Mrs Hastings, "I do not despair – " & you perhaps like the faithful Maria may feel still more certain of the happy Event.*' The 'Maria' referred to here is the Austens' cousin Miss Maria Payne who, '*seems to have been almost permanently resident at Daylesford, presumably as Mrs Hastings's companion, and could well be described as 'faithful'* '.[8]

The second extract, from one of Jane's letters to her sister, written in 1808, strongly implies that Jane had visited Hastings's house at Daylesford, and noted its internal features, presumably during one of her visits to Adlestrop. In the letter, she comments,

> '*I cannot help thinking & re-thinking of your going to the Island so heroically. It puts me in mind of Mrs Hastings' voyage down the Ganges, & if we had but a room to retire into to eat fruit, we wd* [would] *have a picture of it hung there*'.[9]

This is a direct reference to a painting which Warren Hastings commissioned from William Hodges to illustrate the scene when,

> *'In 1782 Warren Hastings's wife Marian made a hasty and dangerous voyage down the stormy Ganges, travelling 400 miles in three days, to nurse him when he had fallen seriously ill. .... and a large canvas, commonly known as Mrs Hastings at the Rocks of Colgong was the result. This painting, with other Indian scenes by Hodges, was hung in the 'picture room' at Daylesford'.*[10]

This indicates Jane's knowledge that the Daylesford 'picture room' served the purpose of 'a room to retire into to eat fruit', and appears to evidence an in-depth knowledge of Daylesford, including how at least one of its rooms was furnished and used. Hastings had expensive tastes and

> *'furnished the house with rich oriental fabrics and exquisite furniture. Amid the beautiful collection of pieces supplied by Ince and Mayhew stood chairs of carved and gilt solid ivory, as well as bejewelled oriental souvenirs and mementoes. As such the house was an early embodiment of the Regency fascination for picturesque exotica'.*[11]

There is one further piece of evidence of Warren Hastings' intimate links with the Austen family, aside from his relationship with, and generous gifts to, Philadelphia Austen. Hastings apparently assisted Jane's brother Frank Austen through various East India Company connections, resulting in Frank profiting from shipping silver to England from China via India without hindrance from the Navy.[12]

Given the close family connections, and the common courtesy of mutual visits between respectable families in any rural 'neighbourhood', I agree with Huxley that it is likely Jane Austen would have met Warren Hastings on one of her visits to Adlestrop. A few years later, she was certainly overjoyed with his praise for her novel *Pride and Prejudice*, a copy of which had been given to him by her brother Henry.

Referring to feedback on the publication of the novel, Jane comments in a letter to her sister in September 1813 that she has received a letter from Warren Hastings (which she can hardly wait to show Cassandra), remarking, '*And Mr Hastings – I am quite delighted with what such a Man writes about it …. His admiring my Elizabeth [Bennet] so much is particularly welcome to me…*'.[13]

In the same letter to her sister is the intriguing sentence, '*Mr Hastings never <u>hinted</u> at Eliza in the smallest degree*'.[14] This is Jane again referring to the letter from Hastings. The comment is made in the context of her cousin Eliza's death on 25th April earlier that year, and Jane makes this emphasised comment presumably in the knowledge of widespread suspicion about Hastings being Eliza's natural father. Jane was perhaps expecting Hastings to have at least made some passing reference to Eliza's death, even simply out of courtesy in sending his condolences to Jane for the loss of her cousin, regardless of any other connections. There is a sense that Jane felt the absence of this common courtesy had some significance, perhaps betraying Hastings' embarrassment about Eliza.

Hastings remained a high-profile figure for several decades after his return from India and retirement to his Daylesford estate, which he had managed to repurchase in fulfilment of the promise he had made to himself at a very young age. The prominent writer Fanny Burney records meeting him. Her diary entry for September 24th 1785 notes that:-

Mr Locke fetched me himself from Twickenham on Wednesday. I had the pleasure of passing one day while there with Mr Hastings, who came to dine with Mr Cambridge. I was extremely pleased, indeed, with the extraordinary plainness and simplicity of his manners, and the obliging openness and intelligence of his communication. He talked of India, when the subject was led to, with the most unreserved readiness, yet was never the hero of his own tale, but simply the narrator of such anecdotes or descriptions as were called for, or as fell in naturally with other topics.[15]

Fanny Burney had been born on June 13th June 1752 at Lynn Regis [*now Kings Lynn*], Norfolk, not far from Burnham Thorpe, Norfolk, where Nelson was born six years later, on 29th September 1758. Burney was a major literary role-model for Jane and also had something distinctive in common with Jane's cousin, Eliza, namely marriage to a high-status Frenchman. In 1793, aged forty-one, Fanny Burney married Alexandre Gabriel Jean-Baptiste Piochard D'Arblay, adjutant general to Lafayette, the famous French aristocrat and military officer who fought in the American War of Independence, and who was also a key figure in the French Revolution of 1789.

As with Hastings, the focus on Burney's life is restricted here to those elements which touch on other relevant characters and themes. She was something of a trailblazer for female writers, and Jane Austen certainly read, and admired, her work. Burney employed letter-writing by her characters as a literary mechanism, her novel *Evelina*, for example, consisting entirely of letters. Jane Austen adopted this mechanism, employing it in several early works. Indeed, *Elinor and Marianne*, the original version of what would become *Sense and Sensibility*, was initially written in this epistolary form.

A common cause shared by Burney and Austen was support and friendship for Warren Hastings. It is enough here to say that Fanny Burney was an ardent supporter of Warren Hastings at his trial, opposing attacks by Edmund Burke, who she challenged face to face.

The impeachment trial, before the House of Lords, dragged on sporadically from 1788 to 1795, and its high-profile political, economic, and imperial implications made it a focus of much public attention and media reporting. In the spirit of late 18th century and Regency culture, with its strong satirical vein, and appetite for scandal, such 'reporting' included the publication of a series of humorous letters, totally in verse, under fictitious names. Entitled *'from Simpkin the second to his dear brother in Wales containing an humble description of the trial of Warren Hastings Esq. from the commencement to the close of the sessions in 1789'*, it was published in London in 1789, and printed by *'John Bell, British Library, Strand, bookseller to His Royal Highness the Prince of Wales, MDCCLXXXIX'*. The detail in its 152 pages gives some sense of the public attention the trial attracted. The following passage not only gives an indication of its style, but encapsulates many of the key elements of the trial, in terms of its strong underlying party political battles and its allegations of corruption and crimes in India :-

> What a strange world it is, BROTHER SIMPKIN ! we're in
> Of lies, and confusion, of folly, and sin !
> And *the Right* and *the Wrong* seem so twisted about,
> That I'm sure at this distance they can't be found out.
> But PARTY I fear is the cause of the *bastings*
> So lavishly given to poor WARREN HASTINGS.
> And I oftentimes think all the MANAGERS cruel ---
> That their FIRE is *Resentment*, and MALICE the *Fuel*.
> Else why should DICK SHERRY and good MASTER BURKE, **
> On the subject of *Plunder* and DEBTS make such work ?
> Dire spectres of MASSACRES call up to view,
> When they surely might know, NOT A WORD OF IT'S TRUE.
> Indeed I must own that I pity the ears
> Of their LORDSHIPS, the BISHOPS, and DIGNIFIED PEERS ;
> I pity the LADIES, so modest and nice,
> Who heard all the *filthy descriptions of vice*.
> And which, while the SPEAKERS so lavishly paint,
> Some Ladies suppos'd the best thing was – *a faint*.

But even for HASTINGS a *something* I feel,
Which by chance may be wrong -- but my heart is not steel ;
For I see him surrounded, by foes, in his chair,
Who attack him like dogs that *are baiting a Bear* ;
While he's nothing to do, but observe what they say,
And expend the NET SUM OF THREE HUNDRED A DAY !

[** Barely disguised references to Richard Sheridan and Edmund Burke.]

The final line highlights the legal fees involved and just how expensive the trial was for Hastings personally - £300 a day for each day of the disjointed seven-year trial would run into the equivalent of many millions today. It also explains why Hastings was so keen to repurchase the family's Daylesford Estate in the Cotswolds ahead of the trial, for fear that he would possibly never again be in a position to do so. In the event he was eventually acquitted. Hastings' trial defence had been helped by supporting comments from a continual stream of those returning from India, as the Cockerells (shortly to purchase Sezincote) had just done. As Macaulay notes,

'The press, an instrument neglected by the prosecutors, was used by Hastings and his friends with great effect. Every ship, too, that arrived from Madras or Bengal, brought a cuddy full of his admirers. Every gentleman from India spoke of the late Governor-General as having deserved better, and having been treated worse, than any man living. ... Retired members of the Indian services, civil or military, were settled in all corners of the kingdom. Each of them was, of course, in his own little circle, regarded as an oracle on an Indian question; and they were, with scarcely one exception, the zealous advocates of Hastings'.[16]

Jane Austen and her family would have followed the trial with interest, and Jane would have been particularly gratified to know that Burney, as one of her literary inspirations, was also supporting this close friend of the Austen family.

At the time of the above humorous publication in verse, Jane was in her early teens. The satirical style it represents, as well as Fanny Burney's use of epistolary technique in her novels, alongside other innovative contemporary examples, evidence the wide range of literary styles and means of expression to which Jane was exposed in her formative years. It was an era in which experimentation with a variety of new ideas in the arts was flourishing and this is reflected in her own early literary output, with its unrestrained and idiosyncratic 'tongue in cheek' threads of ironic and sarcastic humour. Even in her more mature publishable works – and *Sense and Sensibility* was the first – her penetrating humour persists, albeit woven seamlessly into a richer and more brilliantly designed tapestry.

Further common ground with Burney lies in the similarly guarded ways in which both she and Austen approached potential publishers, neither initially wanting to declare her name or gender. In terms of Burney's approach to getting published – she got her brother to pose as the author – there are striking similarities both with Jane Austen's strategy of anonymity three decades later, and with the Bronte sisters in the next literary generation. This reflects the difficulties for women authors of being treated seriously during this extended period. Indeed, when Burney's *Evelina, or, A Young Lady's Entrance into the World* was published, no author was given. Similarly, Austen's identity was not initially disclosed, and was only revealed after initial success, with her reputation established. However, the publisher of Burney's *Evelina* had at least paid £30 for it, whereas Austen had to effectively self-fund or underwrite *Sense and Sensibility*. In the event, it did make Jane a small profit, as she proudly notes in a postscript to a letter to her brother Frank[17]. Notwithstanding the gender issue, getting published was in any event a challenge for all writers. One of the more fortunate aspiring authors was an unnamed friend of Sir John Dashwood-King who noted with pride (and a hint of surprise) in a letter to Sir John in 1793 that a bookseller had published his book, '*on his own account ... and placarded the Advertisement*'.[18]

Burney's second and structurally more conventional novel, published in 1782, was *Cecilia; or Memoirs of an Heiress*. As Bernstein notes, '*toward the end of it one of the characters says, "The whole of this unfortunate business .... has been the result of PRIDE and PREJUDICE". There is no question that Jane Austen read it and was impressed*'[19], even though, by 1813, when her own novel *Pride and Prejudice* was published, Burney's novels were falling out of fashion.

Given this highly probable link between Fanny Burney and the title of *Pride and Prejudice*, together with Austen's love of Burney's work, I also wonder if the name of the heroine in *Mansfield Park*, Fanny Price, who Austen arguably portrays as mirroring some of her own character, is derived by her as an amalgamation of *Fanny* from Fanny Burney and *Price* from a contraction of Pri(de and Prejudi)ce, evidencing further appreciation by Jane Austen of what she had drawn from Burney's writing.

Hastings, having achieved his long-held ambition to buy back the family's Daylesford estate, proceeded to make alterations to the house, employing the established architect Samuel Pepys Cockerell who, significantly, was later architect to the East India Company. Samuel's immediate Cockerell relatives already had many links with, and personal experience of, the sub-continent and he was therefore a natural choice for this commission, given the Indian source of Hastings' funding for the project and his wish to introduce Indian elements both internally and externally. These Indian design influences were deliberately subtle at Daylesford, particularly externally, but Cockerell's next assignment at nearby Sezincote allowed for an unrestrained and exuberant expression of Indian styling. Working also with Humphry Repton, he relied more substantially on Thomas Daniell, directly utilising the latter's artistic Indian adventures, knowledge, and graphic output.

The Daniell, Repton, Cockerell and Dashwood Connections - Indian Style in the Cotswolds

The radical and dramatic Sezincote project directs us to a second group of characters, notably including Thomas and William Daniell, the Cockerells, Humphry Repton, and the Dashwoods, all of whom once again provide links with Jane Austen and the Cotswolds. This group, three of whom were leading exponents in their respective artistic fields, worked together in creating the extraordinary, and influential, Mughal-style house at Sezincote, which still survives as an iconic monument to the enthusiasm for India and all it represented during Jane's lifetime. Reference has already been made to the various characters involved, and the Dashwoods are explored in much more detail later, but the backgrounds to the Daniells and the Cockerells warrant more immediate detailed descriptions, including evidence of their strong Dashwood connections.

Thomas Daniell, born in 1749, was the son of John Sheppard Daniell, lessee of the Swan Inn in Chertsey, Surrey. As a boy, his humble origins saw him assisting his bricklayer brother, but at 14 he became apprenticed to a coach-builder, Mr Maxwell. Coaches were then enjoying increasing popularity and competition, and the decorative painting of rival coaches was becoming ever more elaborate and sophisticated.

His apprenticeship enabled the young Thomas Daniell to pick up elementary painting skills, and he was obviously seen as having some natural ability because he progressed to working for Charles Catton, coach-painter to George III.[20] In parallel with this, he developed an ambition to become a professional artist, and in 1772 exhibited a flower painting at the Royal Academy. The next year he entered the Royal Academy Schools, and over a 12-year period showed thirty pictures in Royal Academy exhibitions.[21] A major breakthrough, and one pivotal to this story, was Daniell's securing of a prestigious commission in 1781 for six paintings of West Wycombe Park from its owner, Francis Dashwood, the Rt Hon. Lord Le Despencer, 2nd Baronet of West Wycombe.

Thomas Daniell painting of West Wycombe Park, 1781
[By kind permission of Sir Edward Dashwood, Bt.]

Why this important Dashwood commission was awarded to the relatively little-known Thomas Daniell is something of a mystery. One possible explanation is that the heir to the West Wycombe estate, soon to become Sir John Dashwood-King, 3rd Baronet, had married Sarah Moore of Sayes House, Chertsey, the same small town in which Thomas Daniell had been born and brought up. Perhaps, through this local connection, she was aware of his emerging artistic reputation and suggested him to her Dashwood in-laws. Once engaged in the project, and presumably being on site at West Wycombe for some time, it is likely that Thomas Daniell and his artistic skill made an impression on the future fourth baronet, John Dashwood, then just 16 years old. This may explain why, many years later, Sir John Dashwood offered to find accommodation near his hunting lodge in Bourton-on-the-Hill for Thomas Daniell while he was working as a key designer on the Sezincote project.

In a further coincidence, another notable figure loosely linked to this narrative was also, like Thomas Daniell, brought up in Chertsey. That figure was Sir John Soane (born 'Soan'), architect of the Bank of England. He was succeeded in that post by Charles Robert Cockerell, son of Samuel Pepys Cockerell, the architect at both Daylesford and Sezincote at the heart of our Cotswold focus. With many parallels to Thomas Daniell, John Soan had been brought up in very modest circumstances in Chertsey and had also initially assisted his own bricklayer brother. He changed his name from Soan to Soane in an attempt to distance himself from his humble origins, such pretentions being mocked by both the Cockerells and Daniells in later correspondence flowing between Chertsey and London. The ongoing animosity between these individuals is most vividly illustrated by the message left by Soane for Charles Robert Cockerell at the time that Soane relinquished the architect post at the Bank of England to this rival family. When asked by Cockerell's assistant for a sight of his drawings of the Bank of England, Soane replied, '*You'll tell Mr Cockerell I'll not leave a scrap, not a bit of paper to go to the water closet with*'.[22] Soane's resentment of the Cockerells' and Daniells' mischief-making and mockery of him, as he saw it, was clearly deeply felt.

Whether or not the joint Chertsey origins of Sarah Moore and the Daniell family were influential in his appointment, the 1781 commission at West Wycombe Park appears to have focused Thomas Daniell's interest in his future choice of subject type. Thereafter, his artistic output was dominated by landscapes, often incorporating architecture. While the West Wycombe paintings mirrored their subject matter in being rendered in a conventional, formal, and classical manner, the next three years saw Daniell respond to changing artistic fashion, notably the growing enthusiasm for 'the picturesque', highlighted in earlier chapters. He began targeting more romantic, irregular, and dramatic landscapes, including rugged subjects such as Wookey Hole and Cheddar Cliffs (now called Cheddar Gorge) in Somerset, together with Brimham Crags (now called Brimham Rocks) and Mother Shipton's Cave, both in North Yorkshire.

The sites in Yorkshire may not have been chosen at random. There are historic Yorkshire ties between the wider Daniell and Ingilby (or Ingleby) families and there are paintings of the Ingleby home, Ripley Castle, North Yorkshire, in the style of Thomas Daniell, within the Castle. Daniell may even have been invited to lodge there while carrying out his artistic visits to nearby Brimham Crags (between Ripley and Pateley Bridge), and Mother Shipton's Cave in Knaresborough, with Ripley Castle being ideally located between the two.

Through these and other commissions, Daniell was establishing a reputation as a highly competent artist. However, competition for landscape painting commissions in late eighteenth century Britain was fierce, and he was looking for other artistic opportunities, particularly commercial ones. Thomas had also taken on the extra responsibility of looking after his nephew William Daniell. Acting as assistant, William must have shown some early promise because Thomas was confident enough in this embryonic relationship to embark on an ambitious joint artistic adventure: the target was India. It is not clear whether, at that stage, Thomas had identified the two distinct commercial art markets that he and William were to exploit very successfully - one in India and one in Britain - but he was both adventurous and confident in his own ability, and may also have felt that, in any event, this was the only way to make his mark. As outlined earlier, any such Indian venture was by no means an easy option. Aware of the inherent dangers involved, he also knew very well that even in India there would be competition, with several European artists already established there, producing portraits and some landscape paintings for a small coterie of potential purchasers in and around Calcutta. He chose to describe himself as 'an engraver' rather than an artist, as a way of offering something different or perhaps, as Archer suggests, as a way to avoid falling foul of the East India Company's effective quota system for transporting 'artists' to the sub-continent.[23] An East India Company ship was the only realistic way for civilians to get to India at that time, and securing a passage for both himself and William was a significant achievement.

As already outlined, their venture was to have important consequences for the portrayal of India to a receptive audience back in Britain, ready to latch on to almost any new exotic influences at a time of fascination with eastern culture, architecture and natural history, an enthusiasm reflected by Jane Austen's inclusion of several references to India in her novels. While China had for some decades been the main source of imports of Asian goods and artistic influences, India was increasingly fuelling the insatiable domestic appetite for oriental fashion inspiration. Nevertheless, journeys to India at this time still often involved sailing to China first and then doubling back to India. Indeed, this is the route that the Daniells followed in 1785, leaving Gravesend aboard the East Indiaman *Atlas* on 7th April, staying in China for some months, before sailing back westward to India, arriving in Calcutta early in 1786.

Their time in China afforded the opportunity for initial attempts at engravings in a distant country, these early artistic outputs being generally considered competent but lacking the refinement later achieved in India.

Thomas Daniell engraving of a 'Chinese Lady'

The wider Indian sub-continent was still largely unexplored by Europeans, but Bengal and some other disparate smaller regions were subject to substantial intrusion and establishment of trading links.

The centre of British interests in Bengal was Calcutta, and an extract from an account of the town in the 18th century provides an impression :-

One edifice [Fort William], confronting the river, dominated the low-lying horizon, the citadel built by Charnock's successors to defend the infant settlement. There the Union Flag proudly waved from a lofty flagstaff, proclaiming the rule of English law. .... Eastwards lay the Court-house .... southwards the Hospital and Cemetery, whilst on all sides scattered about within easy reach of the Fort were the dwelling-houses of the principal members of the settlement, most of them three-storied buildings, and built in the typical English Georgian style of the period. The whole area was less than one square mile.

However, although sounding very civilised, the account continues :-

Few places in the world could have held less attractions than eighteenth-century Calcutta for the refined and cultured Englishman fresh from home. Though Bengal has sometimes been called a Garden of Eden - for reason of its rich fertility – Calcutta was emphatically no paradise. As late as 1780 …. it was described by a visiting traveller as 'that scattered and confused chaos of houses, huts, sheds, streets, lanes, alleys, windings, gutters, sinks and tanks, which, jumbled into an undistinguished mass of filth and corruption, equally offensive to human sense and health ..'[24]

This reality is worth bearing in mind when considering criticism of Warren Hastings emanating from London by those, famously including Edmund Burke, who had a rosy remote view of India, while never having been there.

The lifestyle of the British East India Company staff also reflects the 'live for the moment' mindset inculcated both by the reality of inherent dangers and the liberating absence of the formulaic social constraints they were used to back in Britain. Members of the British high society in Bengal felt they had a limited time to live it up, and they did just that. They would either die, often because of disease or extravagant lifestyle, or return to Britain after a few years to recover. In India, many gambled for large stakes; Philip Francis, for example, '*was said to have won thirty lakhs (three million) of rupees at whist while losing ten thousand pounds at backgammon. The difference in his favor enabled him, when he retired to England, to be independently rich*'.[25] Dinner was typically taken at about two in the afternoon, with the men then each drinking two or three bottles of wine, and repeating it all in the evening, attended by large numbers of servants.

Calcutta was rapidly being developed at this time, with East India Company and British Government agencies establishing buildings for administrative and trading purposes. As sketched in the account above, these buildings were almost all in a European classical style, in line with much of what was being constructed in Britain, but with more emphasis in India on shaded colonnades and loggias in recognition of the different climate, thereby giving them more authenticity and affinity with classical buildings in their countries of architectural origins, namely Greece and Italy. The double colonnaded south front of the Dashwoods' West Wycombe Park, painted by Thomas Daniell back in 1781 (see image on the back cover), and unusual in England, may well have come to his mind again when he looked at some of the new Calcutta buildings. In any event, producing accurate representations of buildings was well within his compass, and he saw the opportunity for marketing engravings of Calcutta's emerging colonial townscape to the European inhabitants of the town and its surrounding area.

These engravings were popular, even though the quality was not as Daniell would have liked. The engraving technique of 'aquatinting', which even in Europe was only just being developed, proved initially to be very difficult for the Daniells to master. This was made more challenging as they were relying on local Indian artisans to carry out much of the work, which involved processes largely new to these willing but inexperienced craftsmen.

As previously outlined, Thomas and William spent the next 8 years travelling in India at a time of unrest, and their bravery and adventurous spirit, combined with their energy and fortune with good health, enabled them to accumulate an extensive and diverse topographical record of substantial parts of the sub-continent. The influence of their published images of India was seminal and, for a time, the height of fashion in Britain, copied extensively in various media including Staffordshire pottery, as noted previously, and with multiple reproductions of their prints finding a ready market.

On his return from India, as well as completing unfinished drawings and prints, and compiling their major work, *Oriental Scenery*, Thomas Daniell was also in demand in the field of architecture. Significantly, several patrons of these architectural creations had themselves experienced India in this formative era and were beneficiaries of the wealth and status generated – some would say plundered - by their pioneering exploits there. The earliest example of this patronage was Daniell's garden pavilion of about 1801 commissioned by Major Sir John Osborne at Melchet Park, Hampshire, as a tribute to Warren Hastings, with a bust of Hastings as a centrepiece within.

Although this small building was later demolished, it is recorded in images (the one below featuring a male figure explaining the building's features to his female companion, just as evidenced in images of visits to ruins in previous chapters). Its design origins are clearly evident in an element of one of the Daniells' prints of the building at Rhotas.

Daniell print of a building at Rhotas, India   *Thomas Daniell's 'Osborne Pavilion'*

This same pavilion design appears in two other significant places. The first is at Sezincote, the Gloucestershire estate in the North Cotswolds, which had been purchased by the Cockerell family in the late 1790s. It was being heavily remodelled in an Indian style from about 1803, with direct design input from Thomas Daniell himself. Nearing completion at the time, this extraordinary local project would almost certainly have been a topic of discussion during Jane Austen's visit to nearby Adlestrop in 1806.

Thomas Daniell's plan drawing for the fountain pool pavilion at Sezincote

Pavilion at Sezincote

Finally, this same pavilion motif, inspired by that at Rhotas in India, and adapted both at Melchet Park and at Sezincote in the Cotswolds, can also be seen in one of Repton's drawings and plans for the Royal Pavilion at Brighton which Humphry Repton presented to the Prince of Wales (later Prince Regent) in about 1808. These extensive plans leaned heavily on several of Daniell's Indian aquatints, Repton almost directly replicating selected elements. These included designs for an octagon, gateway and aviary all borrowed from Daniell prints. As Archer notes, Repton's *'designs were published as a folio of aquatints in 1808 and included acknowledgments to 'my ingenious friend Mr T. Daniell'.*[26]

Image of Repton's drawings for a small building at Brighton Pavilion, closely matching that at Sezincote

At this stage the Prince Regent was wildly enthusiastic about Repton's plans and stated that, "*Mr Repton, I consider the whole of this work as perfect, and will have my part carried into immediate execution; not a tittle shall be altered ... ".*[27] This enthusiasm was at least partly fired by the Prince's Cotswold visit in 1807 to see the newly constructed Sezincote House, which obviously made a major impression on him even though it was probably not fully completed at the time. One of Thomas Daniell's paintings (executed a few years later) purportedly records the Prince's visit. This Regency visit to a substantial country house, approaching along an estate drive just like Jane Austen's visit to Stoneleigh Abbey a year earlier in 1806, resonates with her fictional description of Elizabeth Bennet's arrival at Mr Darcy's Pemberley in *Pride and Prejudice*.

Part of a Thomas Daniell painting, reputedly portraying the Prince Regent's visit to Sezincote in 1807, his carriage (far right) approaching the house over the Indian Bridge
[Courtesy of the Peake family]

Unfortunately, the Prince's enthusiasm was not matched by his finances, and Repton's plans for the Brighton Pavilion (heavily borrowing from Daniell's drawings) were never implemented. However, a copy of the Daniells' highly influential publication *Oriental Scenery* was held in the Prince Regent's library at Carlton House and borrowed from there by John Nash as inspiration for his transformation of Brighton Pavilion several years later. Unfortunately, Nash's cavalier interpretation of Daniells' images was a travesty of design, authenticity, and taste. It was much ridiculed at the time, and even more so in the Victorian era, one critic describing it as '*a melancholy and ludicrous monument, resembling a group of tea-pots, candlesticks, and extinguishers*' [28], but as an example of Regency flamboyance, and the Prince Regent's character, it has undeniable and enduring iconic status.

Despite Repton's disappointment over the Brighton Pavilion, he had contributed substantially to the overall project at Sezincote with its pioneering use of Indian architecture and garden setting, while acknowledging Thomas Daniell as its real initiator and inspiration. As previously outlined, their patrons were the Cockerell family, directly connected with, and enriched by, their involvement with the East India Company.

For those fortunate enough to accumulate wealth from rapidly increasing foreign trade or the equally rapidly growing domestic industrial and agricultural revolutions, typical priorities were acquisition of property, and demonstration of 'improvements', fashion, and status. These motivations, as previously outlined, were also something of an obsession for Jane Austen as themes which she repeatedly incorporated into her novels, often using them as means by which to mock those who pursued these aims blindly, without the intelligence or knowledge to do so sensitively or tastefully. Although it was a notable exception to these specific criticisms, the transformation of Sezincote provides an insight into how one family, the Cockerells, with newly acquired wealth from their Indian activities, pursued acquisition of this property, and how its development was motivated by just such improvements, fashion, and status. A substantive account, mainly based on the Cockerells' archived contemporary correspondence[29], is outlined below with comparisons, where appropriate, to Austen's own treatment in her novels of property acquisitions, improvements, and associated aesthetic commentary, notably in *Sense and Sensibility*.

As an iconic emblem of the impact of Indian influences on Britain at the turn of the nineteenth century it is no surprise that Sezincote was chosen as a major case study for the University College London research project, '*East India Company at Home, 1757-1857*' (EICAH). Furthermore, and underpinning the importance of the North Cotswold context as the setting into which Indian motifs were imported into Britain, another property case study chosen is none other than Warren Hastings' Daylesford, which has already featured prominently in the chapters above. The Sezincote House case study for the EICAH project cites extracts from my published primary research[30], and a fuller account now follows, not least because it further evidences strong ties between our key characters.

The estate, and historic hamlet, of Sezincote lies between the North Cotswold villages of Longborough and Bourton-on-the-Hill. The house and its estate had been owned during the latter part of the eighteenth century by Lord North, the prime minister best known for presiding over the loss of the American colonies. The Norths had bought it in the late 17th century but, having several other property holdings, they were effectively absentee landlords of Sezincote, simply renting out the estate's land and houses. Documentary evidence indicates that in the late 18th century the tenant farmer had allowed '*the mansion*' itself to fall into a state of significant disrepair, and that it was ripe for development by enthusiastic new owners. The Cockerells fell into this category.

Colonel John Cockerell purchased the Sezincote estate in 1795, with wealth accumulated during his lengthy time in India, having been appointed to the military staff of Governor-General Warren Hastings in 1776. Given this connection, and that John Cockerell's sister Elizabeth Cockerell married John Belli, Hastings' private secretary, the decision by Cockerell to purchase the Sezincote estate was probably influenced by its proximity to Warren Hastings' home and estate nearby at Daylesford. Kingsley goes slightly further, suggesting that

> '*The Sezincote estate may have been found for him by Warren Hastings, the former Governor General of Bengal, whose house at nearby Daylesford was just being completed to the designs of John Cockerell's brother, Samuel Pepys Cockerell, at this time. Certainly Hastings' agent, William Walford, also acted for Cockerell, and helped him build up the estate by buying land in Bourton-on-the-Hill and Longborough*'.[31]

In a draft of his will in 1793, John Cockerell described himself as being, '*of the Town of Calcutta in the Province of*

Bengal, a Lieutenant in the Military Service of the United Company of Merchants of England trading to the East Indies', and at that time his will states '*I give and bequeath the sum of Current Rupees Eighty Thousand of lawful money of Bengal*', but with no reference to property. However, a codicil dated 23 December 1795 adds the phrase,

> '*I am now possessed of certain property and land in the County of Gloucester commonly known as Seasoncote* (which) *I have purchased with my own proper monies the said Estates being freehold ..*' [32]

John Cockerell's short period of ownership of the Sezincote estate is accompanied by considerable documentary evidence of him planning improvements to the mansion house and grounds, during which time the central part of the estate was still leased and occupied by William Phillips, a tenant farmer. Later letters indicate that the Cockerells couldn't wait to get Phillips out, so that they could start restoring the main house. The text of the related correspondence mirrors just the sort of exchanges Jane Austen's characters indulge in when discussing the latest improvements to their estates, including the acquisitive practice of bringing more land into estate ownership, often at the expense of the tenant farmers. The fictional Dashwoods' purchase of East Kingham Farm in *Sense and Sensibility* is a perfect example, and Austen's choice of the name Kingham may not be entirely unconnected to the Cotswolds and the real Dashwoods, as described earlier.

Throughout John Cockerell's tenure at Sezincote, opportunities were being sought to purchase adjoining lands, and to survey what had already been purchased. In an undated communication from Henry Clarke, a surveyor from Shipston-on-Stour, to Walford (the Cockerells' agent), maps of the estate are provided, and on December 4 1795, Charlotte Scott (of Banks Fee, Longborough) was approached by Walford regarding Cockerell taking over more land.

S P Cockerell wrote to William Walford on 14 April, 1797;

' .. I have a letter from my Bro. today dated 22nd March .... he is particularly pleased with the Bourton Purchase, with 'thanks to you for your address & management of it' .... he would have no objection to the same prescription Rep. [repeated] *to the extent of four or five thousand pounds in Bourton ... this depends on your general knowledge of what paper in that Country to watch the opportunity – at the same time if he is knowing to his . or even what you call a willing purchase, nothing can be effected in the Market at a Modest Price – this is therefore for yourself ...'* [33]

In other words, Walford was being instructed to buy further suitable property in Bourton-on-the-Hill, but not to publicise that they were in the market for such purchases, as this would increase the price. In the letter, there was also a separate instruction to Walford that,

'No leases more than from year to year shall be granted of the Moreton Land for as Mr Cockerell wants to get land in Bourton he will certainly in case of an Inclosure there wish to exonerate his Land from Tythes by Land in Moreton.' [34]

This determination to acquire additional land again strikes a chord with the actions of the fictional John Dashwood in relation to the estate at Norland in *Sense and Sensibility,* and in the real world it is Dashwood property at Bourton-on-the-Hill that was the Cockerells' next target, though not ultimately acquired. In September 1797, S P Cockerell wrote to William Walford, from Broadstairs; '*I thank you for your attention to the little Estate adjoining Seasoncote ... I don't know where he* [John] *is at present but he was expected at Seasoncote these 10 days past. ... I have given up all ideas of the Dashwood property*'.[35] The Dashwood referred to here is Sir John Dashwood, 4th Baronet of West Wycombe, then living at Bourton-on-the-Hill, within sight just to the north of Sezincote.

But it wasn't just expansion, land-swaps, and consolidation of their local property holdings that John Cockerell had in mind. In the short time between the purchase of Sezincote in 1795 and his death in 1798, John Cockerell had already planned, and started to implement, improvements to the existing house and grounds, using as his architect his brother Samuel Pepys Cockerell.   Certainly, on 10 November 1797, two years after his purchase, John Cockerell wrote to William Walford, from 'No. 49 Conduit Street', London :-

> *'I may express my thanks to you and explain as concisely as I am able my future plans for an Establishment at Seasoncote. To fix my residence there is rather more than I dare promise – but I shall keep it in View.*
>
> *In this consideration the release of Phillips's farm I esteem a most pleasing Event, and on no account would I consent to its being resumed; nor to let the Farm as a separate one.*
>
> *My brother wrote you the sketch of the Grounds I proposed to keep in hand, as Annex to the Mansion which encircles me within a stone bound wall, to extent of about 80 or 90 acres I think and keeps clear of all the Farms , roads etc.*
>
> *I have many conceits and fancies in regard to Seasoncote for a residence ... I propose to throw down every fence, and open up the whole, as park, I ... shall take up my residence [at Stow or Moreton] for a month at least, to form all my plans for the grounds, and the furnishing and finishing of the house, which on Phillips' quitting will probably undergoe further alterations and conversions. Do you know if in Stow, Longborough, Bourton or Moreton there is any*

Cabinet Workman whom I might encourage with some orders for Seasoncote house, in furnishing the plain sort of work I shall want mostly – for bedrooms, servants &c?.' [36]

Clearing areas around the main house to improve its setting is again typical of the period, and mirrors both Austen's descriptions of changes at the fictional Dashwood property at Norland in *Sense and Sensibility*, and the similar taking down of trees and opening up parkland by the real Dashwoods at their ancestral West Wycombe estate. As well as being very much in line with the improvement of farms and estates being progressed in Austen's lifetime, it also coincided with the ongoing enclosure of common land, the legal process of consolidating fragmented landholdings into single large acreages in the hands of a few wealthy individuals. Austen makes reference to such land-grabbing and sweeping away of ancient landscapes, with barely disguised dismay. The visual impact could be dramatic. In relation to the very particular enclosure of the Bourton-on-the-Hill medieval open fields, the Revd. Samuel Warneford's wife, Margaret, noted succinctly that, *'The enclosure has altered the face of the country'*.[37]

Austen's fictional John Dashwood uses the cost of such improvements and consolidations in his pathetic plea of poverty in *Sense and Sensibility,* claiming that, *'The enclosure of Norland Common is a most serious drain'* (on his finances), even though it would obviously massively increase his overall wealth. Land, once enclosed, produced far higher yields through economies of scale and facilitation of new farming methods. It was claimed in the contemporary papers proposing enclosure at Bourton-on-the-Hill, that it would roughly double crop yields.

To return to Sezincote, more comments about the tenant farmer Phillips and plans for the house and grounds, is referred to in a letter from John Cockerell to William Walford.

'My dear Sir, As my Brother is expected in London by the 8th of Nov. at latest, I should be glad you let me

know by that time what has been done in regard to the Cottages at Bourton, if you have anything to communicate respecting Seasoncote let me know that also. ..... Cheney will probably have told you that he proposes taking a considerable quantity of land into Hand when Phillips quits .... By the bye, <u>Mr Clarke</u> is ... asking to draw upon us for his Bill for Surveying & Mapping, I think sixty odd pounds, & without getting any approval of his Bill.

My Brother talks of doing something to the Grounds, the Ponds etc & to make it now a Comfortable Residence, do you know any Body in your neighbourhood or in that Country capable of laying down a sensible general Plans for the purposes - & an Intelligent Garden ... [and] afterwards ... would ... put it into execution .... Perhaps you may know of such a chap, it would be more certain than hiring one here in London.'[38]

Walford wrote to John Cockerell,

'I think I can get you something like the Person you want by way of a general Plan for dropping the Grounds and doing something to the Ponds, but Daylesford [Warren Hastings' estate] *has given me a Dread of such kind of works ... Sir Henry Dashwood* [a relative of Sir John Dashwood] *who lives at Bourton-on-the-Hill speaks much of a Person who has done work for him. The Estate is growing daily in Reputation and is well worth looking at, but the House should now be made visible'* [39]

Whether or not Repton is being referenced here – and he certainly was engaged in due course at Sezincote - the final phrase in this quote implies the removal of trees and other vegetation around the main house, once again very much mirroring Repton's approach at West Wycombe Park for the

Dashwoods, as well as Jane Austen's fictional Dashwoods' treatment of improvements at Norland in *Sense and Sensibility*.

Here again we have visual, picturesque, improvements being given a high profile. These were important components of, and contributors to, the fashionable models of contemporary country estates, illustrated by the striking impression made on Elizabeth Bennet by glimpsed views of Pemberley when entering and driving through its parkland, in *Pride and Prejudice*, as noted above.

On a more practical and prosaic note, a postscript to a letter from S. P. Cockerell to W. Walford, then staying at the White Hart Inn, Chipping Norton, adds, '*I don't think the House* [Mary Hart's in Bourton-on-the-Hill] *should be sold off again – it will do very well for Seasoncote Labourers, & there are no Cottages for them there.*' [40] Bourton-on-the-Hill apparently housed many of those working on the Sezincote project, and Thomas Daniell certainly lodged there.

Ongoing problems with Phillips, the tenant farmer, provide some interesting social insights. Cockerell comments that,

> '*Cheney complains that Phillips is going to inoculate his Children at Seasoncote which will keep the workmen from beginning till it is over – I hope you will prevent it, he is a Surly Brute & we have already lost a great deal of time from his ill temper & unaccommodating spirit, for which he shall suffer if he does not mend his manners.*' [41]

Inoculation, mirroring other oriental influences at Sezincote and neighbouring Batsford, had been introduced from the East, Chinese doctors having noticed that people who had suffered a mild form of smallpox often survived during later epidemics. They developed a method of inoculation which gave a mild dose of the disease and offered protection from a severe attack. However, it was not free of risk, and around this time, Edward Jenner, also based in Gloucestershire, was pioneering the safer procedure of vaccination (from *vacca*, the latin for cow), using a small dose of cowpox, instead of smallpox.

A diary entry of Dr James Woodforde, of Norfolk, for March 7, 1791 gives further contemporary social context,

> '.... *the smallpox spreads much in the parish. Abigail Roberts's husband was very bad in it in the natural way ... His children are inoculated by Johnny Reeve, as are also Richmond's children near me. It is a pity that ... the poor in the parish were not inoculated also.*'[42]

More directly relevant context is provided by an entry in a letter of 1792 sent from George Martin, looking after the Dashwood's Bourton-on-the-Hill hunting lodge, to John Dashwood at his London address,

> 'We rejoice much to hear that your little ones have so well got over the small pox & shall be more glad to hear when you & Mrs Dashwood intend to change your present gay scene for the rural delights of Borton.'[43]

Inoculation was only accessible to the reasonably well-off. It was big business; one doctor inoculated 2,514 people over an eleven year period, and substantial fees were levied. If Phillips, the short-term lessee of Sezincote House and later one of the farmhouses, was a 'surly brute', he evidently wasn't a poor one if he was able to plan for inoculation of his children

Whether or not Phillips actually went ahead with these inoculations is not known, but problems with getting rid of him, and his apparent neglect of the farm, continued to trouble the Cockerells, as evidenced by the following letter of 28 April 1798, from John Cockerell to William Walford.

> '..... *Phillips appears preparing to some disputation I fear ... he must not remove the stacks ... He has quitted the Farm in a very slovenly state ... not a blade of grass hardly .. I am at work on the Grounds, Clearing of Weeds &tc. and shaping the Bank from the Building. I shall probably have my brother here in a few days ... to inspect the remains of the Old House, which is woefully ruinous indeed.*'[44]

These problems had obviously been largely resolved when, in May 19 1798, Cockerell wrote, '*I am most glad to have got free from Phillips – on any terms ...* ', and building work, under the direction of S. P. Cockerell, commenced that year. On the 8 October, a letter from John Cockerell to Walford reads,

> '*I was at Seasoncot a fortnight since to settle my further plans of operation there, which I have completely done & Cheney is proceeding with all dispatch upon the Stables, the Garden Wall will be built in the Spring & in the meantime the planting about the House is to proceed – I think you will hardly know the place again from this great improvement made to it.*' [45]

As previously noted, the idea of improvements and land acquisitions at this time was not only entrenched in the mindset of those with the necessary resources, but was seemingly regarded by some as not only as a natural desire but almost as a duty and responsibility. The words that Jane Austen puts into the mouth of her fictional John Dashwood, regarding improvements and purchase of additional land at Norland in *Sense and Sensibility,* reflect just such a mindset –"*The land was so very desirable for me in every respect, so immediately adjoining my own property, that I felt it my duty to buy it. I could not have answered it to my conscience to let it fall into any other hands.*" [46] In the context of the novel it is clear that Austen is mocking such "duty" and "conscience".

At Sezincote, the continuing desire to build up landholdings in the neighbouring Bourton-on-the-Hill parish, ahead of an anticipated enclosure of the medieval common fields, is evidenced by a letter from S P Cockerell dated 11th October, 1798, commenting that,

> ' ... *I understand there is much talk of enclosing the open ffield of Bourton & therefore it is very material to be [acquisitive]...... in respect to the Commonable Rights.*
>
> *PS I have some intention of visiting Seasoncote in November with my sister.*'[47]

However, building work appears to have been suspended in November, and shortly afterwards John Cockerell suddenly died.

The Cockerells' hasty scramble for additional land in the 1790s was largely done to position themselves favourably for the imminently anticipated enclosure of the open fields. In fact, this haste turned out to be somewhat premature because the enclosure at Bourton-on-the-Hill was locally resisted for many years and didn't receive its necessary Act of Parliament until 1821.

Meanwhile, on John Cockerell's death, his brothers Samuel and Charles, and sister Elizabeth, were joint executors of the will and also its joint beneficiaries. Charles Cockerell, having also made his fortune in India, bought out his brother's and sister's shares in Sezincote. While retaining his brother Samuel Pepys Cockerell as architect, Sir Charles conceived a far more ambitious and radical plan involving a complete redesign of the house in an Indian, and more specifically Mughal, style. The other two contributors to this ground-breaking architectural enterprise were, like S P Cockerell, highly fashionable professionals in their respective artistic fields, namely the landscape architect Humphry Repton, and the topographical artist Thomas Daniell.

Samuel Pepys Humphry Repton Thomas Daniell
Cockerell [NPG D5801]
[NPG D12191]

This contemporary celebrity design team worked together at Sezincote to transform an essentially classical Georgian villa into something far more radical. As Musgrave puts it when referring to the project and these three designers,

> '*The Indian movement in this country had its nerve-centre at a house near Moreton-in-Marsh in Gloucestershire called Sezincote. ... Here were gathered, as at a sort of Regency Bauhaus, all the prophets of the new enthusiasm*'.[48]

Each of these three 'prophets' had substantial involvements with key figures in our story. Repton's impact locally was already evident both at Adlestrop Park and Adlestrop Rectory, and at Longborough, for members of Jane's maternal family, the Leighs, and she explicitly named him in *Mansfield Park*. Samuel Pepys Cockerell had earlier been employed by Warren Hastings at Daylesford, introducing some Indian influence into the architecture. Later to become architect to the East India Company, and with his family's India connections, S P Cockerell would seem to have been an obvious choice for the Indian style at Sezincote. However, S P Cockerell, unlike his brothers, had no direct experience of

India, and relied heavily for Sezincote's Indian detailing on the third of the celebrity designers, Thomas Daniell, whose experiences in India, and resulting published images, have already been outlined.

The choice of style for his house may appear a natural one for Charles Cockerell, given that he had accumulated his wealth during his time in India. However, to adopt an uncompromising Indian exterior was an extremely unusual choice, with none of the other numerous returning 'Indian nabobs' choosing this architectural style for their new or substantially remodelled country houses. Indeed, the now deceased John Cockerell had been planning a low-key architectural approach, using a classical style, and with good reason: there were negative perceptions about these returning nabobs, with their rapidly acquired Indian wealth and associated suspicions of corruption. A level of resentment was understandable among those whose own wealth was largely hereditary and built up over much longer timescales through traditional home-based, largely landowning, means. Most of the returnees therefore deliberately tried to slot seamlessly into English society by adopting the accepted fashionable styles for new and remodelled country houses. The predominant 18th century style was classical, although increasingly challenged around 1800 by neo-classical and gothic-revival designs. By contrast, Oriental influences – mainly Chinese in the 18th century – were generally restricted to the garden or to interiors. As already noted, the Chinese pagoda in the gardens at Kew is a good example of the former, and the influence on interiors is reflected in Chinese-design wallpapers and interior decoration at various country houses across Britain. There are very few examples of Oriental impacts on the exterior appearances of the country houses themselves.

Sezincote House, early C19 print

Sezincote remains the only Indian style country house in Europe, and Charles Cockerell's choice was patently an innovative and bold one. He and his architect brother S P Cockerell were clearly not as sensitive about the Cockerell family's acquisition of wealth in India as others were, and indeed perhaps wanted to set a trend that they thought others would follow. Repton was massively enthusiastic about the possibilities of this new fashion and encouraged embracing it wholeheartedly as a deliberate and distinct break from familiar architectural styles. Having seen Daniell's drawings and prints, Repton notes that,

> *'a new field opened itself; and ... I was pleased at having discovered new sources of beauty and variety, which might gratify that thirst for novelty, so dangerous to good taste in any system long established; because it is much safer to depart entirely from any given style, than to admit changes and modifications in its*

proportions, that tend to destroy its character. ... I should recommend the use of such Indian forms or proportions, as bear the least resemblance to those either of the Grecian or Gothic style, with which they are liable to be compared'. [49]

Had Repton's coherent and authentic vision for the remodelling of the Prince Regent's Royal Pavilion at Brighton (based on Daniell's aquatints and design detailing at Sezincote) been executed, as it so nearly was, this authentic style, combined with the Prince Regent's enthusiastic commendation, would perhaps have been established more widely, even if only for a few years until the next wave of fashion overtook it. John Nash's much inferior pseudo-Indian-style Brighton Pavilion, eventually executed several years later, quite rightly failed to generate much positive contemporary architectural commentary, was lampooned by many, and fortunately had little influence. By contrast, the relatively few examples in Britain of significant Indian-inspired architecture were more directly and positively influenced by Daniell's artistic output and therefore generally with greater authenticity. Although never securely established in England, the Indian style did fit a broader fashion trend for 'the picturesque', which is why the Daniells' images, in the form of prints and various visual derivatives, were so successful for a period of twenty or thirty years at the beginning of the nineteenth century. Although declining in popularity from the late 1830s, they appealed both to romantic sensibilities and to the demand for exotic travel imagery.

As Archer remarks,

'Through their aquatints Thomas and William Daniell undoubtedly made a significant contribution to that elegant synthesis of styles which characterised the late Georgian period ... the popular vision of India still remains that created by [Daniell's] *Oriental Scenery. Bearing repetition here, a contemporary admirer wrote*

of that great work, "The East was clearly reflected as the moon in a lake".' [50]

This takes us back to the role of the picturesque in portraying India, reflected in the title of Thomas Daniell's own 1810 volume, *A Picturesque Journey to India by the Way of China*, '*in which Thomas Daniell summed up in a masterly manner the attitude of the Picturesque Traveller engaged on a Picturesque Tour of India*'.[51]

However, to describe the Daniells' work as falling solely within 'the picturesque' would be misleading. It also had elements of the 'sublime' and 'exotic'. As outlined, the term was in any event susceptible to many different interpretations, and Jane Austen's rather flexible attitudes to the picturesque perhaps reflect this. Labels attached to artistic styles were, as with so many aspects of the Regency period,

> '*constantly being defined and redefined. The colossal, all that was dark, melancholy or terrifying* [themes satirised in Northanger Abbey] *was linked with the sublime; romantic disorder, irregularity, intricacy and singular shapes were seen as 'picturesque' – strange new architectural forms, tropical flora and fauna, 'native' manners and customs all conjured up the exotic.*' [52]

All three influences occasionally intermingled in a single work of art, as seen in some of Thomas Daniell's Indian images, and Archer concludes, ' ... *Here was a medley of romantic, picturesque, sublime and exotic Indian elements which were quite unfamiliar to the British*'.[53]

Thomas Daniell executed a series of paintings of Sezincote a few years after its completion and these are in a gentle picturesque style and, true to picturesque philosophy, adopt optimal viewpoints. As always with his work, they incorporate great attention to detail, as did Jane Austen's writing. It is interesting that the other artist invited to paint

Sezincote and its surroundings was John Martin, the foremost exponent of the 'sublime' at this time who, like Thomas Daniell, had started his artistic career as apprentice to a coach painter. The contrast between their respective portrayals of Sezincote further pushes categorisation of Daniell's style towards the picturesque. However, there is no sharp dividing line, and to the extent that certain Daniell images had sublime potential, this potential was exploited by John Martin in some of his other works, for example *Belshazzar's Feast, 1820*, in which, *'the heavy pillars show the influence of Thomas Daniell's aquatints of the rock-cut temples of Western India'*. [54]

To summarise, there never was any common agreement on precisely what qualified as 'picturesque'; Jane Austen used it in her novels even when elements of the sublime were in play, and in any event the term itself evolved subtly alongside constantly changing fashions in this period. Once the Regency period and sentiments faded, the meaning of 'picturesque' gradually moved further away from its late 18th century origins, becoming even less specific, and more loosely applied. One example is a mid-20th century series of 50 Ogden's cigarette cards entitled 'Picturesque Villages', where the term picturesque arguably means little more than generally attractive. Nevertheless, it is neatly appropriate that number 14 in the series is Bourton-on-the-Hill in the Cotswolds, which features strongly here.

PICTURESQUE VILLAGES

A SERIES OF 50

14

BOURTON-ON-THE-HILL, GLOUCESTERSHIRE

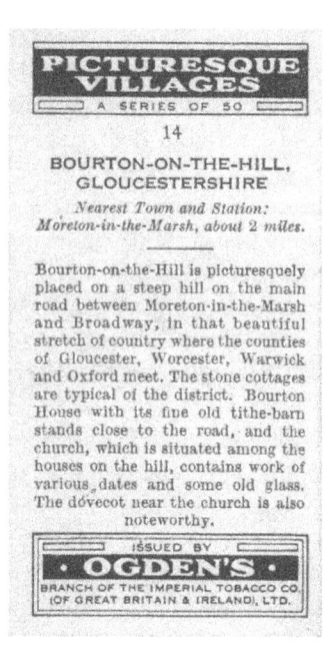

Nearest Town and Station:
Moreton-in-the-Marsh, about 2 miles.

Bourton-on-the-Hill is picturesquely placed on a steep hill on the main road between Moreton-in-the-Marsh and Broadway, in that beautiful stretch of country where the counties of Gloucester, Worcester, Warwick and Oxford meet. The stone cottages are typical of the district. Bourton House with its fine old tithe-barn stands close to the road, and the church, which is situated among the houses on the hill, contains work of various dates and some old glass. The dovecot near the church is also noteworthy.

ISSUED BY
· OGDEN'S ·
BRANCH OF THE IMPERIAL TOBACCO CO.
(OF GREAT BRITAIN & IRELAND), LTD.

Ogden's cigarette card featuring Bourton-on-the-Hill No. 14 in a series of 50 'Picturesque Villages'

There is clear evidence that the house on the left in this cigarette card image is where Thomas Daniell stayed and worked while engaged in the Sezincote project alongside Humphry Repton and Samuel Pepys Cockerell. The deeds of this same house also contain direct reference to Sir John Dashwood-King, 4th Baronet of West Wycombe Park, who resided in Bourton-on-the-Hill for about 30 years in the period either side of 1800. The connections are striking, and it is probably no coincidence that during this period the artist Thomas Daniell who had, earlier in his career, painted the famous views of West Wycombe Park for the 2nd Dashwood Baronet, in 1781, was the designer of the Indian architecture and detailing of much that was executed at Sezincote, less than a mile to the south of Bourton-on-the-Hill. The Daniells, Cockerells, and Dashwoods appear to be closely associated throughout. As explored in more detail in the next and final chapter, it has been asserted by a leading Jane Austen academic that the fictional location 'Barton' in *Sense and Sensibility* may well be an allusion to Bourton-on-the-Hill, this being the village in which the real Sir John Dashwood-King had a hunting lodge and to which he banished his wife. This theme is paralleled in *Sense and Sensibility* with the fictional Dashwood females effectively disinherited and consigned to the small west country village of 'Barton'. If Austen intended to signal connections with the (West Wycombe) Dashwood Baronets, a more tenuous possibility for the choice of the village name 'Barton' is that it may be an allusion to Bart., the common shortened version of Baronet. Alternatively, perhaps Austen came up with Barton as an amalgam of Bourton (the location of Sir John Dashwood's hunting lodge) and Bart. (his Baronet status). In any event, because of these various potential connections, including the deliberate and central use of the Dashwood name by Jane Austen in *Sense and Sensibility*, the activities of the real Dashwood family members in the 18th and 19th centuries are explored in more detail in the final chapter.

CHAPTER TEN
'Hell-Fire Jane' – *Sense and Sensibility* & the Dashwoods

Hell-Fire Jane is the title of a journal article by Professor Janine Barchas in which she outlines her proposition that Jane Austen's *Sense and Sensibility* can only be properly appreciated in the context of an understanding of the real, and high-profile, Dashwood family history, including its role in the notorious Hell-Fire Club. She also, as noted at the end of the previous chapter, suggests that the place-name *Barton* in the novel may allude to Bourton-on-the-Hill where the 3rd and 4th Dashwood baronets had their hunting lodge.

Sense and Sensibility was the first of Jane Austen's novels to be published. This important literary milestone, in 1811, came some 15 years after she had developed the first draft of the novel, then called *Elinor and Marianne* and written in the form of letters between the two sisters. She read this early draft version to her family sometime before 1796, according to her sister Cassandra[1], and subsequent real-life events appear to have had an influence on the transformation of the draft version into the published novel *Sense and Sensibility*. These events include the activities during Jane's lifetime of the 4th baronet, Sir John Dashwood-King, some of which added more layers to an already rather scandalous Dashwood family reputation, thereby rekindling the well-documented notoriety of the 2nd baronet, Sir Francis Dashwood, including his eccentric behaviour, his blatantly lewd gardens, and his hosting of the infamous Hell-Fire Club at West Wycombe.

The Dashwoods' activities were, in true Regency style, exploited by the various gossip media outlets of the day, principally journal articles, pamphlets, and cartoons. In reality it is arguable whether the lifestyle of Sir John, the 4th baronet, and his behaviour towards his wife in particular, were very different from those of many of his peers, but with the name Dashwood already on the predatory media radar he was an easy target at a time when any such news of impropriety was enthusiastically pounced on and devoured. There is a compelling case that the portrayal of these various activities in the public domain influenced the names, structures, and storylines in *Sense and Sensibility*, and that the novel incorporates significant strands which draw directly and substantially from the real-life Dashwood family history and its contemporary media profile. To understand this profile and contemporary public perception, the family story is now sketched out.

The early history of the Dashwoods was briefly traced in Chapter 2, up to their purchase of the West Wycombe estate in 1698. In a parallel with the Cockerells' experience at Sezincote a century later, where Charles Cockerell bought out his siblings and embarked on radical alterations, Sir Francis Dashwood, the first baronet at West Wycombe, bought out his brother Samuel's share for £15,000 and embarked on dramatic changes to the estate. These alterations included pulling down the existing Elizabethan house and building a red-brick house half-way up the hill. When Sir Francis Dashwood (*Lord Le Despencer*) died in 1724 he was succeeded by his son, another Francis, to whom can be attributed most of the fame linked with the Dashwood name, and its disreputable connotations. Much was hoped of this Despencer heir, as expressed in some anonymous 'Lines addressed to the Hon. F Dashwood intended for his Natal Day', retained in the Dashwood family papers :-

May Blooming health, (sweet Boy) guard thy Infant years;
May Wisdom, thy tender Mind with Virtue rear

'Hell-Fire Jane' – Sense and Sensibility & the Dashwoods

'Till ripening Nature, shall to perfection bring,
Great Despencer's Virtues, that in thee shall spring:
May thy Mother's beauty, in thy Person shine,
And all thy Sire's goodness adorn thy Mind.
Belov'd - long may'st thy Live – lamented Die,
And Death gently lead thy Soul to Immortal Joy. [2]

However, 'virtue' was not to be his dominant characteristic. Indeed, Sir Francis Dashwood (1708-81), 2nd Baronet, developed into

'one of the odder and more extravagant characters of his age'. He was a leading figure in founding 'the Dilettante Society, ... the Divan Club, the Lincoln Club and, most famously, the Hell-Fire Club. To ... this last "riotous profane club", as Boswell called it, members brought along ladies of "cheerful, lively disposition to improve the general hilarity of the company".[3]

Of these societies and clubs, the Dilettante Society was generally regarded as respectable, and typically met during the day in London. An invitation card[4] in the Dashwood Family Papers is addressed to Lord Le Despencer (Francis Dashwood's official title), Charles Street, Berkley Square and reads, '*My Lord, You are earnestly desired to attend the Committee of Dilitante on Tuesday next at eleven o'clock in the Morning, May 7th 1764, Star & Garter Pall Mall*'. Its members were prominent figures, most of whom had been on the Grand Tour, and Greece and Italy in particular, the Society's main purpose being the promotion of ancient Greek and Roman art. It was influential in the establishment of the Royal Academy but even within this Society there were controversial figures who challenged normal behavioural conventions, and Francis Dashwood was certainly one of these. In 1743, Horace Walpole believed he saw within the outwardly respectable agenda of the Society a different driving motivation, namely *"..a club, for which the nominal qualification is having been in Italy, and the real one, being drunk: the two chiefs are Lord Middlesex and Sir Francis Dashwood, who were seldom sober the whole time they were in Italy"*.[5] Nevertheless, the Dilettante Society retained a degree of honourable intent and social standing.

The Hell-Fire Club was somewhat different, not least in its more secretive and discreet meeting places, and its membership tending to have more radical and political interests. Probably formed in the 1740s, the Club reputedly met initially at the George and Vulture Inn in the City of London, as well as the members' own houses, before settling at a dedicated meeting place at Medmenham Abbey, a converted Cistercian abbey, on the River Thames just six miles from West Wycombe. Medmenham housed the Club during its most active phase, from about 1750 to the late 1770s, but eventually all evidence of its activities was rigorously removed, possibly because of increasingly negative public media coverage. This may also reflect a decline in Sir Francis Dashwood's motivation and appetite for the type of activities the Hell-Fire Club had indulged in. Some meetings had moved, according to local tradition, to the caves at Wycombe, dug out at the instigation of Francis Dashwood. These caves, now known as the Hell-Fire Caves, had been a by-product of excavations to provide material for building a two-mile section of the London to Worcester turnpike road between High Wycombe and West Wycombe. Also known historically as The King's Way, because it linked the historic royalist cities of London, Oxford and Worcester, this turnpike road was one which would become very familiar to the next two Dashwood baronets, as they shuttled in coaches between London, West Wycombe and their more modest hunting lodge at Bourton-on-the-Hill in the Cotswolds, lying further north-west along the same turnpike road. As an aside, Francis Dashwood made legal enquiries as to whether he could avoid turnpike fees by employing the imaginative and devious idea of avoiding turnpike gates by diverting around them using short tracks across his own land. The legal opinion he received firmly rejected this.[6] The digging of caves at West Wycombe continued even after sufficient hardcore for the local section of the road had been quarried, partly to keep labourers employed in the poor harvests between 1748 and 1754. This extension of the project also enabled later construction of enormous caverns, including one called the 'Banqueting Hall', used by the Hell-Fire Club, infamous for alleged black Masses and other satanic rituals.

The Hell-Fire Club membership featured numerous prominent individuals, including the radical John Wilkes, the poet Paul Whitehead, Sir Henry Vansittart (and his brothers Arthur and Robert), Sir Thomas Stapleton, Sir William Stanhope MP, William Hogarth, and the Earl of Sandwich. Paul Whitehead was a particularly close friend of Sir Francis Dashwood, so much so that when he died in 1774, his will included the unusual instructions that his heart be removed from his body, and that

> '*I give to the Right Honble. Francis Lord Le Despencer my heart aforesaid together with fifty pounds to be laid out in the Purchase of a Marble Urn in which I desire it may be Deposited and placed, if His Lordship pleases, in some corner of his Mausoleum as a memorial of its once warm Attachment to the Noble Founder*'.[7]

The Dashwood Mausoleum, within the West Wycombe estate, had been built in 1765, probably designed by the architect Nicholas Revett, who worked with Sir Francis through till the latter's death in 1781. Paul Whitehead had been the secretary of the Hell-Fire Club, and Sir Francis had secured him a minor government position. They were certainly kindred free spirits, with few concessions to what we would now term political correctness.

Another close friend of Sir Francis Dashwood was Benjamin Franklin, an important figure in sensitive Anglo-American affairs in this period, who is also reported to have attended the

Hell-Fire Club occasionally. In 1774, possibly inspired by Benjamin Franklin's visits and friendship, another American connection resulted in Sir Francis commissioning and erecting on top of the sawmill in West Wycombe park, a life-sized lead statue of William Penn (1644-1718), a Quaker who had gone to America to escape persecution and who was pivotal in founding the state of Pennsylvania, which bears his name. Penn had worshipped, and is buried, at Jordans Friends Meeting House in Chalfont St Giles, not far from West Wycombe. Having been locally well-known and admired as a colonial pioneer, Sir Francis Dashwood clearly wished to commemorate William Penn, perhaps at the suggestion, and with the encouragement, of his friend Benjamin Franklin. Subsequently, Penn's statue, by John Bacon, was removed at the end of the eighteenth century, during a remodelling of the estate by Sir John Dashwood-King, the 4th baronet. It was transported, appropriately, to Philadelphia, Pennsylvania, where it has stood in the grounds of the hospital since 1804. A replica has recently been commissioned and erected in the original West Wycombe position.

Members of the Hell-Fire Club, as well as sharing Sir Francis's love and appetite for culture and the arts, also shared his passions for food, drink, sex, dressing up, politics, blasphemy and the occult, an interesting remit for a club whose official name was 'The Order of the Friars of St. Francis of Wycombe', and whose members were referred to as the Monks of Medmenham, or the Franciscan Brotherhood. The Club spawned multiple accounts and rumours about its activities, many probably exaggerated. Their 'chapter meetings were described in a book of 1779 entitled *Nocturnal Revels*', which outlines

> '*the clothes worn and the admission ceremony. No vows of celibacy were required either by the ladies or the "Monks", "the former considering themselves as the lawful wives of the bretheren during their stay within the monastic walls; every Monk being religiously*

scrupulous not to infringe upon the nuptial alliance of any other brother. .... The offspring of these connexions are stiled the Sons and Daughters of St Francis and are appointed in due order officers and domestics in the Seminary, according to their different abilities, or by drawing lots".'[8]

Whatever actually happened at the Hell-Fire Club meetings, they acquired a notorious public reputation, and Jane Austen would undoubtedly have been aware of this. One of the Club's 'mottoes' was *Love and Friendship*, words incorporated on clothes and badges worn by both male and female Club members. Intriguingly, the 15 year-old Austen's first recorded short novel, not published till long after her death, had the slightly misspelt title *Love and Freindship*, and was noted in her manuscript as being finished on June 13th 1790. This simply adds to the body of evidence, albeit some only circumstantial, for her use of Dashwood-related names and connections.

Sir Francis Dashwood built up an impressive and diverse library at West Wycombe, including one of the earliest copies in English of the Kama Sutra, presented to him, and inscribed, by one of the Hell-Fire Club members, Sir Henry Vansittart, who had been Governor of Bengal – another strong link to India, which exerts its influence on so many characters encountered here. In line with the flexible morals evidenced by his Hell-Fire Club involvement, and his well-recorded sexual appetite[9], Sir Francis's personal tastes and his propensity to shock were just as obviously, and more publicly, exemplified by the extraordinary gardens, landscape features, follies, grottoes, and caverns he established at West Wycombe. Their blatant sexual imagery was scandalous at the time and attracted just the sort of reaction which Sir Francis no doubt intended, such was their provocative nature, reflective both of his rather wild and eccentric character, and of his diverse and often contradictory tastes. It should be remembered, for example, that alongside the bawdy elements of his lifestyle, he served as

Chancellor of the Exchequer, jointly produced a revised version of the Book of Common Prayer with Benjamin Franklin, and devised a Plan of Reconciliation with the American colonies.[10] Both of these latter initiatives, details of which are set out in *The Dashwoods of West Wycombe*[11], evidence his close collaboration and friendship with Benjamin Franklin.

Sir Francis Dashwood, 2nd Baronet of West Wycombe
[National Portrait Gallery 1345]

'Hell-Fire Jane' – Sense and Sensibility & the Dashwoods

Sir Francis Dashwood was a man with great influence, both as Chancellor of the Exchequer (1762-3) and joint Postmaster General (1766-1781), during the premiership of Lord North. There are many letters between the two, and one early debate on the postal system concerned whether there should be an obligation to deliver letters sent to every single part of the country. In November 1775, a case of delivery at Hungerford was reported to the Treasury, with the "private opinion" of the Attorney General, Thurlow, that

> '*the* (Post) *Office was not bound to deliver Letters beyond the Stage or Post House* (of which there were about 440 nationwide at the time). *But if the Construction of the Act* (of 1711) *is once carried beyond that, I know of no Construction which will . . . . entitle them to refuse carrying Letters to every Hole and Corner of the Country*'.[12]

The principle of universal delivery, which we now enjoy, was only later established in the Royal Mail postal system. Sir Francis Dashwood's letters make it clear, as with all his diverse interests and activities, that he was not only completely open to new ideas, but also committed to, and enthusiastic about, implementing them. It appears that in his role as joint Postmaster General he was involved in the introduction of mail carts and mail coaches in place of the rigid reliance on individual horseback delivery. He requested a quote for the cost of a prototype 'post cart' and this is evidenced by a document[13] in the Dashwood Family Papers.

The contrasting aspects of his character and interests are summarised by Barchas in a concise passage of her journal article *Hell-Fire Jane*, highlighting his role in promoting the revival of classical architecture in Britain, his activities in poor relief, drainage and road building, as well as his political career, while contrasting these aspects with his activities as '*an infamous libertine*'.[14] Expanding on these contradictions, or complexities, in his character, and with reference to the Hell-Fire Club, Barchas notes that,

'the club was, like the cultures it imitated, a mass of contradictions, combining the grossest of outrages with the most refined study of classical architecture in its time: "nuns" were brought in from London's brothels to participate in sexual lewdness that took place amidst England's finest and most elaborate re-creations of Ionic architecture and Italianate design'.[15]

Some features of Sir Francis's gardens at West Wycombe survive, and these are supplemented by descriptions of their original conceptions and forms as provided in various texts. Not surprisingly, the most blatantly shocking elements of Sir Francis's gardens are barely mentioned by the 11th baronet, another Sir Francis Dashwood, in '*The Dashwoods of West Wycombe*' (1987); nor do they feature in the official National Trust guidebooks of 1978 and 2001. These publications understandably fail to enlighten the reader on any aspect of its outrageous mid-18th century garden planning and concept. However, a candid description of, and commentary on, some of its features is included in Barchas's article, highlighting its sexual associations, citing for example the Temple of Venus garden building, perched on a belly-like mound with its anatomically shaped doorway beneath leading to a small womb-like grotto, dubbed 'Venus's chamber'.

Temple of Venus, West Wycombe Park

Also, on an island in a central lake [*see image in Chapter 8*],

> ' ...stood a Temple of Music, designed by Nicholas Revett, another club member, which the Hell-Fire club used as a frequent meeting place. [It was the subject of one of the Thomas Daniell paintings commissioned in 1781 by Sir Francis.] Although music's reputation for inciting wantonness was traditional, Marianne's musical self-abandonment in Austen's novel [Sense and Sensibility] might obliquely invoke the Music Temple's history as the site of Dashwood bacchanals.' [16]

Barchas gives additional and more explicit detailed descriptions[17], not repeated here, but there was a clear theme, and intent to shock, in Sir Francis's garden design, the clearing and sanitising of which was carried out by future baronets.

In summary, Sir Francis Dashwood's characteristics - extrovert, exuberant, energetic, enigmatic, eccentric, entertaining and educated - gave West Wycombe a style and reputation that continually attracted other radical and high-profile figures of the age. The notoriety of the physical activities at West Wycombe perhaps overshadow the intellectual and cultural aspects, but there can be little doubt that to have spent time there would have been rewarded with excitement and vibrant intelligent conversation about a diverse range of topics including the arts, politics, philosophy, travel and religion. Sir Francis died in 1781, and with his passing as the ringmaster of an idiosyncratic and dazzling individual creation, the curtain came down on West Wycombe's transient and dramatic period of fame. Its legacy is evident in an enduring fascination for Sir Francis's excesses. The year of his death, 1781, was also the year in which Thomas Daniell executed the Dashwood commission to produce the six paintings of West Wycombe referred to earlier.

These paintings form a valuable visual record, capturing many details of the mid eighteenth-century estate Sir Francis had created, before changes made when the 4th baronet inherited in 1793 deliberately neutralised much of his original design concept. These later changes to the estate were part of a fashionable transformation, with Humphry Repton as the lead designer.

Sir Francis had no legitimate issue, the estate then passing to his half-brother, Sir John Dashwood-King, the 3rd baronet. The addition of King to the Dashwood name derives from his mother Mary King, the third wife of the first baronet. He *'took an interest in his estates at Willoughby, Welton and Dunston in Lincolnshire, where he continued the policy of draining and enclosing the land and converting it from useless bog into good farmland. His impact on the house and estate at West Wycombe was minimal'*.[18] As outlined previously, the name Willoughby will immediately strike a chord with readers familiar with *Sense and Sensibility*, and the question as to whether this is anything more than just another coincidental link is considered elsewhere.

The third baronet (whose image is second from the left on the front cover) made few changes to the West Wycombe estate, and was not always resident, but social events continued, albeit more conventional in nature than some of Francis's more scandalous gatherings. The vicar, Richard Levett, writing to the third baronet's son (also called John) at Bourton-on-the-Hill on 31 January 1793, noted :

> *We have had three Balls, Shrimptons, Sir John's and your Humble Servants; attendants between 30 and 40, dinners from 12 to 15 couple, and would you believe it, I cut a caper amongst them till one o'clock in the morning, when we all retired to Elegant Suppers, sung till between 3 and 4; your sister Lechmere stay'd at the ball at Sir John's till past 12 o'clock when she retired to her room, and in three hours produced a fine boy, named John, both well.*[19]

Although it is not clear when the Dashwoods first established a base in the Cotswolds, we know that the 3rd baronet had used the hunting lodge at Bourton-on-the-Hill before his son took it over in the 1780s. They shared a passion for hunting, and their specific focus was on the pursuit of hares, the main quarry at the time, with foxes only more rarely found. A later Dashwood baronet notes that '*Sometimes there were so few foxes that they were trapped by keepers elsewhere and sent in a bag to be released in the foxhunting country*', giving as an example the contents of a contemporary letter from West Wycombe to Bourton-on-the-Hill, in which, '*Sir John wrote to his son John:*

> *I have a Fox for you which was caught yesterday morng. It would have been sent by last nights Coach; but the Coachman (on complaint of ye passengers) refused to carry it; therefore I desire you will appoint a date early next week for a person to meet my man at ye Angel in Oxford; Sind has brought a Badger for Geo. which shall accompany the Fox. My hounds are so very slow they dwell so long upon ye scent that I have*

no sport .... I wish you would get me a Couple of harder running hounds and send as soon as possible.'[20]

The 'Geo.' referred to is his young grandson, John Dashwood's eldest son George, born at Bourton-on-the-Hill in 1790, and later to become the 5th baronet.

Already fairly elderly, Sir John Dashwood-King's time as third baronet was relatively short. He died in 1793, and his eldest son John inherited, becoming the fourth baronet of West Wycombe. Often referred to simply as Sir John Dashwood (i.e. dispensing with the formal '-King' suffix), he is central to our story. In the period immediately prior to inheriting the baronetcy and the West Wycombe estate in 1793, John Dashwood and his family were firmly entrenched at Bourton-on-the-Hill in the Cotswolds, but John had gradually taken over estate management of West Wycombe during the last few years of his father's life. The 3rd baronet, in a letter dated 14th October 1790 from West Wycombe to John at Bourton, in relation to some transfers of money, comments that, ' ... *I will settle with you very soon probably for the last time as I wish to retire and leave the Management and trouble of the Estate to you*'.[21]

John Dashwood was born in 1765, ten years before Jane Austen. His inheritance of the West Wycombe estate and other properties as 4th baronet in 1793 coincided with Jane Austen's development of *Elinor and Marianne,* the prototype for *Sense and Sensibility* in which the Dashwood family name is centre stage, with Austen's fictional John Dashwood a pivotal figure. Painting a picture of the real John Dashwood, his life, and lifestyle is therefore worth exploring to gauge how these may have influenced the published version of *Sense and Sensibility*.

Using the most accessible literary sources to establish John Dashwood's character, one immediately encounters differences of opinion. A twentieth-century descendant, the 11th Baronet, provides a fair and balanced commentary, including for example that John '*had few of the qualities or the vices of his*

'Hell-Fire Jane' – Sense and Sensibility & the Dashwoods

fun-loving and cultured half-uncle (Sir Francis) .... not entirely surprising as the blood of the Puritan poet John Milton flowed through his veins. He did, however, have a passionate love of country pursuits'.[22] Although Barchas acknowledges this latter passion and his reputation as a keen huntsman, she introduces him as '*The notorious Sir John Dashwood (ca 1765-1849), fourth baronet*'.[23] However, it is not clear that his lifestyle or behaviour, for example obsessively pursuing his country interests, and allegedly maintaining a mistress, were reprehensible by the standards of the day. In any event they are counterbalanced by other more positive evidence. With regard to his marriage, it certainly appears that Sir John Dashwood, for a short period, reacted badly to rumours of his wife Mary Ann's friendliness with the Prince Regent but, as noted elsewhere, he was not alone in this: Nelson had exactly the same concerns, and was even more infuriated about the Prince's attentions to Emma Hamilton, who reacted just as Mary Ann did, bitterly refuting in a letter any such imputations. The Prince's frequent uninhibited attentions to attractive females, usually selfishly and thoughtlessly conducted, were renown and it is understandable that Sir John Dashwood, Nelson, and others, fretted about the potential damage to the reputations both of their respective partners and, perhaps more pertinently, themselves.

The National Trust online thumbnail sketches of the West Wycombe Baronets, picks up on this one short episode in Sir John's marriage and, without providing substantiating evidence, extrapolates it into a comment on the whole marriage, as follows :-

Sir John, 4th Bt. is chiefly remembered as a keen huntsman and on his inheritance he established a pack of hounds at West Wycombe Park. Rumours of his wife's affair with the Prince of Wales led to an unhappy marriage and he died alone in 1849 in lodgings in Baker Street, London.[24]

This assertion of 'an unhappy marriage' is not supported by the evidence and is at best misleading. Documents in the collection of Dashwood Family Papers, including copious details in Sir John's personal diaries, paint a very different and more positive image of their long marriage. Furthermore, the culmination of Sir John's life in reduced circumstances was due to other wider family tragedies, not the state of his marriage. The extract above is also misleading about the location where he established his nationally famous pack of harrier hounds – it is well documented in numerous sources that this was at his hunting lodge at Bourton-on-the-Hill in the North Cotswolds. West Wycombe was never his main hunting base.

It is clear from Sir John's diaries that he not only socialised with his wife at their various homes and rented accommodation, both in London and the country, but he also makes frequent references, for example, to family anniversaries and joint visits to the opera. Most significantly, there are numerous records, spread over many years, of social meetings with his wife's parents, the Broadheads, and other family members, so any suggestion of a persistently unhappy marriage appears unsubstantiated, at odds with the evidence, and wide of the mark.

Further fleshing out his personality and counterbalancing what amounts to a character assassination by other commentators, entries in the Dashwood Family Papers lodged at the Bodleian Library also include, as outlined earlier, his notebook entitled *'Sentimental Tour by Sir J Dashwood Bart.'*, indicating a more sensitive side to his character.[25] Throughout his extensive travel notes on this 'Tour' there are many detailed comments on the views and the aesthetics of the varying scenery, indicating a rather more refined and complex character than acknowledged by other portrayals. On a similar theme, there are also references in his domestic personal diaries to a variety of interests, including visits to the theatre, subscriptions to the Antiquaries of Evesham, and numerous charitable donations to his local church at

Bourton-on-the-Hill, not least for its repair, involving substantial payments for stonework, glazing, whitewashing, and carpentry referred to in a letter of 1802.[26] These particular payments were to tradesmen in the village, notably to members of the well-known local families, Halls and Pooles, the former owning the local quarry, and the latter being prominent carpenters. He also made very generous gifts, including those to a '*poor woman & children*', '*a poor man who had lost his mill by fire*', in 1795, and to '*Bourton poor women & children*' in 1796.[27] There are many other such entries evidencing his positive engagement with, and support for, his local community. One intriguing set of entries comprises a series of payments of £10 for *Mrs Martin's Nurses Fees*', seemingly on a quarterly basis. The vicar at Bourton-on-the-Hill at this time was Joseph Martin, and a George Martin appears to have been acting as Sir John's agent or steward at Bourton. His generosity extended to wider interests, and much later, for example, he made a major donation of property to the Worcester Infirmary in 1815.[28]

Jane Austen's Regency Dashwoods

Portrait of Sir John Dashwood-King, 4th Baronet of West Wycombe
[By kind permission of Sir Edward Dashwood, Bt.]

Overall, the evidence indicates that he was well educated and had genuine wide-ranging interests. If he attracted a certain amount of disrepute it was a shadow of that attaching to his 'Hell-Fire' half-uncle, Sir Francis, and any notoriety was almost certainly exaggerated, or at least more obviously noticed, simply because of that earlier Dashwood family reputation. Indeed, it may be partly because of this reputation that he seemed to have an aversion to the West Wycombe estate, and spent most of his time away from it at Bourton-on-the-Hill in Gloucestershire, at Halton in Buckinghamshire, or in London. He and his wife rid the West Wycombe estate of some of its more ribald features and he later tried to sell it off, only being stopped by his son, whose inheritance interest in the property could not easily be dispensed with.

Before elaborating on his life and its links with Austen's Dashwoods in *Sense and Sensibility*, it is worth noting that the Indian links with the Dashwoods' West Wycombe estate and the Hell-Fire Club, mentioned above, appear to have some significance in relation to the later connections between Sir John Dashwood and the Cockerells (who returned from Bengal and purchased Sezincote in 1795). Sir John Dashwood's substantial time at Bourton-on-the-Hill, from 1788 or before, and through to 1817, spanned the period when the Cockerells were remodelling the neighbouring Sezincote House in an Indian-style, reflecting their substantial involvement with the sub-continent. Furthermore, Sir John is also recorded as arranging accommodation in Bourton-on-the-Hill for those working on this refashioning of Sezincote, barely a mile to the south. The connections are striking, and surely not simply coincidental.

The Dashwood family records note that,

'*after his marriage in 1789 to Mary Anne, the daughter of Theodore Broadhead of Monk Bretton in Yorkshire, Sir John continued to live at his hunting lodge at Bourton on-the-Hill which is set amidst the most beautiful rolling Cotswold hills in Gloucestershire. It was at Bourton that his eldest son, George (later the fifth baronet) was born in 1790 and there also that he set about establishing his pack of harriers*'.[29]

Exactly when Sir John Dashwood-King first lived at Bourton-on-the-Hill is not recorded, but it was his main residence from at least 1788, and certainly until 1817, when his departure is well documented, as set out later. Evidence of it being his main residence is provided by contemporary legal documents referring to him explicitly as 'Sir John Dashwood King of Bourton-on-the-Hill', both in 1799 and 1814. The following archive references are in the Centre for Buckinghamshire Studies :-

DEEDS. Bundle 6: Counterpart Lease. WEST WYCOMBE (V) Mills in West Wycombe. (i) Sir John Dashwood King of Bourton on the Hill, co. Gloucester, Bt. (ii) Michael Lewis Fryer of West Wycombe, papermaker. Water grist mill, paper mills, mill pond, messuage. 5 cottages. Date 1799. Reference D-D/6/171.

DEEDS. Bundle 8: BOND. Sir John Dashwood King of Bourton on the Hill, co. Gloucester, Bt., and John Watson of Chipping Norton, innkeeper, bound to Michael Ciorgan, Thomas Bradley Paget, and Edward Matthews . Date 1814. Reference D-D/8/26.

We also know that another Dashwood relative lived here during the period in question, because in a letter of 9th November 1797 from Walford, the Cockerells' agent for Sezincote, to John Cockerell, he refers to '*Sir Henry Dashwood who lives at Bourton-on-the-Hill*'. Perhaps significantly, the two forenames Jane Austen employs for her fictitious male Dashwood characters are Henry and John. The most likely candidate for this real-life Henry is Sir Henry Dashwood (1745-1828), 3rd baronet of Kirtlington Park, Oxfordshire, from the other high-status branch of the Dashwood family, whose debts in 1775 had amounted to the enormous contemporary sum of £25,000, which his father had to pay off. After Henry came into his inheritance he sold most of the family estate to pay further debts, so perhaps he was living temporarily at Bourton-on-the-Hill with his relatives, who were putting him up out of loyalty. In addition, there is a reference in an old Encycopaedia Britannica (under the entry for '*The Harrier*') to Sir John's father having lived at Bourton, so it appears to have been a Dashwood family base for some time. Having credited the 4th baronet for '*what may be termed the living model of the present improved harrier*' (hunting dogs bred specifically to chase hares) it notes that,

> '*Sir John kept them more than thirty years, at Bourton-on-the-Hill, Gloucestershire, near the four-shire stone on the Oxford and Worcester road, where his father kept them before him; hunting partly in the vales of Warwickshire and Worcestershire, and partly over the Cotswold Hills, which latter country is famous for the stoutness of its hares, ...*[30]

This insight into Sir John's reputation as a huntsman and breeder of harriers, and the fact that Bourton-on-the-Hill had also been the site of a hunting lodge for his father (the 3rd baronet) is corroborated by the following :-

> *I was, at this period of my life, much in the habit of sojourning, in the winter months, with Sir John Dashwood King, at his hunting seat at Bourton-on-the-Hill, half-way between Oxford and Worcester, and where his father had a hunting seat before him. I had carte blanche, and it just suited my book, for the following efficient reasons :—Sir John is a man after my own heart; the society was good; the tap unexceptionable (Raikes's best); and capital accommodation for the nags, at the training-stables on the Hill, where there is the best winter exercise-ground in the world—in short, where horses gallop and sweat with the thermometer at zero. It was also not very badly situated for foxhounds .... and Sir John's harriers, perhaps the best the world ever saw, hunted three days a week, and shewed most extraordinary*

sport. In fact, it required a good man, on a good horse, to see the end of a Cotswold hare, once driven out of her latitude by this beautiful pack.[31]

Sir John Dashwood-King on horseback with a harrier hound
[By kind permission of Sir Edward Dashwood, Bt.]

For part of this period it is known that he let his main property, West Wycombe Park, to the Marquis of Donegall. However, with Halton Manor, in Buckinghamshire, and several other properties also available to him, including his Hanover Square house (and others that he moved to in London), the reasons for establishing and retaining as his favourite home a relatively modest hunting lodge at Bourton-on-the-Hill rather than the magnificent mansion at West Wycombe, or his other properties, are not entirely clear. Finances were undoubtedly a factor, but perhaps not an overriding one. Possibly of most importance was the simple fact that hunting was his obsession and that the quality of the hunting country in the North Cotswolds was far superior to that around West Wycombe or Halton. His much documented high profile in hunting circles is inextricably linked with Bourton-on-the-Hill, largely attributable to his development there of the Bourton Hunt.

We are fortunate in having substantial evidence of Sir John Dashwood-King's lifestyle, largely from the details in the Dashwood Family Papers lodged at the Bodleian Library. These indicate that he travelled frequently between Bourton, West Wycombe, Halton, and 'Town' (as London was referred to by those whose other bases were provincial). The hunting season was paramount for Sir John, and from the evidence of his diary he tended to stay at Bourton more than at any one of his other 'homes' during this period each year, and certainly made a point of spending most of December and the Christmas period there. The majority of his archived incoming mail was addressed to Bourton-on-the-Hill, and legal documents also give this as his permament address. His accounts feature multiple entries recording use of the local services in the village, including general provisions, carpentry, shoemaking, malt milling, tailoring, a bakery, saddlery and stabling, as well as employment of local servants. It should be remembered that at this time the village (occasionally referred to as a '*town*' in contemporary documents) had nearly twice as many inhabitants as it does now, and was a thriving self-sufficient community, as many such rural settlements were. Bourton's location on a main travel route underpinned its vibrancy. Almost every property doubled as a business as well as a home, with tremendous diversity of trades and services, together supplying all the needs of the community itself as well as the many travellers using it as an overnight staging post on the main road between London, Oxford, and Worcester. As previously noted, this busy road was known as 'the King's Way', an informal name particularly appropriate during the Civil War, the latter two cities having been generally loyal to, and strongholds for, Charles I and the Royalist cause after Parliamentary London had turned against him.

Sir John Dashwood-King's diary entries for the first few weeks of 1794 give an idea of his typical movements between his base at Bourton-on-the-Hill, West Wycombe, and London, as well as revealing links with Jane Austen's relatives. For the start of that year, his diary entries indicate he was at the following locations :-

January1st & 2nd	Town (i.e. London)
3-6th	West Wycombe
7-14th	Bourton-on-the-Hill
15-18th	Town
19th	West Wycombe
20-25th	Bourton-on-the-Hill
26-27th	West Wycombe
28-29th	Town
30th-2nd Feb	West Wycombe
3-4th	Bourton-on-the-Hill
5th	To *Addlestrop* (assumed to be just a day visit)
6-7th	No entries (assumed to be back at Bourton-on-the-Hill)
8th	*Hunt at 'Dolphin's'* (this is Eyford Park)
9-12th	Bourton-on-the-Hill
13th	*Hunt at 'Dolphin's'*
14th	*for Mrs Leigh*
15th	*Hunt at 'Dolphin's'*
16th	Bourton-on-the-Hill
17th	House Addlestrop
18-20th	Bourton-on-the-Hill

Of particular note are the entries for the 5th '*To Addlestrop*', the 14th '*for Mrs Leigh*', and the 17th '*House Addlestrop*', surely indicating frequent high-status social contact, and friendship, with the prominent Leigh family members (Jane Austen's close relatives) at Adlestrop, just a few miles from Bourton-on-the-Hill. During Jane's own stays at Adlestrop, such social contacts would undoubtedly have been a subject of conversation.

So, during this period in early 1794, Sir John Dashwood was at Bourton-on-the-Hill for 32 days (including day visits and hunts to nearby Addlestrop and Eyford), with 11 days at West Wycombe, and 8 days in London. This is fairly representative of his constant movements between the three, and notably with a pattern of rather longer stays at Bourton-on-the-Hill, at least in the winter months. West Wycombe, conveniently situated between London and Bourton, appears to be treated largely as a stopping off point on his transitions between the two, allowing him to deal with estate business on his many short stays there. Looking through his diaries, he did spend longer in London in the summer months ('the season'), fitting with the normal fashionable pattern for those with houses both in Town and in the country, and not least because it was out of the hunting season.

There are copious records of Dashwood's time at Bourton, including such mundane account items as the '*Morton Turnpike*' fees, and '*Chimney Sweeper*' charges. He paid rent to Mr Bateson, but the recorded[32] quarterly amounts of £10 seem extremely modest, and we can only guess at the reason. To give some context, his accounts note that the costs of travelling using '*Post Horses*' for a single journey from Bourton to London was just under £6, and in December 1795 he paid local Cotswold suppliers just over £37 for malt and just over £22 for hops, for what was clearly substantial brewing activity at his Bourton home.[33]

Touching briefly on his income, this would have come predominantly as revenue from the Dashwoods' extensive property holdings, but also from dividends on various investment stocks, as recorded in his accounts. Of particular interest, given the Dashwoods' historic oriental trading interests, are dividends recorded from '*South Sea Stock*' and '*East India Co's Anns*' [Annuities], together paying about £160 quarterly. One particular item of income is evidenced in 1808, when he sold just over 10 acres of land (presumably from his Buckinghamshire estates) to the Grand Junction Canal Company, for the substantial sum of £1,338, to enable construction of part of what is now the Grand Union Canal.

Although we know he eventually left Bourton-on-the-Hill in 1817, and then made his main home at Halton in Buckinghamshire, it is clear from his diary entries for December 1816[34] that he was still spending much of his time at Bourton right through until his final departure, including Christmas and New Year :-

Dec. 9th 1816	*Left Halton for Bourton*	*Slept at Oxford*
10th	*Arrived at Bourton*	
18th	*Left Bourton for Town*	*Slept at Oxford*
19th	*Went to London by Star Coach*	
24th	*To Bourton* [through till at least 4th January, 1817]	

Having sketched his lifestyle at Bourton-on-the-Hill, and having flagged his possible inspiration for Austen's fictional John Dashwood, we need to consider whether his 'hunting lodge' in the village had any resonance with Jane Austen's fictional Dashwood cottage at 'Barton', described in *Sense and Sensibility,* given that Barchas tentatively suggests that 'Barton' may be an allusion to Bourton-on-the-Hill. While she proposes nothing more than a possible connection in the names, other similarities (for example, either in type of property or character of the location) are worth investigating.

A hunting lodge could be anything from the size of a very large cottage to something more like a compact country house, and it would be expected that Sir John Dashwood would have required a property of some status at the upper end of this spectrum. It should immediately be noted that the village house in Bourton-on-the-Hill now called Dashwood House is a red herring, this house being of more recent date, and with its name having been adopted only a few years ago, simply and randomly as a result of the name's attraction to the owner having seen it featured in *The Book of Bourton-on-the-Hill, Batsford & Sezincote* (2005).

The most likely suspects as the Dashwood hunting lodge must be the two historic manor houses in the village. The quotation '*Sir John Dashwood King ... will give you a Bed or get you one at Mr Batesons*', rules out the 'Westminster' Manor House in the upper north-west part of the village, where Bateson lived. The other manor house was Bourton House, the most obvious candidate, but there is no record of its occupancy at the time to confirm or reject this.

However, among other candidates in the village is the property now called Porch House, not least because its 1806 deeds include reference to an acre of land in the possession of Sir John Dashwood-King Bt. In 1806, it was being transformed from operating as a traditional farmhouse to becoming a purely domestic dwelling, albeit with a tannery operation continuing on part of its village site. About 70 acres of lands in the open fields associated with the property were sold to the Cockerells of Sezincote that year, and a year earlier, in 1805, a 21-year lease to run the tanyard on part of the site, now the Lower Churchyard, was granted to a '*John King, Gentleman*'. The signature '*John King 1808*', matching that on the tanyard lease, is etched into one of the internal faces of a window in the house, and alongside it is etched, '*Mr. T Daniell '03* '. The latter certainly tallies with the artist

Thomas Daniell's active involvement at nearby Sezincote, c.1803 and later. However, despite these intriguing connections, it was still an extremely modest property for someone of Sir John's status, and the possibility that he was living there seems a remote one. Before dismissing it, the connections just outlined are further explored.

Thomas Daniell was a key figure in the design of Sezincote, working closely with the Cockerells, and, as noted already, Daniell had also been commissioned for paintings of the Dashwoods' mansion at West Wycombe Park in 1781. Could 'John King', the name of the 'gentleman' running the tanyard, be an alias for Sir John Dashwood-King, who was trying to keep a low-profile? This must be decisively ruled out; it is inconceivable that he could have achieved such anonymity even if he had wanted to – his activities in Bourton-on-the-Hill were well-known locally and were frequently in the wider public domain via hunting and other sporting journals, as well as more general publications. Alternatively, perhaps John King, gentleman, was another grandson or other relative of Mary King, Sir John Dashwood-King's grandmother. Without something more than the circumstantial evidence accumulated above, these possibilities must be rejected in favour of a more likely candidate as Sir John's hunting lodge.

It would have been far more natural for him to have occupied a property in keeping with his status, certainly one that was seen as such, and Bourton House is the prime suspect. The inventory of items at the public sale in 1817 (cited later), when Sir John eventually left the village, indicates that his base at Bourton-on-the-Hill was of considerable scale, and with substantial storage space, which narrows down the village contenders. The nature and volume of the furniture, the long ladders and the brewing equipment mentioned in the inventory would fit with the scale of Bourton House and its sizeable brewhouse. This latter facility would tally with the large amounts of malt and hops Sir John Dashwood-King was purchasing in Bourton (as evidenced by his 1795 accounts), itself indicating that he was supporting a large household of family and servants, which Bourton House and its group of ancillary buildings could certainly accommodate.

A further piece of evidence does at least restrict the search to that part of the village south of the main road cutting through the settlement. This evidence is provided by a contemporary travel publication, "*A New and Accurate Description of All the Direct and Principal Cross Roads in England and Wales*" by Daniel Paterson (15th edition, published in 1811). It tracks the road from '*Moreton in the Marsh*' through '*Bourton on the Hill*' and on to '*Broadway*', and along the way remarks on the principal personages living at various points left and right of the road. It notes that before reaching the village of Bourton, to the left, and one and a half miles from the road, is '*Season Cot, C Cockerell Esq.*' , a clear reference to Sir Charles Cockerells' Sezincote estate. This is followed by the phrase '*In the village on the left Sir John Dashwood, and on the right -- Batson Esq.*'. Again these locations and orientations in relation to east-west passage along the road fit with Sir John Dashwood-King living at Bourton House, and with Bateson living in the 'Westminster' Manor House further up the village.

And another source provides further evidence :-

The most complete pack of harriers that I ever saw, or, I believe, any other man ever saw, was that which hunted the Bourton-on-the-Hill country, and kept many years by Sir John Dashwood King, of West Wycombe Park, Buckinghamshire. As that part of Bucks is not fit for hunting, Sir John had a house, for nearly twenty years, as his father had before him, in the village of Bourton-on-the-Hill, in the county of Gloucester, about a hundred yards below the training stables, where he and his family spent the winter months, and where he had excellent stabling, and good

> *accommodation for his hounds. There was one great advantage attending this situation, which was, that the country above his house was an excellent hill country, and that below it a fine vale—comprising part of Warwickshire, Oxfordshire, and Worcestershire, being close to what is called the fourshire-stone, where four counties meet. This enabled him to make his fixtures according to the state of the weather and the season, which he always did for a week or ten days before hand, issuing cards of appointment, after the manner of fox-hounds.*[35]

Finally, a letter (referenced earlier) written from Bourton-on-the-Hill by George Martin to John Dashwood Esq. (before he inherited the baronetcy) and addressed to 23 Argyle Street, Oxford Street, London, includes the following passage :-

> *I have just been at your House. In the latter end of next week (weather permitting) we shall admit the scythe into a fine crop of grass opposite your house. Walton and one more will cut it in about ten days time.*[36]

So, pulling all these pieces of evidence together, Sir John Dashwood's house was within the main village settlement, on the south side of the road, with training stables further up the hill, and with large open fields of '*grass*' for haymaking '*opposite*'. It was also of a scale to accommodate considerable quantities of furniture, needed long ladders, and had substantial brewing capacity. Knowing the village very well, I believe Bourton House is the only property which fits all these pieces of contemporary evidence and is therefore the prime candidate as the Dashwood 'hunting lodge'. Having established a degree of confidence, does Bourton House have any resonance with the fictional Dashwoods' Barton Cottage in *Sense and Sensibility*?

'Hell-Fire Jane' – Sense and Sensibility & the Dashwoods

Bourton House

Bourton House is a compact country house of considerable presence and architectural quality – it is now a grade II* listed building - and on the face of it there is no apparent physical similarity between this property and the term 'Cottage' which Austen assigns to her Dashwoods' Barton property. However, Austen herself notes that '*as a house, Barton Cottage, though small, was comfortable and compact*', but specifically commenting that it failed to satisfy the term '*cottage*' because '*the building was regular, the roof was tiled*' and '*on each side of the entrance was a sitting-room, about sixteen feet square, and beyond them were the offices and stairs*', together with '*four bedrooms and two garrets*'.[37] Rather than the image the term 'cottage' conjures up, Austen's own description of her fictional Barton Cottage does begin to feel far more like a substantial house and formal symmetrical piece of architecture, closer to the reality of Bourton House. In any event, the fictional name Barton may have been chosen by Austen simply as a hint at the real Sir John Dashwood's Bourton base. As it happens, the topographical location, with valley below and hills above, loosely matches elements of Austen's description of Barton. Austen positions Barton as being in

'Devonshire', but this may just be a deliberate means of disguise.

As far as individual characters are concerned, given her interest in genealogy and the peerage, and from her stays with relatives at Adlestrop, Jane Austen would, beyond reasonable doubt, have known about the various local Cotswold dignitaries. Frequent correspondence between her Hampshire home and Adlestrop would also have provided further information and local gossip about high-profile figures in the neighbourhood, and Sir John Dashwood at Bourton House was arguably the most prominent and high-status such figure. The prominent 'Sir John' character she creates in *Sense and Sensibility* (Sir John Middleton) lives at Barton Park, described as being '*large and handsome*', about half a mile distant from the Dashwood females' property in Barton, and screened from view by the projection of a hill. In the real world, about half a mile from Bourton House is Batsford Park, also a large and handsome house. At the time of Austen writing *Sense and Sensibility,* Batsford Park (demolished in the 1880s, and rebuilt in its current form in a more prominent position) would have been similarly screened from view as described in the novel. The allusions are tantalising, and as set out in some detail earlier, there is also a striking match between the characteristics, lifestyles, and behaviours of the real Sir John Dashwood and her fictional Sir John Middleton. As previously stressed, Austen's allusions are never direct copies, instead being subtle and disguised, involving adoption and transpositions of names, characteristics and events.

'Hell-Fire Jane' – Sense and Sensibility & the Dashwoods

Batsford Park, early C19 print

In summary, there is a credible case that Austen's local knowledge of the Dashwoods at Bourton-on-the-Hill and its immediate environs in some way influenced her choice of the village name of Barton for her Dashwoods' *Sense and Sensibility* country retreat. It also appears more than coincidence, given her access to local information, that the character portrayals of her created 'Sir John' and his wife, together with their fictional home being named Barton Park, closely mirror what she could readily have known of the real Sir John Dashwood and his wife living at Bourton House, with Batsford Park the nearest substantial house and estate. Perhaps Austen is just juggling several closely-linked allusions. It is also tantalising that Austen chose Palmer as the name for prominent characters in *Sense and Sensibility* given that Bourton House was the home of Richard Palmer in the late sixteenth century – his initials and the date 1570 being carved into the front of Bourton House's Grade I listed tithe barn. If, during her stays at Adlestrop, Jane Austen visited Bourton-on-the-Hill or was told of its past, her keen interest in history and genealogy may explain her adoption of this historical Palmer name.

The case for any such name and property allusions having been deliberately mixed up and disguised in *Sense and Sensibility* depends on Austen having had knowledge and some interest in these people and places, and there is substantive supporting evidence for this, some already outlined. As well as all the compelling circumstantial evidence which Barchas provides for Jane having a natural and lively interest in the Dashwoods' broader activities, Sir John Dashwood-King's activities and neighbourhood contacts during his lengthy period of residence at Bourton-on-the-Hill are illuminating. His diary entries for 1794, partially set out above, record several connections with people and locations in the neighbourhood. The most relevant entries are references to both '*Addlestrop*', and to '*Mrs Leigh*', confirming his contact with the neighbouring prominent Leigh family, Jane Austen's close relatives. A further local link with the Leighs is evidenced by the fact that John Dashwood, before he inherited the baronetcy, funded works to the Leigh vicarage at Longborough, just two miles south of his Bourton-on-the-Hill home. The letter in the Dashwood family papers from Thomas Leigh at Adlestrop, dated November 8th 1790 (and set out in the Introduction) refers to this payment by John Dashwood.[38]

The Leighs, with different branches of the family at both Longborough and Adlestrop, were long-time patrons of the church at Longborough. Jane's visits to her Leigh relatives at Adlestrop would have involved conversations about local people and events in the neighbourhood, no doubt supplemented between visits by the frequent letters that passed between Jane's Hampshire home and Adlestrop. Given the Leigh's direct social connections with the high-profile figure of Sir John Dashwood-King (4th Baronet of West Wycombe) living at nearby Bourton-on-the-Hill, it must be beyond reasonable doubt that his activities in the local area would have been a topic of interest to Jane and her relatives. We cannot rule out the possibility that, during one of her several visits to Adlestrop, Jane may have actually met Sir John, or his wife Lady Mary Anne Dashwood. In any event, the latter name strikingly resonates almost precisely with Jane Austen's choice of name for Marianne Dashwood in *Sense and Sensibility*.

Returning to Sir John's diary for 1794, there are other notable personal entries. On March 20th, for example, he records '*Presented to the Queen at St James's* ' Palace, and on November 16th his entry reads, '*My second daughter was born*'. Many entries record meetings with named individuals. Two of particular interest are for Friday May 16th and Saturday May 17th, reading respectively '*Lady Rushout*' and '*Mr Hastings*'. The Rushouts' family seat was at Northwick Park, very close to his home at Bourton-on-the-Hill, the Rushouts being very much part of Sir John's local hunting and social network. In the continuing tight network of connections, the Rushouts have links with both Sezincote and Longborough, whose church housed the impressive Leigh memorial tomb of Jane's direct ancestors. Jane would surely have been taken to visit this memorial tomb by her Leigh relatives during one of her stays at nearby Adlestrop, and the high-status Cockerell and Rushout families would no doubt have been discussed in the light of Jane's genealogical interests. Given the other evidence for Jane's adoption and adaptation of names from this North Cotswolds area, the Rushout name may well have led to her using the closely related name Rushworth for a key character name in *Mansfield Park*.

The entry '*Mr Hastings*' on Saturday May 17th in Sir John's 1794 diary is a clear reference to him meeting another prominent figure in his North Cotswold circle, namely Warren Hastings at Daylesford, again evidencing a social network involving those with close links to Jane Austen and her family. Once again it seems almost inevitable, given Jane's inquisitive observations on such things, that on her visits to Adlestrop, very near to Warren Hastings' Daylesford estate, she would have picked up numerous stories about this network of local high-profile figures, including Sir John Dashwood-King.

There is also clear evidence from his diaries and letters that Sir John had frequent direct contact with not only the Leighs at Adlestrop and the Rushouts at Northwick Park, but also with the high-profile Cockerells at Sezincote. The relationship between Charles Cockerell and Sir John Dashwood-King was a very close one judging by the contents of a letter of 1808 from Charles to Sir John, which opens,

> *'I hope you will excuse the application I am going to refer to you which your kindness to my family ever since I have known you induces me to think you will excuse'*. It continues, *'I am going to Paris on Monday* [and explains he has failed to secure sufficient ready funds] ... *I beg the favour of you to advance me an hundred pounds. It would save me some anxiety.'* [39]

In summary, the Dashwood, Leigh, Rushout, Hastings, and Cockerell families were prominent ones in this North Cotswold neighbourhood, and there would have been natural and frequent contact across this upper end of the local social network. Sir John Dashwood-King is explicitly evidenced as having contact with each of these local neighbours. Hunting, while not the only element of such contact, nevertheless played a significant networking role, and Sir John was at the heart of that particular web.

While Sir John was very much at home in the North Cotswolds, which catered ideally to his main rural interests, his main inheritance in 1793 had been the family estate at West Wycombe Park, which at that time held a particular fascination for Jane Austen because of specific family connections. As already noted, West Wycombe was never really to Sir John's liking, and indeed he attempted to sell the estate in 1806, only being thwarted by the trustees acting for his eldest son, George. Initially, however, he had made changes to the gardens, with the involvement of Humphry Repton, during the time Jane Austen was sporadically developing and revising *Sense and Sensibility* in the period from the mid 1790s through to its publication in 1811. As the 11th Baronet records,

> *To begin with he embarked enthusiastically on the park and gardens and called in Humphry Repton in 1795 to advise on improvements to the landscape. Repton found the gardens, especially the lake, overgrown and obscured by large trees. He also objected to numerous features which he considered ridiculous, such as the spire on top of the tower of a folly which from far off was intended to look like a church and was called St Crispin's after the patron saint of shoemakers (one of whom lived in the folly), and the statue of William Penn which Sir Francis had placed on top of the sawmill in the park. These were soon removed, as were the statues of Venus and Mercury from Venus's Mount, which Sir John and Lady Mary Anne perhaps considered to be unduly erotic.*[40]

The original William Penn statue can be seen in the photograph below in its current location in the grounds of Philadelphia Hospital, Pennsylvania. As previously noted, a replica has been commissioned and resurrected in its original position at West Wycombe.

Jane Austen's Regency Dashwoods

C18 statue of William Penn,
Philadelphia Hospital, Pennsylvania
[Originally positioned on top of the
sawmill at West Wycombe Park]

After his initial involvement, '*Repton made further visits – two days in 1798 are recorded, for which he charged 10 guineas plus travelling expenses of £2 12s. 6d., and again in 1799. He set his proposals out in his customary Red Book but this, sadly, has disappeared. We only know from his introduction to the* Theory of Landscape Gardening *about some of his plans for West Wycombe.*'[41] Evidence for his involvement is provided by documents in the Dashwood Family Papers lodged at the Bodleian Library in Oxford. The main evidence is Repton's letter to Sir John Dashwood-King, effectively his invoice for work done, extracts from which were quoted at the head of Chapter 3.

Barchas remarks that, '*Austen .... may even have known of Dashwood's hiring Repton to alter West Wycombe Park to improve his hunting with dogs. In fact, these alterations bear an uncanny resemblance to those described by the fictional John Dashwood in* Sense and Sensibility.' [42] While I agree that the nature of the alterations in both cases has sufficient similarity to suggest a connection between fact and fiction, I am not convinced that the alterations to West Wycombe had, as their main motivation, improvement in their suitability for hunting; hunting was conducted primarily on wide expanses of open country rather than on a landscape garden setting or the immediate (and aesthetically-designed) parkland around a country house.

In any event, there is strong evidence that Austen would have been aware of Repton's work, particularly at Adlestrop, West Wycombe, and Sezincote. A paragraph from Barchas's article, in relation to Austen's likely awareness of Repton's work, adds another persuasive link. In it she references two of Repton's publications which contained reports of his work for Sir John Dashwood, namely *Sketches and Hints on Landscape Gardening* (1796) and *Observations on the Theory and Practice of Landscape Gardening* (1803). In the latter, Repton covers his work at both Adlestrop and West Wycombe in the very same chapter, and Barchas asserts that even if Jane Austen was focusing mainly on the work at her relatives property in Adlestrop she would have also seen mention of West Wycombe.[43] Whatever the depth of her familiarity with Repton's work – and she did after all cite him specifically in *Mansfield Park* - Jane Austen would almost certainly have been interested in West Wycombe in its own right anyway, because of friend and family connections to that important estate, as outlined later.

West Wycombe Park, print c.1800

The changes Sir John Dashwood-King made at West Wycombe were drastic, and arguably unnecessarily destructive. As Barchas notes, what Repton did was to '*cut down a great many trees, at the request of Sir John Dashwood*'[44], and this strikes a chord with the passage (previously quoted) in *Sense and Sensibility*, in which the fictional John Dashwood notes, in relation to establishing a new greenhouse, that :-

The old walnut trees are all come down to make room for it. It will be a very fine object from many parts of the

> *park, and the flower-garden will slope down just before it, and be exceedingly pretty. We have cleared away all the old thorns that grew in patches over the brow.*[45]

Clearly Austen is using this passage as an example of wanton destruction of a long-standing natural environment, itself already having some inherent picturesque merit, and its replacement with an artificially constructed picturesque composition in line with the latest fashion. By way of contemporary fashion comparison, the reference to incorporation of a flower-garden within an estate setting, but visible from the house, chimes precisely with Repton's proposals at Sezincote.

Although Sir John made major changes at West Wycombe, he never really enjoyed residing there, and it is through his passion for hunting in the Cotswolds that other aspects of his life story emerge. His reputation is recorded in numerous hunting journal extracts of the time, and this links with him mixing in high social circles. Dashwood family commentary notes that,

> *Sir John sent some of his hounds to the Prince of Wales. G. Leigh wrote from Crichel in Dorset in about 1795: "the couple of Beagles His Royal Highness had from you turn out very well – we have had some very good sport with them since their return to Critchell." And Sir John wrote in 1799 lamenting "being unable to come to Crichel – I should be happy to avail myself of your Royal Highness kindness towards me but my pack is now complete as I would wish and my choice of whelps as promising as I could desire". ... He had also made a name for judging horses and helped to select horses for the Prince of Wales and for King George III. The New Sporting Magazine went so far as to describe him as "certainly the best master of Harriers England ever saw and one of the best judges of horses".* [46]

The royal connections are relevant in relation to the Dashwood's media profile, as will shortly be apparent.

Sir John's passions for country pursuits and animals include something he shared with Warren Hastings, namely an interest in rare or non-indigenous breeds, no doubt an obvious topic of conversation when they met, as we know they did. As outlined in Chapter 7, Hastings had instructed his emissary to Tibet, George Bogle, to bring him '*goats which produce the shawl wool*', yaks, and '*animals .... that may be remarkably curious*'.[47] He later brought some of these back to Daylesford from India. Sir John Dashwood's similar interest is evidenced, for example, by his diary entry for August 16th 1816, which included reference to 7 Spanish Ewes, 1 Spanish Ram, and 3 Spanish Lambs. There had previously been the acquisition of '*Five Estremadura Pigs*' imported from the Iberian Peninsula by ship from Lisbon to Gosport, as outlined in a letter of 2nd September 1811.[48] Among other things this letter advised that Sir John needed to complete a form confirming that the pigs were for private (rather than commercial) use so as to avoid a £40 Tonnage duty, and also advised that he should send a '*Light Waggon*' to collect them to save on the £10 carriage charge which the author of the letter had been quoted.

These pigs clearly represented a specialist interest for Sir John, but his greatest passions remained his pack of harriers and his horses, the latter primarily for hunting but also for racing. As the 11th Baronet records, the 4th baronet's

> '*love of horses also involved Sir John in racing in a modest way, and from 1811 to 1835 he entered horses at Aylesbury, Cheltenham, Northampton, Epsom and Goodwood. But his horses did not have the success of his hounds. Of five horses which he owned between 1819 and 1838 only The Little Master came in second at Aylesbury in 1819, whilst in 1833 Cinderella came third in the Goodwood Stakes and in October that year won at Epsom*'.[49]

Sir John appears to have had a particular fondness for the racing at Goodwood and extracts from his diary entries in the summer of 1835 evidence not only his frustrations with the deficiencies of his own racehorses, but also provide insights into family social life, as well as a particular horse racing link back to his Bourton-on-the-Hill former residence:-

Tuesday 28th July

... started for Goodwood Races with Mary [his daughter], *her two girls & Augustus* [Mary's husband]. *– my two fillies ran, & nothing could be worse than there* [sic] *running.*

Wednesday 29th July

To Goodwood Races – very little company there – and only two races. Lord Villiers's Nell Gwyn was a great favourite – saw the Duke of Portland and conversed with him.

Thursday 30th July

To Goodwood Races, which was well attended – Mr Theobald's horse Rockingham won the Cup, cleverly. .. walked with Sir Charles Morgan on the course. Saw Pawlett & Adamson and tried to sell Porcupine [one of his racehorses] *to the latter. This day much annoyed at having ran or trained my fillies.*

Friday 31st July

... slept very ill – not many persons going to the Goodwood Races. Heard this evening that Lucifer had beaten Rockingham whose jockey after winning by an hundred yards if he had pleased, was inattentive and Lucifer went by him & won. .... Sent my trunk by carrier to go to Town [London] *by Chichester Coach.*[50]

It is the two references to Rockingham, a famous racehorse of the day, that link back to Bourton-on-the-Hill. Witnessed first hand by Sir John Dashwood, as noted above in his diary, Rockingham won the prestigious Goodwood Cup in 1835, and among many other successes had won three other important races back in 1833, as a three year old, namely 'The Shorts' a one mile sweepstake at the York Spring meeting, the Doncaster Cup, over a distance of two miles and five furlongs, and most notably of all, the St Leger Stakes at Doncaster on 17th September. In the latter race, with a field of twenty runners, Rockingham was fifth choice in the betting at odds of 7/1. The jockey was Sam Darling, who for most of the race held Rockingham up at the back of the field. He gradually moved the colt closer to the leaders in the straight, but still appeared to be blocked in behind the leaders. A furlong from the finish Darling found a way through, and Rockingham accelerated impressively past Mussulman to win by two lengths. Sam Darling had also been the jockey when Rockingham won 'The Shorts' success at York in the spring.

*Sam Darling on 'Rockingham',
winner of the Great St Ledger Stakes, 1833*

'Hell-Fire Jane' – Sense and Sensibility & the Dashwoods

In the 1830s, Sam Darling was the Lester Pigott or Frankie Detorri of his day, and was based, as Sir John Dashwood had been, at Bourton-on-the-Hill. For several years Sam Darling lived in the house next to the church, and his grave is in the churchyard just outside this house, which happens, perhaps not coincidentally, to be the one with reference to Sir John Dashwood-King in its deeds, and with the Thomas Daniell and John King window etchings outlined earlier. Given the Bourton-on-the-Hill connections, Sam Darling may well have ridden one or more of Sir John Dashwood's racehorses. In his retirement from horse-racing, Sam Darling was landlord at the main village pub, named The Horse and Jockey in the early 19th century, and now called The Horse and Groom.

The Darling family involvement in horses and horse racing at Bourton-on-the-Hill, interlinked with the Dashwoods, is evident from the 1780s onwards. In 1788, an account of payment[51] for saddlery work done by K Collett for John Dashwood Esq. (before he became the 4th baronet) has as its first few entries:-

		£	S	D
Apr 12	*for menden a hors brush*	0	0	1
	for 2 new Dog Cople Straps	0	0	8
May 1	*for 2 new pleats an new pleating on new pad an menden Mr Darlens Sadle Runing Sadle Broke at Borton hill Race*	0	6	6

Allowing for the author's shorthand and misspellings, "Mr Darlens" should almost certainly read "Mr Darling's" just as "menden" should be "mending", and the entry gives us a direct reference to this Mr Darling being a jockey in a horse race at or near Bourton. Seven years later, an entry[52] in Sir John Dashwood-King's accounts for 1795 refers to stabling duties performed by the Darling family:-

*Nov. 16   Darling keep of Horse
            from Augt. 20 to Novr. 7th*   10: 10: 6

From these two records and the later known fame of Sam Darling and his descendants, it is clear that the Darling family were involved in the care, training and racing of horses over a long period in and around Bourton-on-the-Hill at the time that Sir John Dashwood was living there.[53]

In summary, all of the above demonstrates Sir John Dashwood's high profile in the area and having rather veered off the direct trail of the Jane Austen and Dashwood connections, we now resume that detective work. As intimated earlier, Jane Austen, on her visits to the Leighs at Adlestrop in 1794, 1799 and 1806, and from constant correspondence with relatives there, would in all probability have heard much of the local news and gossip concerning prominent neighbours, including Sir John Dashwood and his family. This would have included local elaboration of the nationally publicised, and mildly scandalous, gossip that while Sir John travelled freely between Bourton-on-the-Hill and his other properties including West Wycombe, his wife Mary Anne, who in the early years of their marriage had similarly been free to spend time both in London and a variety of country residences, had been banished by Sir John in 1800, at least for a short period, to his house in Bourton-on-the-Hill. The reason for this was her friendship with the Prince of Wales, who was notoriously free with his affections and seemingly unconcerned about the effects this had on the parties involved.

Whether there was any substance in Sir John's suspicions about his wife's behaviour, it is certainly true that they each had connections with members of the royal family. Sir John and the Prince of Wales had a joint interest in hunting, with Sir John, as noted, having provided some beagles to the Prince. And he and Mary Anne jointly socialised with members of the royal family at parties in London. Although these were general social gatherings, the Dashwoods clearly had opportunities for personal contact with the royal family and, intriguingly, Mary Anne appears to have had a particularly close personal relationship with the Prince of

Wales' sister, Princess Elizabeth, one of George III's daughters. The main evidence for this is twofold.

Firstly, in the National Portrait Gallery collection is a sketch of Lady Dashwood, [cross-referenced D17291 in the NPG cataloguing system as *Mary Anne Dashwood (née Broadhead), Lady Dashwood*] by Henry Bone, with the legend, '*Lady Dashwood for HRH Princess Elizabeth 1803*'. Other of Bone's similar sketches feature legends giving the names of the sitter and that of the person who commissioned the work, a good example being Bone's sketch of Lady Harriet Cockerell (National Portrait Gallery ref. NPG D17654) which has the legend, '*Lady Cockerell after Cosway for Sir Chas. Sept. 1809*'. As it happens, the '*Sir Chas.*' who commissioned this latter sketch is the very Sir Charles Cockerell introduced in the previous chapter, with Sir Charles and Lady Harriet Cockerell living at Sezincote, just a mile away from Mary Anne Dashwood's Bourton-on-the-Hill residence to which she had been banished by her husband.

Lady Dashwood
[National Portrait Gallery D17363]

Lady Cockerell
[National Portrait Gallery D17291]

So why would Princess Elizabeth commission a sketch of Lady Dashwood? It suggests not only that Princes Elizabeth knew Mary Anne, but that she had sufficient interest to commission the work. Also, in order for the sketch to be made, Mary Anne Dashwood would obviously have had to agree to sit for it. There is clearly some level of personal relationship between the two.

And there is a second, but very different, artistic link which would also have required Mary Anne Dashwood's agreement, and which further suggests their close relationship. This involves Princess Elizabeth's own artistic endeavours. Rachel Knowles reports that :-

> *Princess Elizabeth, the third daughter of George III and Queen Charlotte, was a notable designer and artist. She painted a trellis on the ceiling of the Picnic Room in Queen Charlotte's Cottage at Kew.*
>
> *Elizabeth designed the hermitage at Frogmore - a small round building with a thatched roof situated in the south west corner of the garden. She also painted the Princess Royal's closet at Frogmore in imitation of rich japan [yet another oriental influence]. She was responsible for the decorations at the lavish entertainment given by Queen Charlotte at Frogmore in August 1799 to celebrate the recovery of the Princess Amelia.*[54]

These works were essentially all within the royal domain, and very private. However, Princess Elizabeth wanted some of her artistic work to be publicly accessible, while not using her own name as the artist, as this would have been deemed inappropriate for a member of the royal family. To gain public exposure, it appears that Princess Elizabeth obtained agreement from Mary Anne to use the pseudonym 'Lady Dashwood'. Rachel Knowles notes that,

In 1795, a series of twenty-four prints was published under the name of Lady Dashwood from drawings by Princess Elizabeth entitled "The Birth and Triumph of Cupid". In La Belle Assemblée, the set of engravings was alternatively called "The Progress of Cupid". They were engraved by PW Tomkins, the court engraver, who had studied under Bartolozzi, and were published at the King's expense. The prints inspired Sir James Bland Burges to write an epic poem in the style of Spenser. The plates were republished with the poem under the title "The Birth and Triumph of Love" in 1796 and met with considerable acclaim.[55]

This is yet another contemporary example of the Dashwood name rarely being out of the public spotlight at the very time Jane Austen was working on, and revising, *Sense and Sensibility*.

Given the portrait of Lady Dashwood commissioned by the Princess, and with the Princess using the name Lady Dashwood as a cover for her own artwork, it is clear that HRH Princess Elizabeth and Lady Mary Anne Dashwood, who were of a very similar age, were at least close friends, and seemingly on fairly intimate terms. The consequence of this is that Mary Anne would probably have had easy informal access to Elizabeth's brother, the Prince of Wales, and vice versa. Knowing the Prince of Wales's nature and reputation, if Lady Mary Anne Dashwood did indeed spend time in his company on a pleasant informal basis, however innocently, this may explain the origins of rumours circulating, and reaching the ears of her husband Sir John Dashwood.

In any event, Mary Anne strenuously denied any serious relationships with the Prince, later George IV and, during one of her husband's absences, wrote to him on 15th March 1801 from Bourton-on-the-Hill, where she had been temporarily banished :-

My Dear Dashwood

The change in your conduct towards me is quite sufficient torment for me to endure without any addition indeed so little comfort do I expect from your letters that since I have been ill I very often keep them by me some time without opening them – your reproaches are very ungenerous I have never acted in any way towards you to deserve such a total change in your conduct towards me and if you will not believe this after all the earnest and repeated assurances you have had from me I repeat I had much rather not live with you as long as you as my protector treat me in such a way at least that makes life supportable.

Had I been fortunate in a Mother I wd long since have flown to her for protection every one has their faults and I dare say I have mine but give me leave to ask you if you have ever devoted one hour to my amusement or comfort. I stay at home and take care of your Children indeed I now consider myself in no other light than head Nurse in your family.

Enough of this miserable. I am miserable.[56]

Sir John Dashwood was not alone in being concerned about the Prince of Wales's attentions to other men's wives or lovers, as noted earlier. Nelson is reported as being

> 'desperately concerned that Lady Hamilton might in his absence fall prey to the lust of the Prince of Wales. …. The thought of the Prince of Wales enjoying himself at 99 Piccadilly, to which the Hamiltons had moved from Grosvenor Square, drove Nelson almost frantic with rage and jealousy'.[57]

Lady Hamilton's response to a letter from Nelson expressing concern that the Prince should even be invited to her house, very much mirrors Lady Dashwood's letter above, namely an exasperated denial :-

As for the P. of W., I know his character, and my confidence is firm as a rock till you try to irritate me to say hard things, that you may have the pleasure of scolding me ...[58]

Nelson's relationship with Lady Hamilton was extra-marital, and even acknowledging that attitudes to, and expectations of, marital relationships were very different at that time, it was nevertheless painful for the respectable and honourable Lady Nelson, while still married to Nelson, to be forced to accept the reality of his passionate attachment to Emma Hamilton. It is clear from this and many other contemporary accounts that Mary Anne Dashwood was not the only wife to feel abandoned or disregarded at certain times in her marriage. Indeed, the Dashwoods' own daughter Mary, during the early years of her marriage to Augustus Berkeley, appears to have suffered far more callous treatment than her mother had experienced.

Augustus had served as a Captain in the Tenth Royal Hussars at Waterloo in June 1815, but a few weeks after the battle his widowed mother wrote to Sir John Dashwood warning him about her son's irresponsible tendencies and strongly discouraging the intentions for his marriage to Mary (Sir John and Mary Anne Dashwood's daughter)[59] :-

Dear Sir

Finding that Henry is going on a visit to you I take the opportunity of sending this with the enclosed note which I have written to Augustus Berkeley – you will learn by it that I have applied to the Duke of York for a troop for him but with very little chance of success. Since I had the pleasure of seeing you and Lady Dashwood, Augt wrote to his brother to know if I would receive him - and I heard from my eldest son that if I did not, he did not know what he would do – as he was without money and must continue so till the first of November; of course my door were open to him

– he came here with one Servant and a Gig – and has remained very quiet – but you will judge my surprise at hearing from one of his brothers today - that he has <u>two</u> Horses and <u>four</u> Servants in France – <u>one</u> of them with <u>two</u> Horses and his baggage left in the middle of the Prussian Army almost without money, and not knowing a word of any language excepting English – the other Servant with <u>two</u> <u>Horses</u> <u>left at Paris to wait his pleasure</u>, so that in fact he has now <u>five</u> Horses and <u>three</u> Men Servants – you must judge of your Daughters prospects, you will judge of his! And you may easily think how unhappy such thoughtless conduct must make me who worked for them as I did in my Husband's life. In thus detailing my son's conduct to you I act from duty – you shall not be deceived if I can help it – nor shall your Daughter – I have not mention'd the subject to him, or to Henry, nor do I intend to do it, but you are quite at liberty to do so if you choose it – pray present me kindly to Lady Dashwood tell her I hope we shall one day meet in happier days

I remain (dr. sir)

Yours sincerely   M Berkeley

Cranford House

Aug 11th 1815

The references to the Prussian Army and Paris relate to the aftermath of Waterloo, with the presence abroad of many British and Prussian forces and supplies persisting long after the battle in June of that year.

The '*enclosed note*' to her son, to which she refers, reads as follows[60] :-

Dear Augt,

Tho' I think nobody can behave worse than you have done towards <u>me</u> and <u>towards</u> yourself yet the *same anxiety I have always felt to serve you still continues. You will see by the enclosed letter what you have to expect. If you have any thing further to offer I will write to the Duke of York again – But it must be clearly understood that my endeavours to serve you have nothing to do with your marriage with Miss Dashwood. I most strongly disapprove of that for both your sakes. ... and nothing can move me from acting up to the letter which I addressed to Sir John Dashwood.*

Your affectionate loving mother

M B

July 30th (1815)

In answer to this I had a letter saying he never would give up Miss Dashwood praying me to consent that he would wait any time - at the same time he keeps five Horses and three Men Servants, this is surely madness.

Nevertheless, Augustus Berkely did marry Mary Dashwood, but in most unusual circumstances, presumably precisely because of the parental opposition, as the following letter from from Sir John Dashwood to Mrs Berkeley, relates[61] :-

Dear Madam

If I could have imparted to your Ladyship any pleasant occurrences I should not have delayed a moment making a communication to you. I have to perform a duty – (and not otherwise than a painful one, & I have in consequence deferred it). It is to inform your Ladyship of the marriage of your Son Augustus with my Daughter. The ceremony was performed in the presence of my two Sons, during my absence from home, and without Lady Dashwood's knowledge. I need not dwell on this subject – each of us must poignantly feel all that disappointed hopes and warm attachments can give rise to.

I have the honor to be your Ladyship's Obed. & faithful (servant?)

J Dashwood King

Mary would soon regret this seemingly impetuous marriage, as Augustus appears to have perpetuated what his mother portrays as her son's selfish and headstrong nature. Mary later wrote to her father, Sir John Dashwood King, as follows[62] :-

Sept 20 (Sept 20th or Sept 1820?)

My dear Father,

I am sorry that you should have been troubled with any unfortunate quarrel of mine. I know not what Augustus writes to you but this I can safely say – I had made up my mind to bear all for the sake of my Children excepting two things, one that I never would have <u>any</u> <u>one</u> under my own roof that Augt. was behaving ill with – nor would I visit any one I thought he was devoted to – which in the case of Mrs Vansittart <u>was</u> <u>the</u> <u>case</u>, the idea of Augustus saying "no human mind can bear up under unjust accusations" is of a piece with the rest of his deceitful conduct. He knows himself guilty therefore is determined to crush me, for finding him out – and I only pray that however spurious his representations may be, you will at last do me the justice of attending <u>equally</u> to my statements, as you do to his –

I can hardly write for my hand trembles with agitation – I know very well what I have to endure, and my hopes in Heaven rest upon my conduct as a wife to Augustus – how he has rewarded me God only knows, of course I have never said any thing to you of *his brutal conduct as I married him against your consent, therefore I brought it on myself – if he wishes to get rid of me, would it not be more manly to do it without trying false pretence? His flirtation has been going on for nearly a twelemonth [sic]. I never gave him an ill word on the occasion but when it came to his writing her letters of course then I knew it was <u>as suspected</u> & refused to dine at her house during the Goodwood Races, as he always goes every where without me, for when in Town, did he ever think of asking me to go to Almacks, the Operas, or any other place of amusement he frequented; no! All <u>his invitations</u> he accepted & went without me, en garcon, therefore this dinner would not have been remarkable, nor would <u>he have wished me</u> to have gone, but to quiet the suspicions of General Crosbie (her Father) who is now in a state of misery about this said flirtation, as Mr Vansittart is a downright Idiot, it of course made General Crosbie more uneasy suspecting his daughter – Augustus never calls upon any of the neighbours, where he <u>ought</u>, but whenever the husband was out, then he called upon Mrs V. Even when he knew he was to meet her at dinner the same day. These are not surmises, I have had an interview with her Father, he knew what I said was true, at one Ball General Crosbie went & took her away from Augustus & cut him – now surely you cannot believe Augustus "suffers under unjust accusations". You talk of working up my mind to a pitch of frenzy – I believe Augustus <u>has been trying to do this</u>, by his insulting conduct adding insult to injury. We are all imperfect Beings it is true, but if I am to be blind to the faults of Augt. in God's name let him have a little mercy to me, & not upon the slightest omission of mine, rate me, as if I have committed a crime – if I am to have as much forbearance towards him let him be a little kinder in his conduct to me – he, who treats me with the greatest* *neglect & harsh way can be <u>so devoted,</u> so attentive to others – these things cannot pass unnoticed by any woman who is fond of her husband. After losing all his money at Epsom he brought me down here, & returned to Town at the end of a week, & spent the little remainder he had left in attending upon this Lady, hiring a Horse to ride with her & getting her invited to all the Balls, among others that odious Mrs Walker, he made her invite Mrs Vansittart & Sister & omit the General, now as this General did not pretend to contradict, I know it to be true, this was during this fortnight he (Augt.) spent after he left me here. Now when I refused to dine at the Vansittarts I did it in a mild way to Augustus, nothing to make him fly out, had he not been guilty – he said if I did not "meet the Lady in General society, the only way he wanted to meet her, he would separate from me" This I have under his own hand-writing – he likewise wrote me another letter from Portsmouth (on his way to Norris Castle) saying "before this last explosion (meaning when I found the letter to Mrs Vansittart) he was fully determined not to be reconciled to me unless I visited at Northlands (the Vansittarts), & now he feared it was impossible, therefore our estrangement in this world must be final". <u>This letter I have.</u> I mention to show <u>who</u> asked for our separation, <u>for I did not</u> – tho' I felt myself aggrieved – Now the letter he wrote to Mrs V. I have, & as he guts out the love parts, and shows it, I have sent Lady Berkeley the real copy in his own hand-writing, that she may show Lord Segrave & Frederick. No doubt he will send a (supposed) Copy to you, therefore I enclose a Copy of the <u>original</u>, - which shows what his intentions towards her were.*

It is worth recording that Mary's father was sympathetic, and in the *"Heads of the intended will of Sir John Dashwood King baronet"*[63], having left a considerable amount '*In trust for his daughter Mary Berkeley for her life*', Sir John specifically added (as an inserted alteration) the words '*for her separate use*', no doubt to ensure it couldn't be squandered by her husband.

Two intriguing names crop up in the above letter. The first is Vansittart, the family already referenced in connection with India, the Hell-Fire Club, and the 2nd Dashwood Baronet. The second is the Vansittart's historic family home Northlands. Could the strong Vansittart-Dashwood connections in the late eighteenth century, and long before the above letter, have influenced Austen in her choice of the slightly amended name Norland Park, appearing in the second sentence of *Sense and Sensibility*? Well maybe, but there is a more direct link, namely an entry in the Dashwood family archives[64] recording payment by Sir John for a delivery of goods 'to Norland House', presumably one of the Dashwood properties. Other possible sources of inspiration for Jane's choosing Norland Park as the name of her fictional Dashwood residence are explored shortly.

Over time, Mary Dashwood's seemingly ill-fated marriage to Augustus Berkeley survived, and perhaps even flourished, as they were still together and involved in wider family social gatherings in 1835 as evidenced in the references to the Goodwood Races set out above.

Another marriage involving Sir John and Lady Mary Anne Dashwood's children faced similar initial opposition from the prospective suitor's parents. Although their son Edwin eventually married Emily Hare, the Hares had not been in favour of the marriage, as a letter from Robert Hare to Sir John Dashwood evidences[65] :-

Herstmonceux June 11th 1821

My dear Sir,

Since you left Herstmonceux a fortnight ago, I have been informed of the attachment of Edwin & Emily, of which before I had never heard, nor had either Mrs Hare or Myself the smallest idea that such an attachment existed. I have likewise been told that they had written to you, to request your consent to their union, which you had refused on the reasonable plea that their joint incomes will not be sufficiently large for them to live upon.

I lament as much as you can, that this attachment has been formed between them, & in a worldly point of view, I look upon it as far from being an advantageous match to either party. Had I known before of Edwin's marked regards I should never have thought of inviting him here, but I considered his visit as being entirely on Miss Dashwood's account, & his presence an additional reaction to her in the affair in which all her family seem to have been so much interested. But tho' I did not know of this attachment, yet I understand that you did, & were made acquainted with it when we were at Brighton. If so, provided you disapproved of the connection, surely it was most imprudent & unguarded to suffer Edwin to come here at all, & more particularly to remain under my roof for so many weeks, as it could not but be self-evident that such continued residence in the same house, must increase & strengthen their affection & make it severe & unjust, to endeavour afterwards to separate them. Your eyes, my dear Sir, they well knew, were open to the subject, & therefore .... sanctioning his continuance here, could not but in some degree, lead them to suppose, what their anxious wishes were desirous what might be true, that is, that you did not in reality object to the union, tho' outwardly you professed to do it. Had you fortunately consulted me at first upon this business, & had explicitly declared your sentiments, I should most cordially have co-operated with you in preventing it; & by expressing our mutual reluctance to its taking place, & by separating the parties, it might comparatively speaking have been more easily put to an end to, at that time.

But the case is now very different indeed; & the attachment you mention is too closely woven, & too intricately intertwined, to be broken or unravelled without deeply affecting both of them; & Emily I have no doubt, in her present delicate state of health, would suffer most severely from it. Having considered therefore the subject with attention, & I trust impartially, I have on their applying to me & stating that their happiness depended on their union, & their full determination to live upon their income, advised them to an immediate marriage, & I cannot but presume that almost every other father would have acted in the same manner, where the future welfare & felicity of a beloved daughter, would in all probability, be established, or destroyed, by his decision.

The wedding will take place on Wednesday next.

I shall conclude with a favourite phrase of the late Mr Pitt's "that it is expedient to be governed by existing circumstances".

I am my dear Sir
Yours very truly
Robert Hare

Given Sir John Dashwood's nationally renowned pack of harriers - hounds bred to pursue hares, and very successfully in the Dashwoods' case - it is perhaps fitting that his son Edwin's marriage pursuit of Emily Hare was equally successful. Unfortunately, as with the fate of her namesake creatures, the pursuit may also have ended badly for Emily. Although only circumstantial, the indications are not promising: Edwin caused his parents considerable trouble, requiring frequent financial assistance, and increasingly pursued a dissolute lifestyle, notably involving heavy drinking, which eventually led to his death. A common feature of these two 'Dashwood' marriages is that the males were both in the military, and both appear to have been less than honourable in their lifestyles and behaviours towards their wives.

Such behaviour was sadly not uncommon during this period. In another high profile marriage, the Duke of Wellington's treatment of his wife was blatantly appalling, and a further example was that of Catherine Tylney Long, a rich heiress who, in March 1812, married one of the Duke of Wellington's nephews. Reviewing Geraldine Roberts' novel *The Angel and the Cad: Love, Loss and Scandal in Regency England*, Roger Lewis's heading reads, *"The downfall of the wealthiest heiress in Georgian England at the hands of a feckless husband"*.[66] He comments that, '*It dawned on me while reading this book that here we have, in the courtship and marriage of Catherine Tylney Long and William Wellesley Pole, the archetypal plot and theme of every single English novel, from Jane Austen and the Brontes, to Thackeray, Dickens and Bram Stoker, right up to Iris Murdoch, Barbara Cartland, and the Kingsley Amis of* Take a Girl Like You'. For a long time after the marriage, Catherine stood by him despite him having disposed of her cash within two years. ' *"She loved being with William every day," says Roberts ... But Catherine was lucky to find him on the premises come bedtime. A copper-bottomed scoundrel, he was always off wenching, perfuming himself beforehand from one of his nine perfume bottles of scent*'. Catherine was ruined both financially and emotionally, and William '*showed no remorse over his profligacy, and wanted the children in his care so he could terrorise them for their trust funds. The children were made wards of court and guardianship was granted to the Duke of Wellington, who must have felt that compared with his nephew, Napoleon was a pussycat*'.[67]

It may again be simply coincidence, but the name Tylney, above, closely matches that of Austen's fictional Tilney family in *Northanger Abbey* ; this may therefore be another high-profile aristocratic name that Jane Austen came across and commandeered, employing only a subtle change to the spelling.

Returning to Sir John Dashwood's treatment of his wife Mary Anne, this was not remotely in such a low league as the Tylney Long example above, and their children certainly did not suffer adverse parental treatment. Sir John's enduring attachment and commitment to Lady Dashwood is evidenced by their later settled married life together, and it is clear that his children were also important to him. Indeed, Sir John's diary for 1794[68] include the entries '*14th March – To Town ... with my children*', '*21st March – My Bro. Was married*', and '*16th November – My second daughter was born*', indicating family togetherness and sensitivity. An underlined diary entry much later in his life, in 1835 when at Halton, notes that on Saturday 18th July '*Lady D, & Agnes came from Town dined family party – Henry came after dinner*'[69], evidencing continuity of family sociability, which was seemingly important to Sir John.

However, back in 1801, Mary Anne Dashwood's feelings of being wrongly accused of extra marital friendships would not have been helped by the fact that Sir John, as was common at the time, reportedly had a long term mistress. Worse still, this mistress provocatively insisted on calling herself Mrs Dashwood, eventually allegedly being bought off for a settlement of £100 a year.[70] This latter reference to a specific financial settlement exactly matches that in *Sense and Sensibility*, in which Austen notes that 'Mr Dashwood', when considering what amount would satisfy the Dashwood women, comments that '*a hundred a year would make them all perfectly comfortable*'.

With regard to the real Dashwoods, this whole unfortunate situation was directly alluded to in '*a typical rumour-mongering text of the time,* The Fashionable Cypriad (1798) .... *essentially a published rumour mill about fallen women*'.[71] Its text also pointedly quotes the settlement figure of £100 a year, outlined above. Because this 1798 text relates so strongly to the structure of *Sense and Sensibility*, more details of this particular 'Dashwood ' entry in *The Fashionable Cypriad* are incorporated later in this chapter when exploring remarkable links between the real and fictional Dashwood storylines. Suffice to say that the publicity surrounding the state of Sir John Dashwood's marriage, together with his former mistress's determination to maximise his embarrassment, again only served to keep the Dashwood name firmly in the public arena. In doing so, it perpetuated the sense of notoriety attaching to the Dashwoods which had originated with the scandalous behaviour of Sir Francis Dashwood's Hell-Fire Club at West Wycombe a few decades earlier.

Another unfortunate item of Dashwood news, widely reported in the newspapers and journals of the day, and obviously of major local interest, concerned the death of two of Sir John's staff at his Bourton-on-the-Hill property in 1811. Although there was no blame attached to Sir John either directly or in the way his household was run, nevertheless it was a disturbing and nationally well-publicised incident which would have helped to keep the Dashwood name in the public realm, again with negative associations, in the same year as the eventual publication of *Sense and Sensibility*. One report reads as follows :-

A few nights ago two servants (the huntsman and whipper-in) of Sir John Dashwood King, Bart, were found dead in their beds, at his hunting seat, at Bourton-on-the Hill, Gloucestershire. It appears, that on retiring to bed the preceding evening, conceiving the room where they slept (being over one of the outbuildings) to be rather damp, they had taken up with them, from under a furnace, some live coals in an open coalscuttle, which they left in the middle of the room; but the place having no chimney or vent of any kind, and being closely shut up during the night, they must have been suffocated from the effect of the sulphuric gas. One of them was found in a sitting posture in bed, as if he had been awoke by the oppression of his breath; but doubtless at the moment he was too much overcome either to effect his escape or create alarm.[72]

Such incidents (probably of carbon monoxide poisoning rather than 'the effect of the sulphuric gas' as quoted above) were, however, not uncommon, a memorial tablet in St James' Church, Alveston, Warwickshire, in the adjoining county, recording a similar tragic pair of deaths.

As noted, although unfortunate, these deaths at Sir John Dashwood's Bourton-on-the-Hill establishment have nothing to do with his treatment of staff which, on the evidence of the following extract, appears to have been kind and caring.

> *'Old Dick, as I before observed, died in his service and was succeeded by a younger man who, with his whipper-in, lost his life by putting a chafing-dish of coals in his bedroom, much to the discomfiture of Sir John, who is a very kind master to his servants'.*[73]

Incidentally, the elaborate title page of this publication appears to be typical of the fashion in the early nineteenth century for experimenting with multiple, and completely unrelated, typefaces, absolutely in tune with the Regency era of stylistic invention and novelty.

THE SPORTING MAGAZINE

OR Monthly Calendar

of the Transactions of

The Turf, The Chase

AND

EVERY OTHER DIVERSION

Interesting to the

Man of Pleasure Enterprise & Spirit

VOL.10, NEW SERIES
or Vol.60, Old Series.

Title page of 'The Sporting Magazine'

The Dashwoods' time at Bourton-on-the-Hill was not devoted solely to hunting, and there was full engagement with the Cotswold community of which they were a part, as the contemporary records evidence. Nevertheless, it was Sir John's passion for hunting that made the area so attractive to him, and he appears to have missed it when business forced him to be away, either at West Wycombe or Halton in Buckinghamshire. John Gage, a hunting friend, wrote to him in 1809, '*I know you are longing for Bourton – it is a pity you dislike your part of Bucks so much*'. [74]

'Hell-Fire Jane' – Sense and Sensibility & the Dashwoods

Bust of Sir John Dashwood-King,
4th Baronet of West Wycombe, in later life
[By kind permission of Sir Edward Dashwood, Bt.]

Eventually, however, he made what was presumably the very painful decision to leave Bourton-on-the-Hill. The timing of this closely follows the death of his second son Francis at Bourton in 1817, recorded and evidenced in *The New Monthly Magazine and Universal Register Vol. VII From January to June 1817*. On page 270, under 'Gloucestershire', and the subheading 'Died', appears the entry, "At Burton-on-the-Hill, Francis, second son of Sir John Dashwood King". Perhaps by 1817 it was his son Francis who was mainly residing there. With Francis dead, retaining a residence in the village possibly no longer made sense, or simply now held painful memories. Whatever the specific reason, his son's death there in early 1817 appears an obvious trigger for Sir John's decision to leave Bourton, and the following detailed entry in *Jackson's Oxford Journal* on Saturday 21st June 1817, advertised and described the sale of his household goods in the village when he departed that year :-

Notice of a Sale by Auction on Monday and Tuesday next, the 23rd and 24th June, 1817, of Household Furniture on the premises of Sir John Dashwood-King in Bourton-on-the-Hill, in the County of Gloucester, who is leaving that part of the country.

All that neat and genteel HOUSEHOLD FURNITURE and other effects ; comprising handsome four-post and tent bedsheet, with furniture, flock beds, blankets, quilts and bedding; hair and wool mattresses; neat mahogany set of dining tables, with circular ends, mahogany card, pillar and claw, and dressing tables, fine-toned pianoforte by Broadwood, handsome mahogany drawing room, chamber, cane, other chairs, floor and bedside carpets, easy chair, with morocco cover, several very handsome chintz window curtains, fringed, complete, neat mahogany butler's trays and waters, handsome shaded and oak chests of drawers, capital eight-day clock in oak case, ditto 30-hour ditto ... 10 well-seasoned 120 gallon casks, seven 90 gallon ditto, and 1 hogshead cask, the whole of which are in good state of preservation, a quantity of timber and fire wood, boards, &c, a very capital 16 bushel mash tub, brewing and washing tubs of different sizes, several pairs of steps, 4 long ladders, wheel barrows, leaping bar, 4 large iron boilers, garden role, 2 very good corn bins, nearly new, of large dimensions, 3 smaller ditto, pots, kettles, sauce pans and numerous other articles of household furniture &C. Also about twenty loads of good rotten manure.

The sale to commence at Ten o'clock each morning precisely.

Two years earlier, in 1815, there had been a similar two day sale of goods by Dr Wells who had been renting the Dashwood's country house at Halton in Buckinghamshire, where Sir John was to move after leaving Bourton-on-the-Hill. The catalogue for the Halton sale ran to 16 pages. The fact that the sale of goods at Bourton was also conducted over two days is an indication of its similar scale, and it is clear his hunting lodge was a substantial dwelling and household, again fitting with Bourton House as the probable candidate. In particular, its dedicated and substantial brewhouse (separate from the main house) tallies both with the amount of brewing equipment and numerous large casks itemised above, and also with the substantial purchases of malt and hops in Sir John's accounts, outlined earlier.

Among the items listed in the sale above is 'a fine-toned pianoforte', and this may be the one delivered in around 1790 from Worcestershire to John Dashwood (before he became the 4th baronet), as referred to in a letter to Bourton-on-the-Hill noting,

Sir, Agreeable to your order I have this day forwarded by Smiths Waggon one of my very best Instruments which is such that I have no doubt will give Satisfaction, the terms are as under, & in the course of a few days a

person will visit on you to put it in Tune. .... To an Elegant Patent Piano Forte on a French stand with two pedals and five stops - 25 guineas.[75]

This piano forte was almost certainly for John's wife, Mary Anne Dashwood and, in another possible Austen translation of fact into fiction, it is noticeable that in *Sense and Sensibility* it is Marianne Dashwood whose playing of the piano, sometimes with joy and sometimes with sadness, features in the novel, seemingly used to emphasise Marianne's changing moods and her associated pronounced sensibility.

Music, and particularly singing and playing the piano, were very much part of the middle and upper class social skills expected of ladies in this Regency period, and as well as the piano delivered to Bourton-on-the-Hill, the Dashwoods' clearly maintained keyboard instruments at their other residences at West Wycombe and in London: an entry in Sir John Dashwood's personal accounts for June 15th 1795 reads '*Broadwood & Jones .. hire of Piano forte in Conduit Street & tuning Harpsichord at W. Wycombe .. £3:12s:0d*'.[76] The focus on music as part of a girl's education is evidenced in a list of school expenses for Sir John Dashwood's second daughter under the heading '*Miss Elizabeth Dashwood's account to June 1810*' which, alongside entries for '*Board & Instruction*' and '*use of Instruments, Maps, Globes*', also includes '*music*' and '*music portfolio*'. In a similar list dated 1783 for Sir John's own earlier schooling, there are no such music expenses although the list, which incidentally itemises his pocket money of three pence a week, does include fees for dancing, writing and French lessons.[77]

Leaving Bourton-on-the-Hill must have been a wrench for Sir John and his family, after so many years there, where their married life had started, and where their son and heir George had been born. Having left Bourton-on-the-Hill, Sir John lived mainly at Halton, but nevertheless kept up contact with his old acquaintances in the Cotswolds, including Lord Redesdale at Batsford Park, Sir Charles Cockerell at Sezincote, and Lord Northwick at Northwick Park.[78]

Although still circulating in high society, including being presented to the King and Queen at St James's, and the Prince Regent at Buckingham House (later Buckingham Palace), as well as dining at Clarence House, Sir John Dashwood's later life was plagued by ill-fortune. Edwin, his second son, died in 1835, through excessive consumption of alcohol, and his youngest son, Henry, who had entered the church, was forced to resign because of sexual scandals, and died shortly after this in 1845. He also lost his daughter Lizzie in 1846, and his granddaughter Amelia in 1847. He had personally run into debt through ill-advised purchases of property, and he died in relative poverty in 1849.[79]

These later events, which would have been reported in newspapers and journals with all their accompanying negative connotations, kept the Dashwood name firmly in the public consciousness. Many readers of *Sense and Sensibility* at this time (well after Jane Austen's death) would have remained aware of, and sensitive to, the novel's allusions to the real Dashwood family members who, since the mid-eighteenth century, had found it hard to keep themselves out of the news.

In setting out key elements of the contemporary Dashwood family narrative, and having touched on several items of its portrayal in the media, there are some close and striking similarities with the main structural elements and storylines in *Sense and Sensibility*. There seems little doubt that Jane Austen drew names and contexts from her own personal, or second-hand, knowledge of contemporary events and individuals. She was also shrewd enough to use particular names (familiar to her readership and with known connotations) as a contemporary mechanism to emphasise specific moral and other messages. I agree with Barchas that this is not to suggest that Jane Austen simply mirrored any particular real life stories or events, but the evidence is compelling that her choice of the name Dashwood deliberately tapped into the contemporary Dashwood family's profile and notoriety, as just such a mechanism in *Sense and Sensibility*.

Barchas opens her article with the assertion that,

'Modern readers of Jane Austen have been reluctant to acknowledge that Sense and Sensibility (1811) rewards, and perhaps even demands, detailed knowledge of one of England's most notorious families in Austen's time – the Dashwoods of West Wycombe Park'.[80]

Her article goes on to set out evidence for this assertion, and the text below blends key parts of Barchas's case with evidence already outlined above. The question as to what, if anything, Jane Austen would have known about the Dashwood family and stories associated with them, has been answered above in relation to the Dashwoods' North Cotswolds activities, but she probably also gained knowledge from a number of other, more colourful, contemporary media references to, and portrayals of, the Dashwoods.

At the end of the 18th century and beginning of the 19th, there was a thriving market in pamphlets, journals and cartoons of varying character, from serious political commentary through to highly personalised caricatures, anarchic satire and gossip-mongering. A litany of perceived scandals provided fuel for the insatiable populist appetite for exposure of the misdemeanours of well-known establishment figures. Warren Hastings, for example, was targeted by such media for alleged corruption and mismanagement of affairs in India. The Dashwoods were also fair game, and by the 1790s the family was already a familiar focus for stories about sexual misconduct, with exotic and erotic undertones, arising principally from perceptions of the secretive Hell-Fire Club, as well as the extraordinary, and blatantly lewd, gardens laid out by Sir Francis Dashwood in the mid 18th century.

The Hell-Fire Club's notoriety, whether fully deserved or not, was well-established, and any further Dashwood family exposures or indiscretions were therefore even more likely to be exploited by the media. Jane Austen, as a well-educated, well-read, and well-connected aspiring writer, would, as Barchas persuasively demonstrates, have had fairly easy access to many of the most popular publications. Even if only browsing these, her family's connections with the Dashwoods – for example, a Dashwood-Austen 'society' marriage in the 18th century – would have made any Dashwood-related stories leap off the page.

There is further specific and convincing evidence that she would have been very well aware of the Dashwoods and at least the basic details of their late eighteenth and early nineteenth century activities. Reference has already been made to Jane Austen's deep interest with the genealogies and histories of the English nobility. Barchas notes that,

> Persuasion (1817), *which opens with Sir Walter Elliot obsessively rereading his copy of* The Baronetage of England (1808), *may provide a clue about how to read* Sense and Sensibility. *As Jon Spence remarks about Jane Austen's own family connections to the landed gentry and peerage, "she was almost as familiar with the book as Sir Walter". In addition to researching her own family history, Jane Austen appears to have been thoroughly familiar with the history of the baronetcy held by the Dashwoods of West Wycombe.*[81]

In outlining the various printed material which circulated about the Dashwoods, West Wycombe, and the Hell-Fire Club, and while accepting there is little direct evidence as to how much of this Jane Austen would have seen, Barchas convincingly demonstrates that the general notoriety of the Dashwoods was widely disseminated and reasonably common knowledge amongst those interested in current affairs, rumours and gossip. Her exploration includes the many books, journals and pamphlets which propagated these rumours from the time the Hell-Fire Club was operating through and beyond the time of *Sense and Sensibility*'s publication.[82] For example, by the time of Austen's draft of *Elinor and Marianne*, twenty editions of Johnstone's novel *Chrysal* had kept West Wycombe scandal in the public consciousness, the novel, for example, being incorporated in an 1801 travel guide to Buckinghamshire. Also, re-publishing of Nathaniel Wraxall's *Historical Memoirs of My Own Time, from 1772 to 1784* in the early decades of the nineteenth century resurrected interest in the Hell-Fire Club's notoriety in the wake of publication of Austen's *Sense and Sensibility*. Against the background of this pervading atmosphere, there were specific Dashwood family events which punctuated the narrative, such as Sir Francis's death in 1781, Sir John's marriage to Mary Anne in 1789, his accession to the title and estate in 1793, and in 1800 the publicity surrounding Mary Anne's alleged infidelity. Throughout all this, Sir John kept a mistress, and had a lifestyle connected with prominent and often colourful characters, including the Prince of Wales (later Prince Regent and eventually George IV). As Barchas concludes, '*in short, during the years Jane Austen composed* Sense and Sensibility, *anyone aware of current events would have been bombarded with mentions of high-profile Dashwoods*'.[83]

For Jane there are also specific Dashwood connections. Sir Robert Austen, of Kent, a relative of Jane's father, married Rachel Dashwood, sister of Sir Francis Dashwood, the infamous second baronet of West Wycombe. It is clear from many letters sent to Sir Francis Dashwood [Lord le Despencer] at West Wycombe that even after her marriage, Rachel Dashwood, now Lady Austen, spent considerable time at West Wycombe with her Dashwood family relations.[84] These letters all conclude with regards to '*Lady Austen*'. One such letter from Robert Dashwood in May 1766 ends for example by offering his '*most humble duty to your Lordship my Lady le Despencer and my Lady Austen*'. Another, having wished Sir Francis Dashwood's wife a speedy recovery sends '*thanks to my Lady Austen for her great goodness to me on this occasion*'.

Also, Jane and her family were intimately friendly with the Lefroys, their neighbours in Jane's early years at Steventon.

'Hell-Fire Jane' – Sense and Sensibility & the Dashwoods

Jane Austen and Tom Lefroy were particularly close, and playfully flirted with each other. In a letter to her sister Cassandra, Jane describes on one occasion dancing with him, and behaving somewhat shockingly, at least by the rigid standards of the day.[85] Significantly (in terms of links with the Dashwoods), Tom Lefroy's paternal grandfather was Anthony Lefroy (1703-1779), a banker in the eighteenth century meaning of the word, incorporating a variety of trading and mercantile investment activities in partnership with Peter Charron. These activities included numerous commercial dealings with Sir Francis Dashwood, 2nd Baronet, resulting in regular shipments of goods from the continent, over a long period, including acquisition of pictures, sculptures, and statuary for the Dashwood's estate at West Wycombe Park.[86] There is also a letter in the Dashwood Family papers[87], dated 22nd April 1754, detailing two half chests and two whole chests of '*good Artemina wine on board the Henrietta*' sent to Sir Francis Dashwood from Lefroy & Charron's trading base at Leghorn (the contemporary English name for Livorno) in Italy. The letters between Anthony Lefroy, Peter Charron, and Sir Francis Dashwood evidence their very close and friendly relationships. Given Jane's close friendship with Tom Lefroy, these notable mid-eighteenth century connections between the Lefroys, the Dashwoods, and West Wycombe were very probably known to her.

In summary, the above family links and her access to contemporary literature, provide strong evidence that Jane would have known about, and had a particular interest in, the West Wycombe Dashwoods. Barchas gives a well-researched analysis of Austen's use of names in her excellent article (and subsequent book), and I set out only one Dashwood example here. With specific reference to the distinction in the novel between what she calls an elected wife and a rejected wife, and the use of the titles 'Mrs John Dashwood' and 'Mrs Dashwood', Barchas notes that the mistress of Sir John Dashwood, 4th Baronet, styled herself as Mrs Dashwood. A rumour-mongering text of the time, *The*

Fashionable Cypriad (1798), employed the fashionable epistolary structure, with one of its 'letters' being headed "Mrs DASHWOOD", and relaying the following :-

> *Mrs Dashwood is the daughter of a respectable farmer, in the county of Sussex, of the name of P__tt. When very young, she was seduced from her family by the then Mr. _____ now Sir John D__w__d, with whom she cohabited for some years, and from whom she continues her present name. Upon Mr. D_____'s marriage with Miss B__dh__d, he settled £100 a year upon his faithful and forsaken Chere Amie, though his father, Sir John, was known to have declared, on this occasion, that he would rather have seen his son, by a thousand degrees, married to his mistress, than to his elected wife.*

As Barchas comments, although parts of the names are left blank (perhaps to avoid legal actions) there is little pretence at hiding the real identities of the characters alluded to, as they exactly match West Wycombe's Dashwood family. Mr John Dashwood (before he inherited the baronetcy and its titles) married Mary Ann Broadhead and only later, on becoming the 4th baronet, became Sir John Dashwood. His father (the 3rd baronet) was, as the above passage accurately notes, also called Sir John. Barchas concludes, '.... *In sum, The Fashionable Cypriad records in print the detailed rumours in public circulation about John Dashwood's abandoned mistress who defiantly took the name of her seducer.*'[88]

Adopting names or titles to which individuals were not entitled had already cropped up in an earlier phase of the Dashwoods' family history. The 2nd Dashwood Baronet's mistress was Frances Barry, and their natural daughter Rachel '*deeply resented her illegitimacy*' and '*pursued a disreputable career as an adventuress after her father's death, styling herself Baroness le Despencer and carrying on a furious pamphlet war with her relations, particularly her aunt, Lady Austen ...*'.[89] Such pamphlets were in the public domain, and given the Dashwood-Austen links in this 'pamphlet war', it may well have been brought to Jane Austen's attention during her formative years.

With reference to the £100 a year which Sir John, 4th baronet, allegedly settled on his mistress, this apparently mirrors payments which, a few decades earlier, the 2nd baronet had settled on his mistress, Frances Barry, for her lifetime, continuing beyond his own death. Indeed, the Dashwood bank account details for the years immediately after the 2nd baronet's death in 1781, have the entries '*1782 ... to Fras. Barry £100*', '*1783 ... to Mrs Barry £100*', and '*1784 ... to Frances Barry £100*'.[90]

Returning to the above indented passage, also significant is the connection between the county of Sussex and the name Dashwood in its opening phrase, indirectly matching the opening sentence of *Sense and Sensibility*, namely '*The family of Dashwood had long been settled in Sussex*'. Once again, this surely cannot be a coincidence, and simply adds to the strong case for the history of the Dashwoods of West Wycombe, and their reputation, having been a rich source for many of the narrative strands and messages in *Sense and Sensibility*. Most contemporary readers of the novel, generally from well-read and well-informed sections of society, would have picked up on at least some of these allusions or undercurrents.

Barchas notes the partial anonymity of the farmer's name in the above passage, and suggests '*Pratt*' as a likely contender. It is perhaps significant that in *Sense and Sensibility* Austen chooses the name Mr Pratt as Edward Ferrars' tutor and Lucy Steele's uncle. Once again, the partially disguised entry in The Fashionable Cypriad passage above is consistent with a name in the novel. The name Pratt also features in connection with a prominent member of the Dashwoods' Hell-Fire Club, namely the MP John Wilkes, whose radical views in edition No. 45 of the North Briton publication triggered his arrest.

The Lord Chief Justice, however, ordered Wilkes's release, and gave the seminal ruling that *'general warrants were illegal, except in cases of treason'* and *'established in England the rights of the individual against general warrants – a very important principle of freedom'*.[91] The Lord Chief Justice's surname was Pratt. [As noted earlier, another Chief Justice, Lord Mansfield, who gave important legal opinions on issues connected with the slave trade, may well have led Austen to adopt the title *Mansfield Park* for her novel in which the slave trade is a key contextual element.]

Finally, the name of another character in *Sense and Sensibility,* Mrs Jennings, may be yet another name garnered from the Dashwoods' history, with the first Sir Francis Dashwood having married Mary Jennings. As with Jane Austen's fictional Mrs Jennings, Mary Jennings also had two daughters.[92]

Overall, it is hard to avoid the conclusion that the Dashwoods of West Wycombe were a contributory inspiration for *Sense and Sensibility* not only in the use of the central family name, but also for names of the novel's other characters, and for some of its underlying themes. A full reading of Barchas's excellent journal article, or her book, is recommended.

On the basis that Austen had a deep interest in the Dashwoods, other more speculative connections can be floated. For example, given Austen's love of wordplay and puns, 'Hell-Fire' Francis Dashwood's building of Mere House, Kent, in 1780, to designs by Nicholas Revett (also involved at West Wycombe Park), may have triggered in Jane's linguistic mind the concept of a mere house, i.e. a house without land, perhaps leading her to choose Norland (also implying an absence of land) as the name for the Dashwoods' home, quoted at the very start of *Sense and Sensibility*. If there is any substance in this speculative connection, the irony that the real Mere House and the fictional Norland Park did have substantial land attaching, represents an additional linguistic contortion which would no doubt have appealed to Jane, given her love of playful use of language.

Mere House, Kent, also leads back to Austen and Dashwood family connections, because it was at Mereworth, Kent, on 4th November 1738 that Sir Robert Austen married Rachel Dashwood, the sister of Sir Francis Dashwood, the 'Hell-Fire' 2nd Baronet of West Wycombe.

Mention was made earlier that as well as John Dashwood-King, 4th Baronet of West Wycombe, having lived at Bourton-on-the-Hill for about 30 years during Jane Austen's life, and leaving there very close to the time of her death in 1817, another Dashwood family member was also residing in Bourton during at least some of this period. He is referred to in the archive documents as 'Sir Henry Dashwood', probably Sir Henry Watkin Dashwood (1745-1828), the profligate elder surviving son of the 2nd Baronet of Kirtlington Park. As noted earlier, he inherited the estate as 3rd Baronet in 1779, but had to sell most of the estate almost immediately to pay his enormous debts. One of Sir Henry Dashwood's sisters was Catherine Dashwood, born in the 1740s and died in 1809, who married a Mr Knightley, another name very familiar to Jane Austen readers: it is Mr Knightley who marries the eponymous heroine in her novel *Emma*. Possibly yet another example of Austen's use of names derived from the Dashwood family history.

In bringing this exploration of the Dashwoods to a conclusion, India may seem to have faded from the scene, but as a recurrent theme it is never far away, and it was Thomas Dashwood (1749-1825), the younger brother of the Sir Henry Dashwood just mentioned above, who was in charge of stationery supplies in India for the East India Company. He is featured in a painting executed in India by Zoffany, entitled *The Auriol and Dashwood Families*, 1783-1787.

Zoffany painting of the Auriol and Dashwood families in India

Zoffany's deliberately structured portrayal provides a wealth of information about the British ruling classes in India at this time, including the perpetuation of British manners and etiquette even in a most unfamiliar environment, far from home both geographically and culturally. It also illustrates the relationships with the Indian population. The feel of the painting is reminiscent of domestic British portraiture in the mid 18th century, intending to show off the control and poise of its sitters, their refined lifestyles, and their status, often incorporating backgrounds which include their estates or land they control. A well known example is Gainsborough's painting of Mr and Mrs Andrews (1750), and this has some resonance with the Zoffany painting in India, with a large tree prominent, verdant background, and with the sitters posed in a relaxed but confident and commanding manner.

The style is therefore a little old-fashioned for the 1780s, but this ties in with a commentary by the museum now holding the painting, namely that, '*Zoffany must have begun the portrait very soon after arriving in Calcutta in September 1783. His work was going out of fashion in London and he hoped to do better among the British in India*'.[93]

'Hell-Fire Jane' – Sense and Sensibility & the Dashwoods

More typical of paintings of India at this time was one referred to earlier by William Hodges, commissioned by Warren Hastings and hung at his Daylesford home in the Cotswolds, as noted in Chapter 8.

In both these paintings by Hodges and Zoffany, there must be a question mark against the authenticity of their portrayals of Indian scenes, including the prominent trees and landscapes. Artistic licence has perhaps been deliberately exercised to give the images a rather softened British feel. For authenticity in depictions of India, Thomas Daniell's images are more reliable. Given this book's aesthetic focus and the associated roles of India and the Cotswolds, Daniell's exceptional contribution to 'the Indian picturesque' and its impact in Britain is acknowledged here by finishing with three of his images. The first is from one of his 6 paintings of West Wycombe Park commissioned by Sir Francis Dashwood, the second is typical of his Indian scenes and the third is one of his paintings of Sezincote House.

Part of Thomas Daniell's painting of the Music Temple, West Wycombe Park

The Chalees Satoon at Allahabad, an engraving from the Daniells' 'Oriental Scenery'

*Sezincote House – detail from a Thomas Daniell painting
[Courtesy of the Peake family]*

Thomas Daniell's active professional career (c. 1772-1817) closely matches Jane Austen's life (1775-1817) and is therefore representative of the main period under consideration throughout this text. His early commission for the Dashwoods at West Wycombe dates from 1781, while the other two images above date from 1795 and c.1817 respectively, the latter commissioned by Sir Charles Cockerell. These three Daniell images taken together therefore provide snapshots of his output spread across four decades of artistic creativity, with the first and last being commissioned respectively by the Dashwoods and Cockerells. As outlined above, the activities of these two families, together with the Hastings and the Leighs, all living within 10 miles of each other at the turn of the nineteenth century, provide close links between Jane Austen, the Dashwoods, India and the Cotswolds.

Postscript

In an editorial article in The Times (Saturday, 22nd June, 2013), entitled 'Persuasion', and subtitled 'There is an obvious female candidate to be depicted on banknotes', the case was put for Jane Austen. Several of the key observations in the article reflect themes touched on in this volume, as the following extracts show :-

No other novelist of her time and of these islands is as fresh to readers today. In part this is because her writings encapsulate a distinctive national trait. Jane Austen elevated irony to art. ......Her reputation has suffered from the widespread misimpression, aggravated by numerous televised costume dramas, that she is the author of period romance. She is in reality the greatest of English comic writers. Like Kafka, and with similarly scant recognition of the fact, she is very funny. Her brilliance rests in the acuteness of her observations. Her irony occasionally strays into acidity and her earliest work betrays implausible plot devices. But the rarity of these idiosyncracies shows her achievement. She wrote about what she knew (it is pointless to condemn her for not referring to the Napoleonic wars), and she emphasised that sensibilities needed to be educated and ordered. .... At the conclusion of Austen's novels, marriage to the right party is an act of wisdom and not unmediated passion, of "smiles reined in and spirits dancing in private rapture". Austen's is a very English genius. It should literally as well as metaphorically be given currency.

The Times, p26, Saturday, June 22, 2013

The current £10 banknote, issued from September 2017, duly features Jane Austen.

Notes

INTRODUCTION

1. *Dashwood Family Papers*, Bodleian Library, C17 F5/22/4
2. From Rachel Knowles website http://www.regencyhistory.net/2012/09/when-is-regency-era.html
3. Jennings, C., *A Brief Guide to Jane Austen*, 2013

CHAPTER ONE

1. Bernstein, J., *Dawning of the Raj*, 1999, p78
2. Ibid, p78
3. Hibbert, C., *Nelson – A Personal History*, 1994, p32-3
4. *Dashwood Family Papers*, Bodleian Library, C2 B2/1/3a
5. Briggs, A., *England in the Age of Improvement*, 1999, p6
6. Ray, R., *Under the Banyan Tree*, 2013, p97
7. *Dashwood Family Papers*, Bodleian Library, C1 B1/1/7
8. *Persuasion*, Wordsworth Classics Ed.1993, p16
9. *Sense and Sensibility*, Wordsworth Classics Ed. 2007, p38
10. *The Song of the Earth*, 2000, pps 8-9
11. Quoted by Bernstein, J., in *Dawning of the Raj*, 2000, p16
12. Musgrave, C., *Royal Pavilion*, 1951, p49
13. *Sense and Sensibility*, Wordsworth Classics Ed. 2007, p38
14. *Northanger Abbey*, Wordsworth Classics Ed. 2000, p80
15. Richardson, J., *The Regency*, 1973, p140
16. Barchas, J., *Hell-Fire Janet Austen and the Dashwoods of West Wycombe*, 2009, pps 27-8

CHAPTER TWO

[1] https://thegenealogycorner.wordpress.com/.../jane-austens-family-tree 27/07/2018
[2] Huxley, V., *Jane Austen & Adlestrop*, 2013, pps 6-7
[3] Ibid, p7
[4] Ibid, p34
[5] Ibid, p35
[6] *West Wycombe Park*, National Trust Brochure, 2001, p31
[7] *Sense and Sensibility*, Wordsworth Classics Ed. 2007, pps 70-71
[8] Tomalin, C., *Jane Austen - A Life*, 2000, p61
[9] Ibid, p111
[10] *Northanger Abbey*, Wordsworth Classic Ed., p50
[11] Tomalin, C., *Jane Austen - A Life*, 2000, p113
[12] *Dashwood Family Papers*, Bodleian Library, C10 B17/4/14
[13] Dashwood, Sir F., *The Dashwoods of West Wycombe*, 1987, p12
[14] *Studies in Dorset History by Maureen Weinstock M.A. F.R.Hist.S. published by Longmans (Dorchester) Ltd 1953 a study of Weymouth Port & Petty Customs Books and the role of Dorchester Merchants.* (freepages.genealogy.rootsweb.ancestry.com/.../Files/Fordington**Dorchester**Co2.html)
[15] *Dashwood Family Papers*, Bodleian Library, C1 A2
[16] Dashwood, Sir F., *The Dashwoods of West Wycombe*, 1987, p13
[17] Ibid, p13
[18] Ibid, p14
[19] Willson, B., *Ledger and Sword*, Vol. II, 1903, pps 8-9
[20] *Dashwood Family Papers*, Bodleian Library, C1 A2
[21] Willson, B., *Ledger and Sword*, Vol. II, p11
[22] Dashwood, Sir F., *The Dashwoods of West Wycombe*, 1987, p15
[23] *Dashwood Family Papers*, Bodleian Library, C1 A1/3
[24] Willson, B., *Ledger and Sword*, Vol.II, 1903, p18
[25] *Dashwood Family Papers*, Bodleian Library, C1 A2
[26] *Dashwood Family Papers*, Bodleian Library, C1 A1/6
[27] *Dashwood Family Papers*, Bodleian Library, C1 A1/5
[28] Dashwood, Sir F., *The Dashwoods of West Wycombe*, 1987, p16
[29] *Dashwood Family Papers*, Bodleian Library, C1 A2
[30] *Dashwood Family Papers*, Bodleian Library, C14 E3
[31] Ibid
[32] Collins, I., *Jane Austen and the Clergy*, 1994, p114

Notes

CHAPTER THREE

1. *Dashwood Family Papers*, Bodleian Library, C21 F7/19/7
2. *Mansfield Park*, Everyman edition, 1993, p40
3. *Emma*, Penguin Books, 1966, p240
4. *Dashwood Family Papers*, Bodleian Library, C18 F6/3/3
5. Huxley, V., *Jane Austen & Adlestrop*, 2013, p2
6. Barchas, J., *Hell-Fire Jane: Austen and the Dashwoods of West Wycombe*, 2009, p12
7. *Dashwood Family Papers*, Bodleian Library, C11 B19/8/2
8. *A Collection of Letters*, The Women's Press Limited, 1978, pps84-87
9. *Love and Freindship*, The Women's Press Limited, 1978, pps26-27
10. *A Collection of Letters*, The Women's Press Limited, 1978, p85
11. Barchas, J., *Matters of Fact in Jane Austen*, 2012, p141
12. Huxley, V., *Jane Austen & Adlestrop*, 2013, pps 7-10
13. Penn, T., *Winter King*, 2012, p287
14. Baldwin, D., *Henry VIII's Last Love*, 2015
15. *Sense and Sensibility*, Wordsworth Classics Ed. 2000, p26
16. Doody, M., *Jane Austen's Names*, 2015, p99
17. Hilton, L.S., Sunday Times, Style section, p59, 17th December, 2017
18. Doody, M., *Jane Austen's Names*, 2015, pp 100-101
19. Ibid, p98
20. *Sense and Sensibility*, Wordsworth Classics, p278
21. Doody, M., *Jane Austen's Names*, 2015, p106
22. Dashwood Family Papers, Bodleian Library, C18 F6/1/3
23. Huxley, V., *Jane Austen & Adlestrop,* 2013, p65
24. Tomalin, C., *Jane Austen - A life*, 1997, p169
25. Ibid, pps 169-170
26. Le Faye, D., *Jane Austen's Letters*, 4th Ed., p95
27. Byrne, P., *The Real Jane Austen*, 2013, p237
28. Tomalin, C., *Jane Austen - A life,* 1997, p170
29. Ibid, p182-3
30. Ibid, p81
31. Ibid, pps 81-3
32. Taylor, C., *Dying – A Memoir*, 2016, p64

CHAPTER FOUR

1. Hibbert, C., *Nelson – A Personal History*, 1994, p45
2. Huxley, V., *Jane Austen & Adlestrop*, 2013, p26
3. Drabble, M., Introduction to 1974 Penguin Classics Ed. *Lady Susan, The Watsons* and *Sanditon,* pps 19-20
4. Ibid. pps 19-20
5. Austen, J., *Love and Freindship – Love and Freindship and Other early Works*, 1978, p6
6. Austen, J., *The Three Sisters – Love and Freindship and Other early Works*, 1978, p104
7. *Dashwood Family Papers*, Bodleian Library, C18 F6/1
8. Tomalin, C., *Jane Austen - A life,* 1997, p183
9. Gordon, L., *Charlotte Bronte: A Passionate Life, 1995*, p12
10. *Sense and Sensibility*, Wordsworth Classics Ed., 2000, p36
11. *Sense and Sensibility*, Wordsworth Classics Ed., 2000, p27-8
12. *Pride and Prejudice*, Wordsworth Classics Ed., 1999, p3
13. *Emma*, Penguin Ed. 1966, Introduction, p29
14. Ibid, back cover
15. Tomalin, C., *Jane Austen - A life,* 1997, p65
16. *Sense and Sensibility*, Wordsworth Classics Ed., 2000, p219
17. *Emma*, Penguin Ed. 1966, Notes, pps 470-1
18. Tomalin, C., *Jane Austen - A life,* 1997, p170
19. *Persuasion*, Wordsworth Classics Ed., 2007, pps 10-11
20. Hardy, T., *The Trumpet-Major*, Macmillan, 1971, p1
21. Collins, I., *Jane Austen and the Clergy*, 1994, p134
22. Dashwood, Sir F., *The Dashwoods of West Wycombe*, 1987, p82
23. *Sense and Sensibility*, Wordsworth Classics Ed., 2000, p 24
24. Ibid, p24
25. Ibid, pps 23-4
26. Ibid, p21
27. Ibid, p24
28. Dashwood, Sir F., *The Dashwoods of West Wycombe*, 1987, p73
29. *Sense and Sensibility*, 2000, p 21
30. Ibid, pps 31-2
31. Ibid, pps 32-3
32. Ibid, pps 94-5
33. Ibid, p24
34. Dashwood, Sir F., *The Dashwoods of West Wycombe*, 1987, p76
35. Le Faye, D., *Jane Austen's Letters*, 4th Ed., 2011, p224

[36] https://oldgreypony.wordpress.com/austen-and-the-picturesque/
[37] 'Angela Carter: Of Wolves and Women', BBC Two, 4th August, 2018

CHAPTER FIVE

[1] *Sense and Sensibility*, Wordsworth Classics Ed., 2000, p 69
[2] Collins, I., *Jane Austen and the Clergy*, 1994, p113
[3] Batey, M., *The Picturesque: An Overview*, Garden History, Vol 22, No.2, The Picturesque, (Winter, 1994), pps 121-132, The Garden History Society
[4] Austen, J., *Love and Freindship*, The Women's Press Limited, 1978, p31
[5] *Dashwood Family Papers*, Bodleian Library, C18 F6/3/1
[6] Walton, J.K., *The English Seaside Resort, A Social History 1750-1914*, 1983, p16-7
[7] Strong, Sir R., *Scenes and Apparitions – The Roy Strong Diaries 1988-2003*, Weidenfeld & Nicolson, 2007, p69
[8] https://parksandgardensuk.wordpress.com/2014/04/04/humphry-repton/
[9] Loudon, J. C., *The Landscape Gardening and Landscape Architecture of the Late Humphry Repton esq.*, Humphry Repton, 1840, p114
[10] Quoted in Hibbert, C., *Nelson – A Personal History*, 1994, p311
[11] *Dashwood Family Papers*, Bodleian Library, C18 F6/3/1
[12] http://www.bl.uk/collection-items/the-tour-of-doctor-syntax#sthash.sKX0Wy42.dpuf
[13] *Sense and Sensibility*, pps 71-3
[14] Ibid, pps 168-170
[15] Ibid, p170
[16] Ibid, p170
[17] Tillyard, S., *George IV – King in Waiting*, 2019, p24
[18] Quoted in *Nelson – A Personal History*, Hibbert, C., 1994, p234
[19] Barchas, J., *Hell-Fire Jane: Austen and the Dashwoods of West Wycombe*, 2009, p6
[20] Doody, M., *Jane Austen's Names*, 2015, p109
[21] Ibid, p101
[22] Bate, J., The song of the Earth, 2000, p8
[23] Ibid, p9

24. Burke, E., *Parliamentary speech about India, 1st December 1783*
25. Macaulay, T. B., *Warren Hastings*, 1907 Ed., p108
26. *The Abolition of Slavery Project* website, http://abolition.e2bn.org/campaign_17.html 16/06/2016
27. Handed out around 1825-1833 by the Sheffield Female Anti-Slavery Society. *The Abolition of Slavery Project* website, http://abolition.e2bn.org/library/1202428800/eastindiasugaradvertsmall.jpg 16/06/2016)
28. http://www.britishmuseum.org/research/collection_online/collection_object_details.aspx?objectId=1477504&partId=1&people=75139&peoA=75139-1-9&page=1 16/06/2016
29. *The Abolition of Slavery Project* website 20/06/2015
30. Introduction to *Emma*, 1966 Penguin Edition, p7
31. Poser, N., *Lord Mansfield*, 2013, Rear Cover
32. Disraeli, B., *Sybil*, 1845
33. Pevsner, N., *The Architectural Setting of Jane Austen's Novels*, p 404, *Journal of the Warburg and Courtauld Institutes*, Vol. 31 (1968), pp. 404-422. Published by: The Warburg Institute DOI: 10.2307/750649. Stable URL: http://www.jstor.org/stable/750649
34. *Northanger Abbey*, Wordsworth Classics Ed., 2007, pps 100-101
35. Bate, J., *The Song of the Earth*, 2000, pps 128-9
36. Ibid, pps 129-130
37. Ibid, p131
38. Ibid, pps 135-6
39. Huxley, V., *Jane Austen & Adlestrop*, 2013, p100
40. *Northanger Abbey*, Wordsworth Classics Ed., 2007, p 80
41. Huxley, V., *Jane Austen & Adlestrop*, 2013, p101
42. Austen, J., *Mansfield Park*, Everyman Edition 1993, p43
43. Doody, M., *Jane Austen's Names*, 2015, pps 31-2
44. Ibid, p33
45. Collins, I., *Jane Austen and the Clergy*, 1994, p76

CHAPTER SIX

1. Quoted in *Dawning of the Raj - The Life &Trials of Warren Hastings*, Bernstein, J., 2001, p33
2. Hibbert, 1994, p6
3. Bernstein, J., 2001, p30

Notes

[4] Macaulay, T. B., *Warren Hastings*, 1907 Ed., p5
[5] Quoted in *Nelson – A Personal History*, Hibbert, C., 1994, p277
[6] Busteed, H.E., *Echoes from Old Calcutta*, 1888, p107
[7] Hibbert, C., *Nelson – A Personal History*, 1994, pps69-70
[8] Briggs, A., *The Age of Improvement*, 1999, p16
[9] Magnus, P., *Gladstone*, 2001, p2
[10] Gibson, M., *Warneford*, undated, p64
[11] Green, D., *Patrick Bronte: Father of Genius*, 2010, p189
[12] Tomalin, C., *Jane Austen - A Life*, 2000, p80
[13] *Dashwood Family Papers*, Bodleian Library, C16 F5/10
[14] Ibid, C15 F4/5
[15] *Northanger Abbey*, pps 81-2
[16] *Northanger Abbey*, Notes, pps 193-4
[17] *Dashwood Family Papers*, Bodleian Library, C14 F/2/1/1
[18] Charlotte Bronte letter to G H Lewes, 12th January, 1848
[19] Lewes, G. H., *The Lady Novelists*, Westminster Review, 1852
[20] Anonymous, *The Progress of Fiction as an Art*, 1853
[21] Blythe, R., Introduction to *Emma*, pps 7-8
[22] Briggs, A., *The Age of Improvement*, 1999, p9
[23] Tomalin, C., *Jane Austen - A Life*, 2000, p83
[24] Drabble, M., *Lady Susan*, *The Watsons* and *Sanditon*l, Penguin Classics Ed., 1974, pps 29-30
[25] Le Faye, D., *Jane Austen's Letters*, 4th Ed., 2011, p308
[26] Ibid, pps 308-9
[27] Ibid, p319
[28] Ibid, p325
[29] Ibid, p326
[30] Irene Collins Obituary, The Times, Friday 14th August 2015
[31] Hibbert, C., *Nelson – A Personal History*, 1994, p228
[32] Revd James Woodforde's journal, *The Diary of a Country Parson, 1788-1802*, quoted in Hibbert, C., *Nelson – A Personal History*, 1994, p157-8
[33] Hibbert, C., *Nelson – A Personal History*, 1994, p144
[34] Nelson, quoted by David Nokes in Tomalin, C., *Jane Austen; A Life*, 1997, p291
[35] https://janeaustensworld.wordpress.com/2015/11/15/the-gracefulness-of-india-shawls-in-the-georgian-era/
[36] Thackeray, W.M., *Vanity Fair*, Wordsworth Classics edition, 2001, pps 15-35
[37] Careless use of scissors also appears in *Sense and Sensibility*, with Edward Ferrars nervously and clumsily handling a pair.

Did Austen have some fixation with scissors, other cutting implements, and their sharpness? Margaret Doody (*Jane Austen's Names*, 2015) certainly highlights the hidden roles of metals and cutting implements in her analysis of names in *Sense and Sensibility* – see Chapter 9

[38] *Dashwood Family Papers*, Bodleian Library, C18 F6/6&7
[39] Vinayah Purohit, *Arts of Transitional India Twentieth Century*, Volume 1, pps 388-389
[40] Ginger, A., *Daylesford House and Warren Hastings*, Georgian Group Report and Journal 1989, 1990, p83
[41] Briggs, A., *The Age of Improvement*, 1999, pps 33-4
[42] Collins, I., *Jane Austen and the Clergy*, 1994, p103
[43] Dashwood, Sir F., *The Dashwoods of West Wycombe*, 1987, pps73-4
[44] Ibid, p82
[45] *Northanger Abbey*, Wordworth Classics edition, Introduction, 2007, pv
[46] Ibid, Facing p1

CHAPTER SEVEN

[1] *Sense and Sensibility*, Wordsworth Classics Ed. 2007, p38
[2] Prior, K., *An Illustrated Journey Round the World*, 2007, p29
[3] Wild, A., *The East India Company – Trade and Conquest from 1600*, 1999, pps 74-6
[4] Ibid, p78
[5] Quoted in Sutton, T., *The Daniells - Artists and Travellers*, 1954, p16
[6] *Persuasion*, Wordsworth Classics edition, 2007, p52
[7] Macaulay, T. B., *Warren Hastings*, 1907 Ed., p14
[8] Wild, A., *The East India Company – Trade and Conquest from 1600*, 1999, p76
[9] Ibid, p77
[10] *Persuasion*, Wordsworth Classics edition, 2007, p16
[11] Quoted in *Nelson – A Personal History*, Hibbert, C., 1994, p340
[12] Bernstein, J., *Dawning of the Raj – The Life and Trials of Warren Hastings*, 2001, p125
[13] Willson, B., *Ledger and Sword*, Vol.II, 1903, pps211-2 & *Oxford Dictionary of National Biography*, Volume 49. Oxford University Press. 2004. p. 534

14 Some dates in Indian cricket history, Wisden 1967
15 Prior, K. (Ed.), *An Illustrated Journey Round the World*, 2007, p8
16 Quoted in Sutton, T., *The Daniells - Artists and Travellers*, 1954, p16
17 Ibid, p16
18 Dashwood, Sir F., *The Dashwoods of West Wycombe*, 1987, p201
19 Sutton, T., *The Daniells – Artists and Travellers*, 1954, p91
20 Lowe, A., *La Serenissima – The Last Flowering of the Venetian Republic*, 1974, p131
21 Sutton, T., *The Daniells – Artists and Travellers*, 1954, p17
22 Ibid, pps 38-9

CHAPTER EIGHT

1 Ray, R., *Under the Banyan Tree*, 2013, p3
2 Sutton, T., *The Daniells - Artists and Travellers*, 1954, pps 47-8
3 Quoted in Sutton, T., *The Daniells - Artists and Travellers*, 1954, p49
4 Sutton, T., *The Daniells - Artists and Travellers*, 1954, p91
5 Ibid, pps 91-2
6 Prior, K. (Ed.), *An Illustrated Journey Round the World*, 2007, p35
7 Ibid, p35
8 Ibid, p55
9 Ibid, p59
10 Ibid, p67
11 Ibid, p67
12 Ibid, p67
13 Ibid, p144
14 Ibid, pps 144-7
15 Sutton, T., *The Daniells - Artists and Travellers*, 1954, p19
16 Archer, M., *Early Views of India – The Picturesque Journeys of Thomas and William Daniell 1786 1794*, 1980, pps 223-4
17 Page, N., *Kipling Companion*, 1984, p?
18 Ray, R., *Under the Banyan Tree*, 2013, p2
19 Ibid, p3
20 Ibid, p4
21 Crinson, M., *Empire Building – Orientalism and Victorian Architecture*, 1996, p21

[22] Ray, R., *Under the Banyan Tree*, 2003, p7
[23] Ibid, p2
[24] Ibid, pps 186-7
[25] Sutton, T., *The Daniells - Artists and Travellers*, 1954, p44
[26] William Daniell quoted in Sutton, T., *The Daniells - Artists and Travellers*, 1954, p69
[27] Ray, R., *Under the Banyan Tree*, 2013, pps 38-9
[28] Quoted in Bernstein, J., *Dawning of the Raj – The Life and Trials of Warren Hastings*, 2001, p16
[29] Quoted in Ray, R., *Under the Banyan Tree*, 2013, p73
[30] Ray, R., *Under the Banyan Tree*, 2013, p100
[31] Ibid, p101
[32] Ibid, pps 108-9
[33] Ibid, p263
[34] *NorthangerAbbey*, Wordsworth Classics ed., 2007, pps 126-7
[35] Ray, R., *Under the Banyan Tree*, 2013, p266

CHAPTER NINE

[1] Bernstein, J., *Dawning of the Raj – The Life and Trials of Warren Hastings*, 2001, pps 32-3
[2] Ibid, p34
[3] Ibid, p48
[4] Tomalin, C., *Jane Austen - A Life*, 2000, p19
[5] Bernstein, J., *Dawning of the Raj – The Life and Trials of Warren Hastings*, 2001, p52
[6] Huxley, V., *Jane Austen & Adlestrop*, 2013, pps 185-6
[7] Le Faye, D., *Jane Austen's Letters*, 4th Ed., 2011, Letter 28, p66
[8] Ibid, p386
[9] Ibid, Letter 55, p144
[10] Ibid, p402
[11] Ginger, A., *Daylesford House and Warren Hastings*, Georgian Group Report and Journal 1989, 1990, pps80-1
[12] Huxley, V., *Jane Austen & Adlestrop*, 2013, p188
[13] Le Faye, D., *Jane Austen's Letters*, 4th Ed., 2011, Letter 87, p227
[14] Ibid, Letter 87, p230
[15] Entry for September 24th, 1785, *The Diaries of Fanny Burney*
[16] Macaulay, T. B., *Warren Hastings*, 1907 Ed., p133
[17] Le Faye, D., *Jane Austen's Letters*, 4th Ed., 2011, Letter 86, p226

Notes

[18] *Dashwood Family Papers*, Bodleian Library, C16 F5/9/9
[19] Bernstein, J., *Dawning of the Raj – The Life and Trials of Warren Hastings*, 2001, p193
[20] Archer, M., *Early Views of India – The Picturesque Journeys of Thomas and William Daniell 1786-1794*, 1980, p10
[21] Ibid, p10
[22] Darley, G., *John Soane: An Accidental Romantic*, 1999, p304
[23] Archer, *Early Views of India – The Picturesque Journeys of Thomas and William Daniell 1786-1794*, 1980, p12
[24] Quoted in Bernstein, pps 9-10
[25] Ibid, p71
[26] Archer, M., *Early Views of India – The Picturesque Journeys of Thomas and William Daniell 1786-1794*, 1980, p232
[27] Summerson, J., *Architecture in Britain 1530 to 1830, Vol. 3, 9th Ed.*, 1993, p454
[28] Quoted by Richardson, J., *The Regency*, 1973, p140
[29] Glos. R.O. D1652
[30] Firth, A., *The Book of Bourton-on-the-Hill, Batsford & Sezincote*, 2005, Chapter 9, 'The Creation of Sezincote House and Gardens'
[31] Kingsley, N., *Country Houses of Gloucestershire, Volume Two*, 1992, p225
[32] All from uncatalogued documernts in GRO.
[33] Ibid
[34] Ibid
[35] Ibid
[36] Ibid
[37] Beckwith, E.G.C., *Dr Samuel Wilson Warneford, LL.D. (1763-1855)*, 1974, p18
[38] Uncatalogued documernts in GRO
[39] Ibid
[40] Ibid
[41] Ibid
[42] Woodforde, J., *The Diary of a Country Parson, 1758-1802*, 2014
[43] *Dashwood Family Papers*, Bodleian, C16 F5/10/9
[44] Uncatalogued documernts in GRO
[45] Ibid
[46] *Sense and Sensibility*, Wordsworth Classics, p170
[47] Uncatalogued documernts in GRO
[48] Musgrave, C., *Royal Pavilion*, 1951, p 49
[49] Archer, M., *Early Views of India – The Picturesque Journeys of Thomas and William Daniell 1786-1794*, 1980, p232

50 Ibid, p233
51 Ibid, p223
52 Ibid, p10
53 Ibid, pps 225-6
54 Ibid, p232

CHAPTER TEN

1. Tomalin, C., *Jane Austen - A Life*, 2000, p109
2. *Dashwood Family Papers*, Bodleian Library, C14 E3
3. Times obituary of the 11th Baronet in its March 11th 2000 edition
4. *Dashwood Family Papers*, Bodleian Library, C5 B11/12/44
5. Horace Walpole, quoted in Jeremy Black, *The British and the Grand Tour*, 1985, p120
6. *Dashwood Family Papers*, Bodleian Library C10 B17/2/13
7. *Dashwood Family Papers*, Bodleian Library, C5 B11/4/6
8. Dashwood, Sir F. Bt., *West Wycombe Caves guidebook*, undated, pps 17-18
9. *West Wycombe Park*, National Trust, 2001, p51
10. Dashwood, Sir F., *The Dashwoods of West Wycombe*, 1987, p65
11. Ibid, pps 66-70
12. Treasury Letter Book (1770-8), pps 90-99
13. *Dashwood Family Papers*, Bodleian Library, C2 B2/3/2a
14. Barchas, J., *Hell-Fire Jane: Austen and the Dashwoods of West Wycombe*, 2009, pps 6-7
15. Ibid, pps13-14
16. Ibid, p16
17. Ibid, pps 14-16
18. Dashwood, Sir F., *The Dashwoods of West Wycombe*, 1987, p73
19. Quoted in Dashwood, Sir F., *The Dashwoods of West Wycombe*, 1987, p77-8
20. Dashwood, Sir F., *The Dashwoods of West Wycombe*, 1987, p74
21. *Dashwood Family Papers*, Bodleian Library, C16 F5/2/3
22. Dashwood, Sir F., *The Dashwoods of West Wycombe*, 1987, p73
23. Barchas, J., *Hell-Fire Jane: Austen and the Dashwoods of West Wycombe*, 2009, p24

Notes

24 https://www.nationaltrust.org.uk/features/introducing-the-dashwood-baronets
25 *Dashwood Family Papers*, Bodleian Library, C18, F6/3/1
26 *Dashwood Family Papers*, Bodleian Library, C21, F7/14/2
27 *Dashwood Family Papers*, Bodleian Library, C18 F6/3/3
28 *Dashwood Family Papers*, Bodleian Library, C18 F6/4
29 Dashwood, Sir F., *The Dashwoods of West Wycombe*, 1987, pps 73-4
30 The Encyclopaedia Britannica, or Dictionary of Arts, Sciences ..., Volume 11
31 The Sporting Review, edited by 'Craven'. Volume III, January 1840
32 *Dashwood Family Papers*, Bodleian Library, C18 F6/3/3
33 *Dashwood Family Papers*, Bodleian Library, C18 F6/3/3
34 *Dashwood Family Papers*, Bodleian Library, C15 F4/2
35 Sporting magazine, Volume 10 new series (or Volume 60 Old series) 1822, p275-277
36 *Dashwood Family Papers*, Bodleian Library, C16 F5/10/9
37 *Sense and Sensibility*, Wordsworth Classics, p20
38 *Dashwood Family Papers*, Bodleian Library, C17 F5/22/4
39 *Dashwood Family Papers*, Bodleian Library, C21 F7/16/3
40 Dashwood, Sir F., *The Dashwoods of West Wycombe*, 1987, p79
41 Ibid, p79
42 Barchas, J., *Hell-Fire Jane: Austen and the Dashwoods of West Wycombe*, 2009, p24
43 Ibid, pps 24-5
44 Ibid, p25
45 *Sense and Sensibility*, Wordsworth Classics, p170
46 Dashwood, Sir F., *The Dashwoods of West Wycombe*, 1987, p76
47 Bernstein, J., *Dawning of the Raj – The Life and Trials of Warren Hastings*, 2001, p16
48 *Dashwood Family Papers*, Bodleian Library, C21 F7/12/16
49 Dashwood, Sir F., *The Dashwoods of West Wycombe*, 1987, p82
50 *Dashwood Family Papers*, Bodleian Library, C15 F4/10
51 *Dashwood Family Papers*, Bodleian Library, C18 F6/5
52 *Dashwood Family Papers*, Bodleian Library, C18 F6/3/3
53 *Sam Darling's Reminiscences*, Mills and Boon, London, 1914
54 www.regencyhistory.net/2012/05/princess-elizabeth-artist.html

55 www.regencyhistory.net/2012/05/princess-elizabeth-artist.html
56 Dashwood, Sir F., *The Dashwoods of West Wycombe*, 1987, p77
57 Hibbert, C., *Nelson – A Personal History*, 1994, p238-9
58 Ibid, p244
59 *Dashwood Family Papers*, Bodleian Library, C16 F5/3/1a
60 *Dashwood Family Papers*, Bodleian Library, C16 F5/3/1b
61 *Dashwood Family Papers*, Bodleian Library, C16 F5/3/5
62 *Dashwood Family Papers*, Bodleian Library, C16 F5/3/10a
63 *Dashwood Family Papers*, Bodleian Library, C18 F6/1
64 *Dashwood Family Papers*, Bodleian Library, C18 F6/5
65 *Dashwood Family Papers*, Bodleian Library, C16 F5/4/11b
66 The Times Saturday 13th June 2015, Saturday Review section, p11
67 Ibid, p11
68 *Dashwood Family Papers*, Bodleian Library, C15 F4/1
69 *Dashwood Family Papers*, Bodleian Library, C15 F4/10
70 Barchas, J., *Hell-Fire Jane: Austen and the Dashwoods of West Wycombe*, 2009, p23
71 Ibid, p22
72 *The Annual register, or, A View of the history, politics etc .., Volume 53*, By Edmund Burke, John Davis Batchelder Collection (Library of Congress)
73 *The Sporting Magazine Or Monthly Calendar of the Transactions of The Turf The Chase And Every Other Diversion Interesting to the Man of Pleasure Enterprise & Spirit* (page 276), Volume 10 New Series, Or Volume 60 Old Series
74 Dashwood, Sir F., *The Dashwoods of West Wycombe*, 1987, p80
75 *Dashwood Family Papers*, Bodleian Library, C17 F5/22/2
76 *Dashwood Family Papers*, Bodleian Library, C18 F6/3/2
77 *Dashwood Family Papers*, Bodleian Library, C18 F6/4
78 Dashwood, Sir F., *The Dashwoods of West Wycombe*, 1987, pps 81-2
79 Ibid p83
80 Barchas, J., *Hell-Fire Jane: Austen and the Dashwoods of West Wycombe*, 2009, p1
81 Ibid, p2
82 Barchas, J., *Matters of Fact in Jane Austen*, 2012, pps 183-190
83 Ibid pps189-190
84 *Dashwood Family Papers*, Bodleian Library, C5 B11/7
85 Le Faye, D., *Jane Austen's Letters*, 4th Ed., 2011, p1, Letter 1, from Steventon, Saturday January 9th, 1796

Notes

[86] Barchas, J., *Hell-Fire Jane: Austen and the Dashwoods of West Wycombe*, 2009, p20
[87] *Dashwood Family Papers*, Bodleian Library, C5 B11/12/16a
[88] Barchas, J., *Hell-Fire Jane: Austen and the Dashwoods of West Wycombe*, 2009, pps 21-2
[89] West Wycombe Park, National Trust, 2001, p56
[90] *Dashwood Family Papers*, Bodleian Library, C18 F6/3/3
[91] Dashwood, Sir F. Bt., *West Wycombe Caves*, undated, p24
[92] Barchas, J., *Hell-Fire Jane: Austen and the Dashwoods of West Wycombe*, 2009, pps 5-6
[93] http://www.holburne.org/zoffany/

Selected Bibliography

Archer, M., *Early Views of India – The Picturesque Journeys of Thomas and William Daniell 1786-1794*, London, Thames & Hudson, 1980

Austen, J., *Emma*, Harmondworth, Middlesex, Penguin Books, 1966

Austen, J., *Lady Susan and Other Works*, Ware, Herts., Wordsworth Editions, 2013

Austen, J., *Love and Freindship and Other Early Works*, London, The Women's Press Limited, 1978

Austen, J., *Mansfield Park*, London, Everyman, J.M. Dent, 2007

Austen, J., *Northanger Abbey*, Ware, Herts., Wordsworth Editions, 2007

Austen, J., *Persuasion*, Ware, Herts., Wordsworth Editions, 2007

Austen, J., *Pride and Prejudice*, Ware, Herts., Wordsworth Editions, 2007

Austen, J., *Sense and Sensibility*, Ware, Herts., Wordsworth Editions, 2007

Baldwin, D., *Henry VIII's Last Love*, Sroud, Gloucestershire, Amberley Publishing, 2015

Barchas, J., *Matters of Fact in Jane Austen*, Baltimore, Maryland, The John Hopkins University Press, 2012

Barchas, J., *Hell-Fire Jane: Austen and the Dashwoods of West Wycombe*, Eighteenth Century Life, Vol. 33, No. 3, Duke University Press, 2009

Bate, J., *The Song of the Earth*, London, Picador, Macmillan Publishers Limited, 2001

Batey, M., *The Picturesque: An Overview*, Garden History, Vol 22, No.2, The Picturesque, (Winter, 1994), pps 121-132, The Garden History Society

Beckwith, E.G.C., *Dr Samuel Wilson Warneford, LL.D. (1763-1855)*, 1974

Bernstein, J., *Dawning of the Raj – The Life and Trials of Warren Hastings*, London, Aurum Press, 2001

Blythe, R., Introduction to *Emma,* Harmondsworth, Middlesex, Penguin Books, 1966

Briggs, A., *England in the Age of Improvement*, Harlow, Essex, Pearson Education Limited, 1999

Busteed, H.E., *Echoes from Old Calcutta*, 1888

Byrne, P., *The Real Jane Austen – A Life in Small Things*, London, Harper Collins, 2013

Collins, I., *Jane Austen and the Clergy*, London, The Hambledon Press, 1994

Crinson, M., *Empire Building – Orientalism and Victorian Architecture*, London, Routledge, 1996

Darley, G., *John Soane: An Accidental Romantic*, London, Yale University Press, 1999

Dashwood, Sir F., *The Dashwoods of West Wycombe*, London, Aurum Press, 1987

Dashwood, Sir F. Bt., *West Wycombe Caves*, West Wycombe, undated

Disraeli, B., *Sybil*, 1845

Doody, M., *Jane Austen's Names*, Chicago, University of Chicago Press, 2015

Drabble, M., *Lady Susan, The Watsons* and *Sanditon (Introduction)*, London, Penguin Classics Ed., 1974

Firth, A., *The Book of Bourton-on-the-Hill, Batsford & Sezincote*, Tiverton, Devon, Halsgrove, 2005

Gibson, M., *Warneford*, undated

Ginger, A., *Daylesford House and Warren Hastings*, Georgian Group Report and Journal 1989, 1990

Gordon, L., *Charlotte Bronte: A Passionate Life,* London, Vintage, 1995

Green, D., *Patrick Bronte: Father of Genius*, Stroud, Gloucestershire, The History Press, 2010

Hardy, T., *The Trumpet-Major*, London, Macmillan, 1971

Hibbert, C., *Nelson – A Personal History*, London, Viking, Penguin Books, 1994

Huxley, V., *Jane Austen & Adlestrop*, Adlestrop, Gloucestershire, Windrush Publishing, 2013

Kingsley, N., *Country Houses of Gloucestershire, Volume Two*, Chichester, Sussex, Phillimore & Co, 1992

Selected Bibliography

Le Faye, D., *Jane Austen's Letters*, 4th Ed., Oxford, Oxford University Press, 2011

Loudon, J. C., *The Landscape Gardening and Landscape Architecture of the Late Humphry Repton esq.*, Humphry Repton, Longmans, 1840

Jennings, C., *A Brief Guide to Jane Austen*, London, Constable & Robinson, 2012

Lewes, G. H., *The Lady Novelists*, Westminster Review, 1852

Macaulay, T. B., *Warren Hastings*, London, Cambridge University Press, 1907 Ed

Magnus, P., *Gladstone*, London, Penguin Books, 2001

Musgrave, C., *Royal Pavilion*, Brighton, Bredon & Heginbothom, 1951

Page, N., *A Kipling Companion*, London, Macmillan, 1984

Penn, T., *Winter King*, London, Penguin Books, 2012

Pevsner, N., *The Architectural Setting of Jane Austen's Novels*, p 404, *Journal of the Warburg and Courtauld Institutes*, Vol. 31 (1968), pp. 404-422. Published by: The Warburg Institute

Poser, N., *Lord Mansfield*, London, McGill-Queen's University Press, 2013

Prior, K. (Ed.), *An Illustrated Journey Round the World*, London, The Folio Society, 2007

Purohit, V., *Arts of Transitional India Twentieth Century, Volume 1*

Ray, R., *Under the Banyan Tree*, London, Yale University Press, 2013

Richardson, J., *The Regency*, London, Collins, 1973

Strong, Sir R., *Scenes and Apparitions – The Roy Strong Diaries 1988-2003*, Weidenfeld & Nicolson, 2007

Summerson, J., *Architecture in Britain 1530 to 1830, Vol. 3, 9th Ed.*, London, Yale University Press, 1993

Sutton, T., *The Daniells - Artists and Travellers*, London, The Bodley Head, 1954

Taylor, C., *Dying – A Memoir*, Edinburgh, Canongate Books, 2016

Thackeray, W.M., *Vanity Fair*, London, Wordsworth Classics edition, 2001

Tomalin, C., *Jane Austen: A Life*, London, Penguin Books, 2000

Tillyard, S., *George IV – King in Waiting*, Penguin Books, 2019

Walton, J.K., *The English Seaside Resort, A Social History 1750-1914*, New York, St. Martin's Press, Leicester University Press, 1983

Wild, A., *The East India Company – Trade and Conquest from 1600,* London, Harper Collins, 1999

Willson, B., *Ledger and Sword*, Vol.II, London, Longmans, Green, and Co., 1903

Woodforde, J., *The Diary of a Country Parson, 1758-1802,* Norwich, Canterbury Press, 2014

Selected Index

Adlestrop vii, vii, x-xiv, xvii, xviii, 4, 19-22, 38, 40, 44, 49, 103-4, 148, 154-7, 213-4, 230, 244, 277, 284, 286-8, 291-2, 298, 338-340, 342, 346, 354
Austen, Cassandra (Jane's mother) xii, 17, 18, 21, 210
Austen, Cassandra (Jane's sister) 21, 43, 50, 53, 82, 213, 215, 325
Austen, Charles 50, 149
Austen, Frank 147-9, 165, 214
Austen, Henry 211, 214
Austen, Jane vii-ix, xi-xiv, xvii, 1-4, 7, 10, 11, 13-15, 17-19, 21-25, 30, 32-3, 35, 38-40, 42-44, 46-7, 49-56, 58-9, 61, 65, 68-70, 73, 76, 78, 82, 85, 87-8, 92, 95-6, 99, 101, 103-4, 107, 111-6, 118, 120-1, 123, 125, 128-131, 135, 137-9, 141, 143-5, 147-9, 152-8, 160, 170, 172-3, 185, 188, 191, 197, 199, 200, 202, 205, 207-8, 210-6, 219-221, 225, 230-1, 233, 235, 240, 242, 248-9, 251, 253, 259, 266, 272, 276, 278, 284, 286-9, 291-2, 298, 301, 312, 321-5, 327-9, 333, 335-344, 346, 348-351, 353-5
Austen, Philadelphia 52, 154, 163, 166, 168, 205, 207-211, 213-4
Barton (*Sense and Sensibility*) 45, 77, 97, 156, 251, 253, 278, 282-5
Bateson, family 277, 279, 281
Bath 12, 22, 51, 70, 72-3, 158, 174
Batsford i, viii, xviii, 156-7, 240, 279, 284-5, 320, 347, 354
Bennet, family (*Pride and Prejudice*) 58, 60, 96-7, 104, 215, 231, 240
Bengal xiv, 31, 52-3, 153, 163-4, 169-70, 206, 208, 218, 226-7, 234-5, 259, 271
Berkeley, family 57, 303-5, 308-9
Bingley (*Pride and Prejudice*) 48, 96
Bogle, George 11, 151, 164-5, 197, 294
Boston 6-7
Boston Tea Party 6
Bourton-on-the-Hill i, vii, xi, xii, xiv, xvii, xviii, 22, 39-40, 48, 77, 79, 81, 89, 129-30,

357

148-9, 157, 206, 234, 236-8, 240-1, 243, 249-51, 253, 256, 265-6, 268-9, 271-3, 275-81, 285-6, 295, 297-9, 301, 314-6, 318-20, 329, 347, 354
Bourton House 77, 279-85, 319
Brandon, Charles 18, 21, 44-5, 75
Brandon, Colonel (*Sense and Sensibility*) 18, 21, 44-7, 61, 66-7, 71, 74, 104, 161, 188, 212
Briggs, Asa 7, 119, 128, 131, 137, 155, 202, 337, 343-4, 354
Brighton Pavilion viii, 3, 11, 145-6, 154, 185, 189, 231-2, 247
Broadhead, family 57, 153, 268, 271, 299, 326
Bronte, family 66, 129, 134-5, 219, 340, 343, 354
Burke, Edmund 91, 107, 188, 191, 216-8, 227, 342, 350
Burney, Fanny 82, 158, 205, 215-6, 219-20, 346
Calcutta 10, 161, 165, 169-70, 179-80, 194, 197-8, 208, 225-8, 234, 330, 343, 354
Canaletto, Antonio 173, 178
Chawton 73, 82, 143
Chertsey 221-3
China 1, 34, 106, 163, 165, 171, 184, 214, 225, 248
Clarke, James Stanier 136, 138-45
Cockerell, family xiv, xvii, 4, 39, 154, 157, 165, 218, 220-1, 223, 229, 233-46,

250-1, 254, 271-2, 279-81, 287-8, 299, 320, 333
Collins, Irene 34, 87, 112, 144, 156, 338, 340-4, 354
Cotswolds vii, viii, xi, xiv-xviii, 4, 14-15, 18-19, 22, 35, 39-40, 49, 76-7, 87, 89, 103-4, 126, 130, 149, 151, 154-7, 180, 188, 205-6, 208, 213, 218, 221, 223, 229-31, 233-5, 249, 256, 266, 268, 271, 273-5, 277, 284, 287-8, 293, 316, 320, 322, 331, 333
Crawford, Henry & Mary (*Mansfield Park*) 51, 58-60, 119-20, 212
Creswicke, family 206, 208
Daniell, Thomas & William viii, ix, 4, 10, 105, 118, 161, 165-6, 171-5, 177, 179-86, 188-9, 194, 197, 200, 203, 206, 220-6, 228-33, 240, 243-5, 247-51, 263-4, 279-80, 297, 333, 344-8, 353
Darling, family 296-8, 349
Dashwood, family v, vii, viii, ix, xii, xiv, xvii, 4, 7, 15, 17, 22, 24-7, 30, 32-5, 37-41, 47-8, 55, 57, 77, 87, 89, 103, 115, 122, 130, 147, 149, 157, 162-5, 180, 193, 197, 206, 221-2, 228, 235-6, 238, 240-1, 250-1, 253-5, 257, 259-68, 271-3, 275, 277-8, 280, 282, 285-6, 291, 298, 303, 305, 309-11, 313-4, 316, 318-25, 327-30, 333, 337-41, 343-5, 347-351, 353-4

Selected Index

Dashwood, Sir Francis, 1st Baronet 26, 31-3, 254, 264, 328

Dashwood, Sir Francis, 2nd Baronet 4, 7, 9, 13, 22, 24, 27, 33-4, 42, 82, 88, 101-2, 193, 197, 222, 251, 253-61, 263, 309, 314, 322, 324-6, 328-9, 331

Dashwood, Sir John, 3rd Baronet 222, 253, 256, 264, 266, 273, 326

Dashwood, Sir John, 4th Baronet vii, xi, xii, 33, 37-9, 48, 57, 65, 76-9, 81, 89, 91-2, 94-6, 118, 130, 133, 153, 157, 203, 220, 223, 237, 239, 241, 250-1, 253, 256, 258, 266-88, 291-4, 296-8, 301-3, 305-6, 308-9, 311-2, 314-5, 317-21, 325-6, 329

Dashwood, Sir George, 5th Baronet 48, 57, 65, 266, 271, 289

Dashwood, Sir Francis, 11th Baronet 78, 172, 262, 265-6, 294

Dashwood, Sir Edward, 12th Baronet ix, 270, 274, 317

Dashwood, Mary Anne 57, 65, 78-9, 81, 153, 241, 267, 271, 282, 287, 299-305, 309, 312-3, 320

Dashwood, family (*Sense and Sensibility*) vii, viii, 11, 15, 24, 33, 39-41, 47-8, 55, 77, 101, 104, 122, 156, 197, 235, 238, 240, 251, 253-4, 266, 271, 278, 282-5, 313, 321, 325-7, 353

Dashwood, John (*Sense and Sensibility*) 53, 94, 99-101, 104-5, 236, 238, 242, 266, 284, 292, 313

Dashwood, Elinor (*Sense and Sensibility*) 24, 54, 80, 100, 284

Dashwood, Marianne (*Sense and Sensibility*) 11, 21, 24, 41, 44-6, 54, 79-80, 87, 100-1, 118, 161, 284, 287, 320

Dashwood, Mrs (*Sense and Sensibility*) 54, 79, 284

Dashwood, Mrs John (*Sense and Sensibility*) 67, 102, 325

Daylesford vii, xiv, xvii, xviii, 4, 40, 104, 125-6, 151, 154, 156, 206, 213-5, 218, 220, 223, 233-4, 239, 244, 287-8, 294, 331, 344, 346, 354

Dorchester 25, 338

East India Company xiv, xvii, 4-9, 26-8, 30, 34, 39, 146-9, 151, 163-5, 170, 185, 191, 194, 198, 206-7, 214, 220, 225, 227-8, 233, 244, 329, 344, 356

Egypt/Egyptian 2, 146-7, 156

Emma 38, 61, 65, 68-9, 72, 74-5, 112, 136, 141, 329, 339-40, 342-3, 353-4

Ferrars, family (*Sense and Sensibility*) 11, 23, 47, 71, 80-2, 87, 97, 104, 118, 156, 327, 343

Franklin, Benjamin 7, 147, 257-8, 260

Gillray, James 109-10, 191-2

Gilpin, William 88-9, 94, 96-7, 122, 199-200
Godmersham 22
Halton 271, 274-5, 278, 313, 316, 319-20
Hamilton, Lady Emma 94, 101, 127, 267, 302-3
Hancock, Eliza 85, 130, 205, 210-3, 215-6
Hancock, Tysoe 52, 207-8, 210-11
Hardy, Thomas 25, 75, 187, 340, 354
Hare, family 57, 309, 311
Harriers 76, 268, 273-4, 281, 293-4, 311
Hastings, Warren xiv, xvii, 4, 11, 30, 39, 125-8, 136, 146, 151, 154, 163-5, 179, 185, 191-2, 197, 205-18, 220, 227, 229, 234, 244, 287-8, 294, 322, 331, 333, 342-4, 346-7, 349, 354-5
Hell-Fire Club & Caves vii, 27, 34, 40, 101-2, 115, 122, 170, 193, 253, 255-9, 262-3, 271, 309, 314, 322-4, 327
Hodges, William 105, 174, 179, 213-4, 331
India/Indian vii, viii, ix, xiv, xvii, 1-12, 14-5, 18, 26-32, 34-5, 39, 50, 52, 58, 85, 87, 91, 105-9, 125-7, 136, 138, 145-6, 161-6, 168-175, 177-194, 197-203, 205-8, 210, 212-5, 217-8, 220-1, 224-230, 232-4, 243-250, 259, 271, 294, 309, 322, 329-31, 333, 342-5, 347, 353, 355-6
Jennings, Mrs (*Sense and Sensibility*) 328

Kew 1, 172, 189, 195, 197-8, 245, 300
Kingham xviii, 103, 125, 235
Leigh, family xi, xii, xiii, xiv, xvii, 4, 15, 17-22, 25, 32, 34, 38, 40, 44, 59, 85, 104, 157, 162, 210, 244, 276-7, 286-8, 298, 333
London 5, 8, 17-8, 25-6, 32, 70, 72, 81, 105, 114, 130-3, 142, 147, 163, 169, 185, 206, 217, 223, 227, 233, 237-9, 241, 255-6, 267-8, 271, 274-8, 282, 295, 298, 320, 330, 349, 353-6
Longborough vii, xii, xiii, xiv, xvii, xviii, 19, 40, 104, 156, 234-5, 237, 244, 286-7
Mansfield Park 19, 37-9, 50-1, 58, 60, 71, 82, 88, 111-2, 119-20, 136-8, 140, 148, 153, 220, 244, 287, 292, 328, 339, 342, 353
Medmenham 34, 101, 115-6, 122, 256, 258
Middleton, family (*Sense and Sensibility*) 42, 77-82, 284
Moreton-in-Marsh xviii, 11, 103, 206, 236-7, 244, 281
Mughal (style) viii, xiv, xvii, 3, 105, 221, 243
Nash, John 145, 189, 232, 247
Nelson, Horatio 4-5, 8, 58, 94-5, 101, 125, 127-8, 145-8, 164, 169-70, 216, 267, 302-3, 337, 340-1, 343-4, 350, 354
Norland (*Sense and Sensibility*) 54, 99-100, 104-5, 236, 238, 240, 242, 309, 328
North, Lord 4-5, 7, 234, 261

Selected Index

Northanger Abbey 12-3, 23, 74, 83, 88, 101, 112, 114-5, 119-20, 130-1, 133, 138, 153, 159-60, 202, 248, 312, 337-8, 342-4, 346, 353

Northwick Park xviii, 156-7, 287-8, 320

Oriental Scenery 179, 189, 200-1, 229, 232, 247, 332

Palmer, Richard 285

Pemberley 19, 60, 114, 231, 240

Penn, William 258, 289-90, 339, 355

Persuasion 10, 13, 22, 51, 72-3, 148, 159, 162, 167, 169, 325, 335, 337, 340, 344, 353

Philadelphia 6, 258, 289-90

Picturesque v, viii, ix, 2, 10-12, 14, 35, 55, 58, 83-4, 87-91, 94-9, 102, 112-3, 116-20, 122-3, 138, 151, 154, 174-5, 177-8, 180-4, 186, 188-90, 195, 199-203, 205, 214, 224, 240, 247-9, 293, 331, 341, 345, 347, 353

Price, Fanny 51, 58-9, 82, 138, 220

Pride and Prejudice 19, 41, 48, 58-60, 67, 71, 74, 82, 88, 96, 104, 112, 114, 134, 214, 220, 231, 240, 340, 353

Prince Regent viii, xv, xvi, 4, 101, 136, 138-40, 142-3, 145, 154, 185, 189, 230-2, 247, 267, 321, 324

Princess Elizabeth 110, 299-301, 349

Redesdale, Lord 157, 320

Repton, Humphry viii, 2, 4, 37-40, 92-4, 119-20, 145, 156, 172, 188, 206, 220-1, 230-2, 239, 243-4, 246-7, 250, 264, 289, 291-3, 341, 355

Rhotas 179, 229-30

Riots 129-30, 133

Rushout, family 287-8

Rushworth (*Mansfield Park*) 38, 60, 287

Sanditon 13, 61, 73, 92, 136-8, 340, 343, 354

Sense and Sensibility v, vii, xiv, 3, 11, 15, 18, 21, 23-4, 33, 35, 39-48, 53-5, 57, 59, 61-2, 66-7, 71, 73-7, 79, 81-3, 87, 94, 97, 99, 101-5, 112-3, 122, 129, 156, 161, 188, 197, 200-1, 212-3, 216, 219, 233, 235-6, 238, 240, 242, 251, 253-4, 263-4, 266, 271, 278, 282, 284-7, 289, 291-2, 301, 309, 313-4, 320-4, 327-8, 337-41, 343-4, 347, 349, 353

Sezincote viii, ix, xiv, xvii, xviii, 3-4, 11, 39-40, 146, 154-7, 165, 172, 188-9, 206, 218, 220-1, 223, 230-50, 254, 271-2, 279-81, 287-8, 291, 293, 299, 320, 331-2, 347, 354

Slavery/Slave trade 106, 108-9, 111, 136, 328, 342

Soane, John 223, 347, 354

Steele, family (*Sense and Sensibility*) 47, 81, 327

Steventon xi, 18, 51, 72-3, 174, 211-2, 324, 350

Stoneleigh Abbey 18-9, 21-2, 44-5, 59, 231
Sutton, Thomas ix, 172-5, 177-9, 182, 344-6, 355
Thackeray, William 8, 50, 150, 312, 343, 355
Trafalgar 8, 10, 73, 148, 169
Vansittart, family 164-5, 170, 257, 259, 306-9
Wales 22, 89, 94, 203, 217, 268, 281
Walpole, Horace 255, 348
Warneford, Revd. 129-30, 238, 343, 347, 353-4
Waterloo 73, 303-4
Wellington, Duke of 4, 145-6, 154-5, 157, 312
Wentworth 21-2, 148

West Wycombe vii, ix, xi, 4, 7, 9, 13, 22, 24-5, 27, 32-3, 35, 37, 39, 41-2, 48, 57, 89, 102-3, 105, 115, 122, 130, 133, 147, 157, 170, 172, 193, 196-7, 222-3, 228, 237-9, 250-1, 253-4, 256-60, 262-8, 270-2, 274-7, 280-1, 286, 288-93, 298, 314, 316-7, 320, 322-9, 331, 333, 337-41, 344-5, 348-51, 353-4
Whitehead, Paul 257
Wilkes, John 257, 327-8
Willoughby, Cassandra 21, 44
Willoughby, John (*Sense and Sensibility*) 21, 42-8, 66, 79, 161-2, 212, 264
Zoffany, John 34, 329-31, 351

Lightning Source UK Ltd.
Milton Keynes UK
UKHW012148180821
389073UK00002B/691

9 781786 236401